MOM to MOM

A Valuable Collection
of
Tips and Hints
for
the Mother-to-Be and New Mother

Lynett Root Cablk

Communication Dynamics
San Diego, California

© 1990 Lynett Root Cablk

All Rights Reserved. No portion of this book may be reproduced—mechanically, electronically, or by any other means, including photocopying—without written permission of the publisher, except for the inclusion of brief quotations for a review.

Cover design and artwork by Linda Brosio
Illustrations by Joan Boyer

Library of Congress Catalog Card Number 90-81088
ISBN 1-878747-05-3

The author of this book does not dispense medical advice or prescribe the use of any technique as a form of treatment for medical problems without the advice of a physician, either directly or indirectly. The intent of the author is only to offer information of a general nature to help you cooperate with your doctor in your mutual quest for health and to help you meet the challenges of motherhood more easily and confidently. In the event you use any of the information in this book for yourself and your child, you are prescribing for yourself, which is your right, but the author, publisher, and distributors assume no responsibility for your actions. If you have any question or concern about the appropriateness or application of techniques described in this book, consult your health-care professional.

Published by
Communication Dynamics
10601-A Tierrasanta Boulevard, Suite 201
San Diego, CA 92124

First Printing May 1990
Second Printing February 1991
Printed in the United States of America

IN APPRECIATION . . .

A book is definitely not a solo project, and *Mom to Mom* is no exception! Had it not been for the enthusiastic, encouraging help and support of so many, this book would have remained only a dream.

A tremendous amount of gratitude goes to these loving, dedicated moms who contributed their own tips, hints, and ideas to help make this resource become a reality:

Linda Bannister	Ann Gaines	Janine Schooley
Sue Brandes	Bonnie Ebel	Joanne Soukup
Linda Brosio	Rose Fioravante	Doreen Seldon
Lori Buschmann	Karen Johnson	D.J. Strauss
Lynn Carlson	Melody Leopard	Jan Sundblad
Eileen Carroll	Joyce Mattson	Peggy Takaaze
Terri Ciosek	Kate McCann	Sue Wexler
Priscilla Cowell	Sandy Price	Stephanie Wooten
Wendy Davis	Terrya Rez	

Many thanks to all of those unnamed who throughout the past four years have helped me develop my mothering skills. I've remembered the tips and the ideas and the hints but not the names or where I read or heard them.

It's said that behind every successful married author there's an understanding, supportive spouse, and that's so true of my husband, Tom Cablk! In the midst of a continuously hectic travel and work schedule, he found time to review sections of the manuscript as they were completed, make some valuable suggestions, and offer some additional ideas.

Reading a manuscript can be a very tedious job. Not only is the reader trying to grasp the ideas being shared, but she is simultaneously trying to catch "typos" and usage faux pas, and make helpful suggestions to better the product. I was very fortunate to not only have a wonderful

Mom to Mom . . .

reader who accomplished that tall order, but she eagerly volunteered to be the proofreader of the final copy as well! My heartfelt thanks to a very dear friend, Terri Ciosek, who accomplished all of this *and* was a constant source of enthusiastic encouragement and support.

Linda Brosio is a very talented, sensitive artist who created the special cover for this book. It was such a pleasure working with her! She, too, was a source of enthusiasm and brought a real love to the project for which I am very grateful.

Joan Boyer, also a talented artist and a friend of many years, had little lead time but provided the illustrations for this book with excitement and gave that much needed encouragement.

Rose Fioravante, better known as "Rowie" to all who love her, has helped with this project in innumerable ways for which I'm very grateful. She is Maryanna's devoted sitter of four years and, because of her pediatric nurse practitioner background, she's also our "resident" source of medical guidance and help. She happily gave many extra hours of discussion time and "sitting" time so that chapters and sections of this book could be regularly completed.

Michael Caparelli, R.Ph., who is a friend and our trusted pharmacist, happily reviewed the section on the suggested contents of a medicine cabinet and equipment to have on hand to care for little ones. His review and his suggestions were very helpful and much appreciated.

Nancy Powers, M.D., who is a specialist in breastfeeding and poor weight gain in infants and is a pediatrician on staff with Wellstart, the San Diego Lactation Program, thoroughly reviewed the chapter on feeding. Her suggestions for improvement and accuracy greatly enhanced the section and I appreciate her assistance very much!

Robert Giarratano, M.D., an obstetrician in private practice in San Diego, reviewed the chapter on pregnancy. I greatly appreciate the time he took to not only carefully review the chapter, but also the care and time he took to explain procedures and various important issues in obstetrics. His feedback, suggestions, and instruction were invaluable!

In Appreciation ...

Frederick Frye, M.D., a pediatrician in private practice in San Diego, enthusiastically reviewed the sections on health and provided several helpful suggestions and additional ideas which are much appreciated!

Grateful acknowledgment is also given to the following publishers and copyright owners for permission to reprint selections from their publications. All possible care has been taken to trace ownership and secure permission for each selection. Any oversight is unintentional and will be corrected in future printings and editions upon proper notification. Excerpts from the following sources are reprinted with permission: *The Baby's Bedtime Book* by Kay Sproat Chorao, ©1984, E.P. Dutton, New York; "Song for a Fifth Child" by Ruth Hulburt Hamilton, © 1958, Meredith Corporation, reprinted from *Ladies' Home Journal* magazine with permission of the author; *Breastfeeding—Third Edition, A Guide for the Medical Profession* by Ruth A. Lawrence, M.D., © 1989, C. V. Mosby Company, St. Louis, MO; *The Natural Diapering Handbook,* © The Natural Baby Company, Titusville, NJ; *Lactation: Physiology, Nutrition, and Breast Feeding* by Margaret C. Neville, M.D., and Marianne R. Neifert, M.D., © 1983, Plenum Press, New York; *The Family Circus is Us* © by Bil Keane, Fawcett-Columbine Books, November 1990; *Growing Parent* and *Growing Child,* © Dunn & Hargitt, 1986 to 1990, Lafayette, IN; *Pediatrics for Parents* edited by Richard J. Sagall, M.D., Bangor, ME; *The Family Bed* by Tine Thevenin © 1987 Avery Publishing, Garden City Park, NY; La Leche League International, catalogue materials, Franklin Park, IL; La Leche League International, LLLI articles appearing in *Baby Talk*, November 1985 and August 1988.

DEDICATION...

Dedications in most books are normally quite short. But a book such as this really requires several dedications accompanied by special explanations.

To my wonderful husband, Tom, who is my constant source of inspiration and encouragement;

To our precious daughter, Maryanna, without whom this book could not have been written;

To two loving mothers in my world, my mom, Mary Root, and my aunt, Nancy Closson, who have been and continue to be beautiful role models of what a loving mother can be.

And to my dear "once-upon-a-time" sitter, Jeanne Caravalho, who continues to be a special part of my family and thoughts of whom recall happy, delightful childhood memories.

Contents

"If Only I Had Known..." An Introduction   **13**
Why This Book ◊ How to Make This Resource Work for You

SECTION ONE
PREGNANCY THROUGH INFANCY

1 Pregnancy—Healthy, Comfortable, and Joy-Full...   **21**

Highly Recommended Resources ◊ Dressing the Part ◊ Promoting the Health of You and Your Unborn Baby ◊ Concerning Your Dental Health ◊ Relieving Common Discomforts of Pregnancy ◊ Traveling While Pregnant ◊ Potpourri of Other Great Ideas

2 Preparing for the Precious Arrival...   **45**

"Must" Reading Before Your Little One Arrives ◊ "Must" Activities Before Your Little One Arrives ◊ Selecting a Pediatrician ◊ Equipment Needed and Not Needed ◊ The Non-Essentials...At This Time ◊ Clothing Initially Needed and Not Needed ◊ The Set-Up—Getting the Nursery Ready ◊ A Potpourri of Ideas to Consider ◊ Shopping List

3 Your Little One's Arrival . . . **91**

Recommended Reading ◊ Two to Four Weeks Before Your Little One's Expected Due Date ◊ If You Have Other Children At Home ◊ While At the Hospital ◊ Returning to Home Sweet Home ◊ Siblings and the Little One's Arrival at Home ◊ Settling In During the First Few Weeks ◊ Potpourri of Other Great Ideas

4 Feeding Time! **115**

Recommended Reading ◊ Breastfeeding ◊ Breast Is Best ◊ You CAN Be Successful with Breastfeeding ◊ Some Helpful Tips Concerning Successful Breastfeeding ◊ Some Additional Thoughts on Breastfeeding from Other Moms ◊ Breastfeeding and the Working Mom ◊ Bottle Feeding ◊ Equipment ◊ An Important Caution ◊ Keys to Successful Bottle Feeding ◊ Introducing Solids ◊ To Begin Introducing Solids ◊ Making Your Own Foods ◊ Additional Suggestions from Other Moms ◊ Preparing for Sitters ◊ For Breastfed Babies ◊ For Bottlefed Babies ◊ For Babies on Solids ◊ For All the Above Categories

5 Daily Care . . . **149**

The Best Advice ◊ Baths and Washing Hair ◊ Clothing and Dressing ◊ Crying ◊ Diapering ◊ Equipment ◊ Playtime ◊ Dealing With the "Not Accomplishing A Thing" Syndrome

6 Sleepy Time . . . **177**

Recommended Reading ◊ Some Sleepy Time Hints for the Newborn ◊ Some Tips from Some of the Experts

7 Health . . .   187

Visiting the Doctor ◊ Caring for the Sick Infant ◊ Administering Medication ◊ A Couple of Helpful "How-to's" ◊ Treating Rashes ◊ Dealing with Hospitalization ◊ Teeth and Teething ◊ Potpourri of Important Suggestions

8 Safety for Little Ones . . .   217

Bath Safety ◊ Car Safety ◊ Childproofing ◊ Furniture and Equipment ◊ Sleepy Time ◊ Miscellaneous Safety Tips

9 Traveling Away from Home *Can* Be Simple . . .   233

Short Trips Around Town ◊ Suggested Diaper Bag Contents ◊ General Tips for Short Trips ◊ Traveling by Car ◊ Out-of-Town Travel with Infants ◊ At the Airport ◊ On the Plane ◊ Packing ◊ Sample Packing List ◊ Blank Personal Packing List

10 Babysitters and Day Care . . .   253

Some Initial Thoughts ◊ Determining Your Requirements ◊ Sources of Sitters and Day Care-Givers ◊ Interviewing Potential Sitters and Day Care-Givers ◊ Suggested Process of Selecting Quality Sitters and Day Care ◊ A Great Babysitting Alternative—The Babysitting Cooperative ◊ Some Things Worth Reviewing with Your Sitter or Care-Giver ◊ Some Suggested Do's and Don'ts ◊ A Closing Thought on Beginning Day Care

Section Two
A Treasure of Great Ideas for Baby from Six Months through Preschool

Activities with Toddlers and Preschoolers . . .   273
Baths and Hair Washing . . .   279
Breastfeeding the Older Baby and Toddler . . .   280
Clothing and Dressing . . .   281
Creating Memories . . .   286
Communicating with Your Little Ones . . .   286
Day Care and Sitters . . .   289
Dining Out . . .   292
Diaper Bag Contents for the Toddler . . .   294
Discipline . . .   295
Equipment . . .   297
Fears . . .   300
Feeding Toddlers and Pre-Schoolers . . .   301
Health . . .   305
Holidays . . .   320
Parenting Suggestions . . .   322
Pets. . .   326
Playtime . . .   330
Preschool . . .   335
Products Worth Knowing About . . .   339
Safety . . .   341
Security Items—Lovies . . .   358
Self-Reliance . . .   359
Siblings and Their Rivalry . . .   359

Sleepy Time . . .   361
Storytelling . . .   362
Teeth and Teething . . .   363
Television . . .   365
Toilet Training . . .   367
Traveling Away from Home . . .   368

SECTION THREE
APPENDIX

A   Scrapbook of Thoughts to Ponder . . .   **381**

B   Indispensable Resources for Moms and Dads . . .   **393**

       Catalogues ◊ Newsletters ◊ Magazines ◊ Lactation Consultants—Regional Listings

C   Bibliography . . .   **405**

       Topics: Breastfeeding ◊ Feeding and Meal Preparation ◊ Newsletters ◊ Parenting Assistance ◊ Sibling Preparation

$$ For Your Tips and Hints . . .   **411**

Additional Clips and Notes . . .   **415**

Index . . .   **431**

Order Form . . .   **448**

11

"If I Had Only Known..."
An Introduction

Why This Book...

If you are a new mom...or about to be a new mom...or have been a mom for a while, I'm quite familiar with the feelings you are now experiencing.

Those feelings began for me in the summer of 1985 when I knew we were going to be blessed with a little one in March of the following year. I had *so many* questions and yet no friends with young children to ask who could provide me with their desperately needed ready answers. After all, I was 38—an "older mother"—and my friends with children were ready or nearly ready to launch their children into college! I definitely couldn't share in *their* hot topics and questions of the day! Any questions I had concerning diaper bag contents, hospital necessities, books a new mom can't manage without, breastfeeding, layette necessities, questions ad infinitum, fell on ears that were now filled with a multitude of teen interests, football cheers, incessantly ringing telephones, and unending requests for, "What's there to eat, Mom??" The cries and squeals of a baby or the giggles and demands of a toddler, were, for them, the sounds of long ago. Any guidance they might have had for me had been long forgotten over the years.

Consequently, like you, I scanned the endless bookshelves of every bookstore I passed throughout my pregnancy. The shelves were filled with hundreds of interesting titles, but...which ones were the best? I was quite lost as to just which ones would give me the best guidance. Some of the books I bought I dog-eared to death. Others, too many for me to count, wound up barely skimmed before being tossed aside.

As the much anticipated day quickly approached, my husband and I delightedly began searching for baby furniture and equipment. Unanswered questions again hounded us. "What's really needed? What will

Mom to Mom . . .

be the most practical?" No one other than the salesperson with poised pen and empty sales receipt in hand was able to give us any "guidance." Needless to say, we made some costly mistakes in selection.

What about a pediatrician? We wondered how to find the one with whom we would feel most comfortable and who would be most supportive as we bumped along uncertainly in the first weeks and months of parenthood. Again, no one other than my obstetrician could offer any assistance; we simply didn't know anyone who used the services of a pediatrician. Again, we made a mistake.

As for other resources that could give needed periodic replenishment and encouragement, I fortunately *bumped* into the ones I devour each month: *Parents Magazine, Growing Child,* and *Growing Parent,* none of which had ever been recommended to me by anyone.

By now you must have the picture . . . I was not nearly as prepared as I had hoped before our little one arrived, right on her due date, in March of 1986! If I had only known then what I know now!

- Had I only known some mothers with small children who could have given me some desperately needed advice and guidance that would have helped me avoid some mistakes and helped me have a more smooth entry into motherhood!

- Had I only known the right books to read *before* our baby was born.

- Had I only known some of the wonderful hints and tips that I discovered simply by accident and by necessity, hints that I was sure every mother must know but I had never read or heard about.

Too often helpful hints and tips that are so urgently needed by new and inexperienced mothers are assumed by many to be common knowledge, so they consequently are never written or suggested or shared. It's because of this unfortunate assumption that this collection of valuable ideas, tips, and hints has been written for you.

"If I Had Only Known . . . "

How to Make This Resource Work for You . . .

This book is divided into three sections for your convenience:

Section One The first section is dedicated to your pregnancy, preparation for your baby's arrival, and your baby's infancy—his first six months of life.

Section Two The second section is dedicated to the "treasure" of other ideas and tips that concern your older baby—seven months of age through pre-school. All the topics in this section are in alphabetical order.

Section Three This last section is the Appendix. It contains a chapter on some thoughts worth thinking about that may have a profound effect on you as they did on me, a list of indispensable resources, the index, and an invitation to submit ideas for the next edition of this book—ideas for which we will pay you.

My ultimate goal is to have this book—this resource—quickly and easily become your handy companion whenever you need some on-the-spot guidance and advice from other moms who have found their way out of the dark.

To ensure that this resource becomes that handy companion, I recommend that you do the following:

1. WRITE *in this book.*

    Write in this book whenever in using a tip or hint found in these pages you find a way to make it even more successful for you. Write notes as reminders for yourself.

    When you discover a hint or tip of your own, write it down in the appropriate section. Blank pages have been included at the end of each chapter in Section One and at the end of Section

Mom to Mom . . .

Two just for this purpose. Then write the tip's topic and page number in the index.

2. *Use this book as a "filing cabinet" for the great ideas that you come across.*

Clip and save other great hints and tips that you find in the newspapers and magazines that you read. Write on pieces of paper the hints and tips that you hear from other mothers and read in other sources. Then tape those clippings and notes at the end of the appropriate chapter and section on the blank pages provided for that purpose.

Write in the hint's topic in the index at the back of the book and include its page number. In that way, you'll always be able to easily locate it. You might also want to "flag" each of those tips and hints by writing somewhere in the pages of its chapter or section a word or phrase that would remind you of it taped elsewhere in the book.

Do *not* worry about spoiling the book's appearance or its "new look." Do whatever you can to mold this resource into a companion that you can't manage without.

Throughout this book you will find many suggestions on books and videos that are especially helpful. They are all listed in the Bibliography in the back of this book with ordering information, when appropriate. For example, although most books are available at the library or at a bookstore, some are only available from La Leche League International or some other source. Consequently, that information is provided in the Bibliography.

I sincerely hope that this resource will give you a tremendous amount of help, support, and encouragement. I wish you all the joy and delight that being a mommy can bring. And, as you cuddle your beautiful little miracle, keep in mind the following thought that was shared with me soon after our little one was born:

"If I Had Only Known..."

Your work will wait while you show your child the rainbow...
but
the rainbow won't wait while you do your work.

Mom to Mom . . .

SECTION ONE

PREGNANCY THROUGH INFANCY

1

Pregnancy—Healthy, Comfortable, and Joy-Full

*A baby is a gift of life
born of the wonder of love,
a little bit of eternity
sent from the Father above,
giving a new dimension
to the love between husband and wife
and putting an added meaning
to the wonder and mystery of life.*[1]

What a conglomeration of mixed emotions you experience at the confirmation of your pregnancy! You may feel boundless delight, you may feel awe in the miracle that's taking place within you, you may feel concern about being a parent . . . the *best* parent, and you may feel bewilderment over just how to prepare—yourself, your marriage, your home, your life. Everyone beams, "How wonderful!" and then they add, "How *different* your life is going to be!"

"Where do I begin? *How* do I begin?" Have you heard these questions echo in your mind? I'm sure you have—I did and every other first-time mother did, too. We all share the same thoughts, the same fears, the same excitement. Yet you are unique and different and these thoughts and experiences are truly uncharted territory for you.

In this chapter and the next, you will find many suggestions to help you enjoy this time before your little one arrives, to help you organize yourself and get you started on your way.

Mom to Mom . . .

Highly Recommended Reading and Resources . . .

You will find that one of the most exciting activities during your pregnancy will be the reading that you can do. Not only can you prepare yourself for nurturing and handling your baby, but through books and videos on pregnancy, you will also be able to visualize what is happening with your baby as it is growing and developing inside of you.

A Child Is Born by Axel Ingelman-Sundberg

> Published in 1965, some of the photographs of expectant parents may seem a bit antiquated. The value that I found in having this paperback on our shelf during our pregnancy was having incredible pictures of a baby's development to look at, marvel at, and be awed by. The pictures are phenomenal and it meant so much to us to be able to look at them and know approximately what our baby was looking like at various stages of development in the womb.

What to Expect When You're Expecting by Arlene Eisenberg, Heidi Eisenberg Murkoff, and Sandee Eisenberg Hathaway, R.N.

> This is another excellent book that guides you through your pregnancy by answering some common questions you may have that don't seem to be answered anywhere else. It even includes a full section of answers to questions that fathers-to-be generally ask.

What to Eat When You're Expecting by Arlene Eisenberg, Heidi Eisenberg Murkoff, and Sandee Eisenberg Hathaway, R.N.

> One of the things we all are very much aware of when we first become pregnant is that our diet must be healthy. But, does that mean an egg a day? *Must* we drink milk four times a day if we can't tolerate it? How many calories must we consume to feed our baby but not become as big as a circus tent? The questions are endless, yet this book will answer them all. It wasn't available for my first pregnancy, but I used it faithfully during my second pregnancy and found it to be a priceless guide.

Pregnancy—Healthy, Comfortable, and Joy-Full...

The Complete Handbook of Pregnancy by George B. Feldman, M.D., with Anne Felshman

> For me, this was an indispensable handbook during my pregnancy. Its information is uniquely organized by stages: preconception, the first days of pregnancy (weeks 1-6), early days (weeks 6-13), on through labor, delivery, and first weeks following birth. It is well researched, easy to read, and the many illustrations are excellent.

Lovestart Prebirth Bonding by Evelyn Marnie

> Eva Marnie, a registered nurse and the author of this book, was our wonderful LaMaze instructor. Not only did she give us direction and support for the birth experience, but she also provided us with a wealth of information about prebirth bonding, a subject in which she has done considerable research. Several of those in our class—both fathers and mothers—made the comment that they wished they had known more about prebirth bonding long before the eighth month of their pregnancy.
>
> *Lovestart* is an excellent book, it will give you some valuable insight, and it will give both you and your husband a feeling of involvement with your baby, long before it is born.

The Pregnancy Exercise Book by Barbara Dale and Johanna Roeber

> Exercise and stretching have never been so important as they are now during your pregnancy. That doesn't mean that you immediately begin to log a six-mile jog around your neighborhood each and every day! It does mean that a healthy exercise routine that you and your doctor agree to is a must for you and for your baby. There are a number of helpful exercise guides for pregnancy on the market, but this one was the one I used and found it to provide especially sound guidance.

Mom to Mom...

While Waiting—A Prenatal Guidebook by George E. Verrilli, M.D. and Anne Marie Mueser, Ed.D.

> This relatively short book is packed with good information. It gives excellent information on working with your doctor, how your baby grows, keeping healthy and fit, and labor and delivery. It also provides a helpful alphabetical listing with brief explanations and simple guidelines on topics about which many women have questions. Although you will probably want to read other books on pregnancy and the birthing process as well, *this is an excellent first book.*

The Miracle of Life, video produced by NOVA

> This 60-minute video takes you on an incredible journey through the human body as a new life begins. Viewers can actually see what happens at the moment of conception, and follow the development of the embryo and fetus, until finally, a baby is born. This Emmy award-winning segment from Nova is beautifully done and it will be of special interest to you as new parents, as it was to us. (It can be borrowed from many local libraries or can be ordered from the La Leche League. See the Bibliography for details.)

As you are probably aware, there is a growing interest in childbirth at home. Several of the mothers who offered their suggestions for creating this resource have experienced home birth. One of them suggests the following:

> *An excellent source for natural childbirth at home is* <u>Childbirth at Home</u> *by Mrs. Marion Sousa. This book is my favorite and prepared me for a relaxed, natural pregnancy and delivery. It answers many questions for the "first time" mom and assured me that childbirth was nothing to fear.*
>
> Linda Bannister
Cotati, California

Pregnancy—Healthy, Comfortable, and Joy-Full . . .

Dressing the Part . . .

Although maternity means the expense of a new wardrobe, the suggestions below may help you get the most from the dollars you spend:

Undies

Bras	Buy new bras as you grow. Depending on your size, you may want to consider a more supportive style such as an underwire. Nursing bras are expensive and aren't necessary until just before your due date.
Panties	Buy panties that are made of soft, absorbent cotton.
Maternity Pantyhose	Until your fourth month, use queen-sized pantyhose. Maternity pantyhose fit best from your fourth month on.
Maternity Slips	Full slips, nylon or cotton, are best. Half-slips tend to be a nuisance.

Wardrobe

- *Buy or sew items that are simple but chic, will easily mix and match as well as easily coordinate with the accessories of your existing wardrobe.*

  Your accessories can be used to make an outfit casual or dressy.

- *Keep the same color scheme that you already use in your existing wardrobe.*

  It helps you keep your personal fashion identity and helps you feel a little less self-conscious about your changing shape.

- *Consider your usual wardrobe needs.*

  What does your work environment require? What does your social life require? What does your leisure life require? Once

Mom to Mom...

you have focused on your true needs, you can work on coordinating a wardrobe that will fit your requirements. Here is a rough guide for you to work with to determine what your needs will be:

Item	Suggested	I need:
Pants/Slacks	2-3	
Skirts	2-3	
Blouses	4	
Blazers	2	
Dresses	2	
Sweaters	2	
Poncho/coat*	1	

* Buy this item only if you will pass through a winter during your pregnancy.

Promoting the Health of You and Your Unborn Baby

- *Follow the "Best-Odds Diet" recommended by the Eisenberg trio as soon as you know you're pregnant.*

  The "Best-Odds Diet" can be found in either of the Eisenberg books—*What to Expect When You're Expecting* or *What to Eat When You're Expecting*. The most complete guidance is given in the second book, since the whole book is dedicated to the subject.

- *Avoid alcohol.*

  A few years ago, the *Journal of the American Medical Association* reported on a ten-year follow-up of children born with fetal alcohol syndrome. The study confirmed that the effects of the mothers' alcohol consumption are long-term. The children included in the study had abnormal facial development while in the womb, which caused misaligned teeth and bites, and problems with their eustachian tube. Intellectually they were defi-

Pregnancy—Healthy, Comfortable, and Joy-Full...

cient and their behavioral and academic problems continued into early adolescence.

... A study conducted in Seattle has demonstrated that even *moderate* drinking of just one alcoholic drink a day can permanently affect a developing baby's mental abilities.[2]

- *Avoid smoking and secondary smoke.*

    The evidence is also clear on the dangers of smoking and secondary smoke. Numerous articles appear in the newspapers and popular magazines that elaborate on the ill effects of smoking and secondary smoke on the unborn child.

- *Use vitamins and drugs (over-the-counter and prescription) with extreme caution. Avoid all non-medical drugs.*

    Many questions that you may have can be answered by an excellent reference guide: *Peace of Mind During Pregnancy* by Christine Kelley-Buchanan. It reviews drugs, chemicals, infections, pollutants, and medical procedures that may cause birth defects. It also provides a listing of resources that can give answers to questions the book itself doesn't answer.

    Remember that many medications change in composition when stored on the shelf and become harmful only with increasing age.

- *Avoid common harmful substances.*

    These are: alcohol (mentioned above), tobacco, *secondary* smoke, marijuana, cocaine, artificial sweeteners,* large doses of vitamin A and C, and Accutane, an acne medication which carries a high risk of causing fetal malformation.

    (*Controversy continues on whether or not artificial sweeteners should be avoided. Before using them, check with your obstetrician.)

- *Be aware of other potential chemical hazards.*[3]

Mom to Mom . . .

For example:
(1) Avoid pumping your own gasoline, if at all possible.
(2) Ask someone else to spray pesticides on your garden or houseplants.
(3) Leave the house if the exterminators arrive.
(4) Postpone painting, remodeling your house, or refinishing furniture.
(5) When using cleaning products, be sure that the rooms are well ventilated.
(6) Avoid cleaning sprays when possible.

- *Find a local hot line for drug and chemical information, keep it handy, and use it whenever you have a question.*

There are many hot lines in the United States that provide pregnant women with information on drug and chemical exposures. To find such a service in your area, ask you obstetrician, local hospital, your state's Department of Public Health or the Science Information Division of the March of Dimes at (914) 428-7100.

- *Be aware of fetal movements from the 28th week on.*

It's a good idea to do a "kick count" each day after the sixth month. A good time to record the first 10 you feel is after the evening meal. A fetus tends to be the most active at that time of day. Doing such a "kick count" involves you in your pregnancy and may be an otherwise unnoticed alarm that could save your baby's life. If you don't notice any movement, contact your obstetrician. Richard W. Swanson, M.D., of the University of Saskatchewan, University Hospital, in Canada, believes that as many as three out of every four non-catastrophic stillbirths could be prevented through such a simple practice.[4]

- *Exercise for your health and the health of your baby, but be sure to follow the guidelines given by the American College of Obstetricians and Gynecologists:*[5]

Pregnancy—Healthy, Comfortable, and Joy-Full...

1. Drink plenty of fluids before, after, and, if necessary, during exercise.

2. Avoid exercise during hot, humid weather or when feverish.

3. Keep your heart rate between 130 and 140 beats per minute, depending on your age. For your own suggested maximum rate, ask your obstetrician.

4. Do not exercise strenuously for longer than 15 minutes at any one session.

5. Avoid any exercise that is performed lying on the back after the completion of the fourth month.

6. Avoid jerky, bouncy movements, as well as either deep flexion or extension of the joints.

7. Include five-minute warm-up and cool-down periods in your exercise routine.

8. Exercise regularly—at least three times a week—rather than sporadically.

Two great exercises that benefit the entire body are swimming and walking. Prior to my pregnancy, walking had fortunately been my favorite form of exercise. I had also heard "via the new-mothers grapevine" that for pregnancy well-being and preparation for delivery, regular walking at a good pace for one's current state of pregnancy was a great way to increase the chances of having a faster, easier delivery. Walking may or may not have had anything to do with it, but I did have a fast, relatively easy delivery!

- *Use regular blankets and comforters rather than electric blankets.*

A study conducted by researchers at the University of Colorado Medical School found that pregnant women who sleep under an electric blanket appear to be more likely to have a miscarriage than those who do not. This included heated water beds as well.

Mom to Mom . . .

> Those who use electric blankets and heated water beds are exposed to low frequency electric and magnetic fields. Such exposure still occurs *even if the blanket is turned off but remains plugged in.*[6]

Concerning Your Dental Health . . .

- *Brush your teeth or at least rinse your mouth with an anti-bacterial mouthwash after each bout of morning sickness.*

  Nausea and vomiting can have a significant effect on the health of your teeth because of acid erosion. If you are prone to frequent bouts of morning sickness, it is especially important that you brush your teeth or rinse your mouth after each bout of sickness.

- *Limit sugary foods as much as possible.*

- *Diligently floss and brush your teeth during pregnancy.*

  > *During pregnancy* [your] *hormone levels increase, particularly the levels of estrogen and progesterone. Due to the higher levels of hormones,* [your] *gums are more readily aggravated by the irritants present in plaque. . . . There is pretty good evidence that the hormones decrease the tissue resistance of the gum to the irritation from the plaque and debris, resulting in an increased amount of gingivitis. . . . If the gingivitis isn't treated, of course, you get bleeding and then this is the lead in to periodontis.*
  >
  > Ronald Gier
  > Professor and Chairman
  > Department of Oral Diagnosis
  > University of Missouri-Kansas City
  > School of Dentistry[7]

Pregnancy—Healthy, Comfortable, and Joy-Full...

- *Visit your dentist <u>very</u> early in your pregnancy for a thorough cleaning which may help prevent the tenderness and inflammation of gums that many women experience.*

Relieving Common Discomforts of Pregnancy...

- *Morning Sickness/Nausea*

    There is something new on the market that is rather revolutionary in helping to alleviate nausea and morning sickness! Acting on information he read in a British medical journal about a pressure point in the wrist (referred to as P6) that seemed to affect feelings of nausea, Dr. Robert Giarratano, an obstetrician in San Diego, designed the Accupreg Bracelet. It's a velcro band with a bead that places pressure on the point on the wrist that seems to affect nausea. In several preliminary studies, the success rate for women wearing one on each wrist appears to be consistently at 80%. The same success rate has been found even with those women who have experienced severe cases of nausea requiring hospitalization.

    If this product interests you, it can be ordered from University Pharmacy by calling (in California) 1-800-445-1373 or (outside California) 1-800-445-4391.

The following suggestions were adapted from some childbirth education literature distributed by Mercy Hospital and Medical Center in San Diego, California:

- *Constipation*
    (1) Exercise regularly.
    (2) Increase fluid intake. (water, milk, juices)
        Drink at least two quarts—8-10 glasses—daily.
    (3) Increase fiber foods such as whole grain breads, cereals, pasta, fresh vegetables, fruit, and dried fruit.
        Be sure to include prunes, dates, and/or figs in your diet.

Mom to Mom . . .

    (4) Eat regular meals.

    (5) Give yourself a *regular* time for a bowel movement every day.

- *Heartburn* (mid to late pregnancy)

  (1) Eat several small meals throughout the day rather than three big ones.

  (2) Eat slowly and relax.

  (3) Limit fats and fried foods which are hard to digest.

  (4) Avoid spicy foods.

  (5) Wear loosely fitting clothes.

  (6) Don't lie down immediately after eating.

  When you do lie down, lie on your side to help the stomach empty.

- *Hemorrhoids* (mid to late pregnancy)

  (1) Prevent constipation.

  (2) Take frequent warm, shallow baths.

  (3) Use cold compresses which will decrease the swelling.

  (4) Sit on a "donut" pillow.

  (5) Keep the area lubricated with a cream or gel (eg., baby oil) to prevent dryness and keep the area from cracking.

- *Shortness of Breath* (mid to late pregnancy)

  (1) Avoid strenuous activity and rest frequently while climbing stairs, etc.

  (2) If reclining, prop your upper body with several pillows.

  (3) Relieve this discomfort with the "rib cage stretch:"

      (a) Stand with your arms at your side.

      (b) Swing your arms up while crossing them in front of your body and then form a circular motion over your head.

Pregnancy—Healthy, Comfortable, and Joy-Full...

(c) Stop the movement when your arms are at shoulder height.

(d) With your thumbs pointing back, swing your arms back slowly three times.

(e) Then extend your arms directly in front of your body and return them to your side.

(f) Repeat three to five times, as needed.

- *Varicose Veins* (mid to late pregnancy)

    (1) Prop your feet up for 10 minutes, two to three times per day.

    (2) Avoid standing for long periods of time. When standing, move about frequently.

    (3) Avoid crossing your legs at the knee *or* at the ankles.

    (4) Wear support stockings.

    Be sure to put them on *before* arising and remove them *after* retiring.

    (5) Never wear elastic garters or knee high or ankle high stockings.

    (6) Do leg exercises daily.
    They will help your blood to circulate better.

Traveling While Pregnant...

General:

- *Check with your doctor on the advisability of your trip.*

    Give him/her all pertinent information as to the mode of transportation, length of trip, and expected stresses. For example, are you planning 12-hour working days... or plenty of relaxation by the pool?

- *Send for these free brochures:*

    "Travel During Pregnancy" (p-055) and "Seat Belt Use During Pregnancy" (p-018) by writing to The American College of

Mom to Mom . . .

Obstetricians and Gynecologists, Resource Center, 409 12th Street, S.W., Washington, D.C. 20024-2188.

These handy brochures will provide information on different types of travel and comfortable use of safety belts during pregnancy.

- *For motion sickness, use club soda or bottled water to relieve nausea . . . or use a medication **approved by your doctor**.*

- *Try to alternate days filled with activity and busy-ness with days of relaxation.*

Due to your pregnancy, you will probably tire more quickly. It's also a good idea to plan on resting for an hour or two each afternoon. You'll enjoy your trip so much more if you're not sluggish, irritable, and "washed-out" due to fatigue . . . and so will your traveling companion!

- *Allow plenty of time between connecting flights and trains.*

From personal experience, it isn't any fun to run for close connections when carrying/pulling luggage while several months pregnant. It's not only exhausting but the strain can be worrisome.

By Car:

- *Always use a safety belt, regardless of the distance.*

The greatest percentage of accidents occur within three miles of our homes, so it's wise to always "buckle up." Basically, the shoulder harness should fit snugly across your shoulders, between your breasts. The lap belt should be placed under your tummy.

- *Plan frequent stops for leg-stretching and restroom visits if you are planning to drive or ride a long distance.*

Pregnancy—Healthy, Comfortable, and Joy-Full...

By Air:

- *The second trimester (4-7 months) is generally best for travel.*

  The first trimester tends to be "rocky" for some women due to nausea and fatigue. The second trimester tends to be the most comfortable for most women, and the third trimester can be uncomfortable due to increasing size and fatigue.

- *Check with the airline about its policy on carrying pregnant passengers.*

  Domestic airlines generally do not allow pregnant women to fly who are past 36 weeks gestation. For foreign airlines, it is 35 weeks. Many also require written permission from the doctor that includes estimated due date.

- *Take written permission from your doctor even if you are only at 29 or 30 weeks gestation.*

  Airline personnel may think a woman *looks* 35 weeks pregnant, when in fact she's only 29 or 30 weeks pregnant. Consequently, the only way you can prove you're not 35 weeks pregnant is with a written statement from your doctor. Remember, an airline can elect to *not* carry you if they feel you are a risk and further along in your pregnancy than you say.

- *Ask for an aisle seat in the non-smoking section when making reservations.*

  All domestic flights of six hours or less are designated non-smoking. Longer flights, however, especially overseas, still allow smoking.

  Being in a non-smoking section and in an aisle seat are important for several reasons:

  (1) You will reduce your exposure to smoke and carbon monoxide.

Mom to Mom . . .

    (2) You may want to make frequent trips to the restroom.

    (3) You will find it easier to get up for some leg-stretching during the flight which is necessary for circulation.

- *Get plenty of rest before the flight.*

- *Wear loose, comfortable clothing and flat or low-heeled shoes.*

- *At check-in, ask if a bulkhead seat or seat by an exit in the non-smoking section is available and, if so, ask to have your seat changed.*

These seats often cannot be reserved ahead of time, as they are reserved for passengers with special circumstances. If you are going on a long, non-stop flight, these seats are preferable, however, because they provide greater leg room. However, bulkheads and some seats by exits have only overhead bins for your carry-ons.

- *Avoid removing your shoes—your feet may swell and it will be difficult to get them back on.*

- *Eat lightly to avoid air sickness and carry a small bag of cheese, bland crackers, and fruit in your travel bag to help combat nausea or pangs of hunger.*

- *Drink plenty of fluid before and during the flight because the pressurized cabin causes dehydration.*

Sometimes it's not possible to get up for a drink (and leg-stretching!) due to air turbulence or carts in the aisle. Consequently, it's a good idea to take along one or two small plastic bottles of mineral water in your carry-on bag.

- *Wear your seat belt below your "fetal bulge."*

Pregnancy—Healthy, Comfortable, and Joy-Full...

Preparing a Sibling for the Arrival of the Little One....

Jan Sundblad, a mother of three girls in San Diego, writes:

> *We always said that they were going to be "a big sister"—not that I was pregnant. We also said, "Daddy and I are having a baby," so that they would have a feeling of our being a family unit rather than individuals.*
>
> *Also, the girls went to the doctor's office with me and were able to hear their sister's heartbeat—that was a special time. Plus my Ob-Gyn was great with the girls. He was willing to take the time to answer their questions.*

Small children who are three years or older will be excited, but will also have some interesting questions. An excellent "lift the flap" book to share with them is *See How You Grow* by Dr. Patricia Pearse and Edwina Riddell. It answers their questions in a clear, gentle way. It doesn't just stop with "where do babies come from," or "how does the baby live in there?" It also goes into questions such as, "What will I look like when I'm grown up?" and "What makes us grow?" I highly recommend it!

Potpourri of Other Great Ideas...

- *Begin a journal soon after you discover you're pregnant.*

    Such a journal will be a priceless gift for your child when he or she is an adult. And, perhaps an even greater benefit, you will enjoy brousing through it throughout your little one's childhood and certainly when he or she is an adult. You'll enjoy reliving many of the delightful things that happened that you would only remember if they were recorded in a journal. What can you write? Below is a list of suggestions to get yourself started.

Mom to Mom . . .

(1) Describe your feelings and those of your husband when you discovered your pregnancy and mark the date when you first knew for sure.

(2) Describe the reactions of various family members when they heard the news.

(3) Tell how the news was announced to the grandparents-to-be and others.

(4) Describe your thoughts and feelings as your pregnancy continues.

(5) If the holiday season passes during your pregnancy, describe things that included the baby yet-to-arrive.

Just after we opened packages on Christmas morning, my husband Tom was talking long-distance with one of our relatives. I overheard him say, "Maryanna received more gifts than we did, and she isn't even born yet!" (We had already named her since we knew the sex of our baby in advance.)

(6) When you write your journal, write it to the child, as though you are actually talking to him or her.

For example, I started what is now a very thick journal for our daughter Maryanna, with these words:

November 11, 1985

These last few months have been very special for us, little one. We still have more than three and a half months until we truly meet you for the first time, yet you have been very much an exciting part of our lives for the last several months. Several very important dates in your life have already passed, even before you are born!

Pregnancy—Healthy, Comfortable, and Joy-Full...

I then went on to tell her about those important dates... July 5, 1985, when a home pregnancy test gave the positive result and what our feelings and reactions were; September 17, 1985, when I had a sonogram and saw her fully formed and moving about, even though I was hardly showing....

Maryanna is only four years old now, but already I love reading and re-reading the early pages of her "book of life."

Another mom had this to say:

> *I kept a journal of my pregnancy. I had more profound thoughts during those nine months than the rest of my life all together! It's a treasure for me and it will be a treasure for Katie later on, whether or not she becomes a mother.*
>
> Terri Ciosek
> Poway, California

- *Call 1-800-MOM-4-NEWS for important information on nutrition, iron, weight gain, morning sickness, and food cravings.*

This toll-free hot line for pregnant women is sponsored by MCN: *The American Journal of Maternal /Child Nursing* and Reid-Rowell, the makers of Zenate, a prenatal vitamin supplement.

- *Begin the bonding process with your baby long before your baby is born.*

Research has confirmed that fetuses feel, hear, see, taste, and perhaps even smell for several months before birth. Consequently many expectant parents spend time every day talking and singing to their unborn baby, as well as playing enjoyable, pleasant music for it. Many mothers concentrate on their thoughts and emotions during their pregnancy, believing that they too carry across the placenta.

Mom to Mom . . .

An excellent book on this topic which I included in the Recommended Resources section at the beginning of this chapter is *Lovestart Prebirth Bonding* by Eve Marnie, R.N., and Certified Birth Instructor. It will give you and your husband some valuable insight into the research done and suggest some things that the two of you can do during pregnancy to begin developing an important bond with your baby.

Another mom suggests the following:

> *Read about prenatal life: <u>The Secret Life of the Unborn Child</u>; <u>Imprints: The Lifelong Effects of the Birth Experience</u> by Arthur Janor; and <u>Babies Remember Birth</u> by David Chamberlain.*
>
> Eileen Carroll
> La Jolla, California

Another mom writes:

> *My husband Harry did his own type of bonding before our girls were born, especially when they started getting active and kicking. We would lie in bed and he would push on my stomach and the baby would kick back. We all had fun with this but it made Harry feel a relationship with the baby I was carrying. The two older girls were able to do the same with our youngest. Each pregnancy was a family affair—everyone was made to feel important.*
>
> Jan Sundblad
> San Diego, California

- *Be thoroughly familiar with the birthing process.*

  The more familiar you are with the birthing process, the more natural it will seem and the more relaxed you will be with the entire experience. Attend birthing classes and read all you can about the birthing process.

Pregnancy—Healthy, Comfortable, and Joy-Full...

Twenty-five to 30% of all deliveries are now by caesarean section, a much higher percentage than may be necessary. However, fetal monitoring is now often used, and the "strip" that it produces doesn't give information that is exactly "black and white." Some situations to which it alerts medical personnel may or may not be risky if left to vaginal delivery, but as an obstetrician has said, "It can be a hard call, and I'm not willing to risk a baby's health or the mother's health if a serious risk appears to be present." He continues by saying, "We [obstetricians] no longer are willing to do difficult, high forceps deliveries because of possible injury to both mother and baby, and the risk with Breech presentations is four times greater when delivered vaginally. And, very premature babies—under 34 weeks—should be delivered by C-section to prevent damage to the fetal head."

Obstetricians in general believe VBACs (vaginal birth after caesarean) are fine in certain situations. For example, VBAC can be permitted if a woman has had only one C-section in the past. The incidence of a rupture of the uterus due to the scar is less than 1%. Consequently, most women who have had a previous C-section can safely undergo a vaginal delivery. However, the incidence of uterus rupture may be greater after two or more C-sections, and therefore, under those circumstances, VBACs are not recommended.

Because the possibility of uterus rupture does exist for a woman who has had one previous C-section, even as slight a possibility as it may be, she must be carefully monitored for her well-being and that of her baby.

If the possibility of a caesarean delivery concerns you, do ask your obstetrician for his caesarean rate and if it seems high to you, ask him why. If you have had a previous C-section, ask your obstetrician what his/her opinions are concerning VBAC.

There are several books available that can give you a wide perspective of caesarean deliveries. Eileen Carroll of La Jolla,

Mom to Mom...

California, suggests that women read *Silent Knife—Caesarean Prevention and Vaginal Birth After a Caesarean* written by Nancy Wainer Cohen and Lois Estner. The La Leche League catalogue describes the contents as follows:

Painstakingly researched and passionately written, this landmark book discusses the current caesarean epidemic, vaginal birth after caesarean, and medical interventions that interfere with natural birth. It also suggests ways to heal the psychological pain of past birth experiences.

---

[1] Author unknown—this poem was copied from a card received into a personal journal without noting an author or company.
[2] *Family Circle Magazine,* July 1989.
[3] Jane M. Healy, *Your Child's Growing Mind: A Guide to Learning and Brain Development from Birth to Adolescence,* Doubleday, 1987.
[4] Charles Orrico, "April Almanac," *Parents Magazine,* April 1989, p. 16.
[5] Marina Raith, "April Almanac," *Parents Magazine,* April 1986, p. 16.
[6] Barry Blackman, "December Almanac," *Parents Magazine,* December 1987, p. 17.
[7] As quoted in an article by Tammy M. Swanson, "Dental Care in Pregnancy," *Baby Talk,* November 1986, p. 38.

Pregnancy—Healthy, Comfortable, and Joy-Full . . .

Clips and Notes . . .

Mom to Mom . . .

Clips and Notes . . .

2

Preparing for the Precious Arrival . . .

*Your baby's hands will touch so much...
your lives, your hearts,
your love.*[1]

Preparing for your little one involves so much . . . as you've already discovered! In the first chapter you read many suggestions about preparing you and your husband for your little one's arrival as well as about the personal things that you can do to take care of yourself and your baby during your pregnancy.

Now it's time to focus on preparing your home. In this chapter, you'll find a multitude of ideas on furniture and equipment that are needed . . . and not needed, clothing and linen that are needed . . . and not needed, on selecting a pediatrician . . . on all sorts of things that you will want to do before your baby arrives.

At the end of this chapter you'll find a helpful shopping list that includes the essentials that you'll want to have on hand. The best time to begin shopping is two months before your baby's expected arrival. By starting two months in advance, you will have some time to comparison shop, pick up things at a leisurely pace, and feel relaxed and completely prepared at least two weeks before your baby's due date. What a relief it is to know that you're prepared, even if your little one should decide to surprise you and come a few days early!

Reading "Musts" Before Your Little One Arrives . . .

Reading some of the books below and browsing through the others listed will give you not only some valuable information and help you

Mom to Mom . . .

prepare . . . , but, if you are a new mother-to-be, they will also give you a tremendous boost in self-confidence for this new experience.

Reading "musts" include one on the day-to-day care of a baby so you'll have some idea of what is involved and one on infant/child development which will give you a feeling for what to expect and what will be needed for normal development.

Your Child from Birth to Five Years of Age by Penelope Leach

> This is a wonderful book that covers both "musts" mentioned above. It was and continues to be one of our most frequently consulted books and it was often mentioned by many other parents who contributed to this resource. It is a comprehensive, authoritative, and outstandingly sensitive guide to child care from birth to age five. What I especially appreciated was its meeting my concern for both the physical and psychological well-being of our child. Its contents progress from birth through the newborn and settled baby, to the older baby, the toddler, and the pre-school child. Its index is an incredible A to Z reference in itself and concludes with an extremely helpful chart on playthings for the newborn on through preschool age.

Your Child from Birth to Adolescence by Penelope Leach

> This is another must for any family bookshelf. As the book cover of the 712-page guide suggests, it is:
>
>> *. . . an A to Z compendium of vital information and comfort for every mother and father—from new parents bringing home their first infant to parents of adolescents soon to strike out on their own. . . . Penelope Leach's full and specific advice always reflects the practice of leading medical authorities, as well as her own immense expertise and experience as a child psychologist, her extraordinary sensitivity to the feelings of both child and parent, and her grasp of*

Preparing for the Precious Arrival...

> *realities—financial, professional, and social—of life today . . . . Just about every problem a parent can face is discussed in this book.*

The overview may sound exaggerated, but it's not. It's a reference that every family should have readily available.

Nighttime Parenting—How to Get Your Baby and Child to Sleep by William Sears, M.D.

This book was invaluable to me, but what a help it would have been had I read it *before* our little one arrived! Unfortunately, I "bumped" into it when Maryanna was 15 months old, but it still was immensely helpful. In *Nighttime Parenting*, Dr. Sears explains how babies sleep differently than adults, how sharing sleep can help the whole family sleep better, and how to help little ones sleep more peacefully.

The Fussy Baby—How to Bring Out the Best in Your High Need Child by William Sears, M.D.

Parents of a fussy baby will need this one within reach! Again, it is one that probably should be read before your baby arrives. I wish I had! Should you have a newborn who spends most of her waking hours crying, you will have a better idea of how to handle it rather than becoming frazzled and not knowing where to turn for advice. Dr. Sears provides a guide to interpreting a baby's cries and includes chapters on coping with colic, feeding, fathering, soothing, and avoiding maternal burnout. He includes plenty of support and reassurance as well as day-to-day survival tips.

The First Three Years of Life by Burton White, M.D.

Although this book tends to be rather academic, I found that it gave me valuable reassurance and encouragement, especially where my instincts were concerned. It also is an excellent introduction to each phase that a baby enters and suggests a

Mom to Mom...

variety of things to do with a baby in various phases of development.

Not having been around babies much at all prior to our baby's birth, I had no idea of what I could or should do to encourage her curiosity. You'll be surprised at how concerned you will be about the boredom your little one must be experiencing! I would see my baby lying on her back or her tummy and I'd worry about her being bored! Dr. White provides all kinds of reassurance—suggesting that everything is new to your baby, so let her simply "sit in" on what you're doing. And, perhaps most important to me, he gave validity to my own instincts such as picking up and carrying my baby as much as she needed was not only O.K., but essential, and that letting a baby "cry it out" was quite detrimental.

The Womanly Art of Breastfeeding, Fourth Edition-Revised 1987 by La Leche League International

I found this book to be the most helpful in preparing for as well as in managing breastfeeding. This latest edition is especially encouraging, nurturing and helpful. It has a new easy-to-access format that makes reading easier and quick reference a breeze! It is filled with the latest information on positioning your baby at the breast, avoiding sore nipples, breastfeeding and working, and breastfeeding when your baby is jaundiced. Two chapters are devoted to breastfeeding in special situations, such as breastfeeding twins, a premature baby or, as in my case, a baby with slow initial weight gain.

Infants and Mothers by T. Berry Brazelton, M.D.

T. Berry Brazelton, M.D., has the best instincts about children and parenting of anyone I have ever read. He approaches children from a developmental point of view, noting that children reach the normal developmental stages at various times and in vari-

Preparing for the Precious Arrival . . .

ous ways, and that their inborn personalities have a lot to do with how they behave and develop. This book was my greatest joy and comfort!

Priscilla Cowell
Portland, Oregon

The First Twelve Months of Life by Frank and Teresa Caplan

This book is a must for every new parent. It includes plenty of photographs and explains a child's development in the first 12 months, divided into "monthly" chapters. This book helps a parent to see the child's progress even in the first two weeks. I was able to see the accomplishments from day #1 and felt much more in tune with my little ones. Also by the same authors: <u>The Second Twelve Months of Life</u> *and* <u>The Third Twelve Months of Life</u>.

Linda Bannister
Cotati, California

"Must" Activities Before the Little One Arrives . . .

- *Attend classes in Baby Care, First Aid, and infant/child CPR given by a local Red Cross chapter and some local hospitals.*

- *Decide whether or not you plan to breastfeed.*

"Breast is best," even if you plan to return to work soon after the baby's delivery or even if you've been told to expect twins! If you are leaning toward *not* breastfeeding, please delay your final decision until you have done some of the recommended reading. Breastfeeding provides many, many benefits, not only for its primary little beneficiary but for you as well.

49

Mom to Mom . . .

- *If you plan to breastfeed your baby, attend a prenatal lactation class sponsored by the hospital where you plan to deliver or given by a certified lactation consultant in your area.*

Had I supplemented my extensive reading on breastfeeding with a prenatal lactation class, I would have been much more confident from the minute our baby was born. I would have definitely known "fact from fiction" when nurses tried to be "helpful" during those few hours that we were at the hospital.

For example, I was told:

(1) "Be sure to give her (my baby) these bottles of glucose water—the doctor ordered it."

Without telling them directly, I refused and just didn't do it because all of my reading had told me otherwise. But, my decision sure made me feel guilty . . . after all, doesn't the *pediatrician* know best?! And, isn't this my first baby? What do I know?!

(2) "Don't keep your baby in bed with you—she should be in her glass bassinet from the nursery!"

Whenever the nurse would leave my room, I'd "sneak" my baby back into bed with me. In the bassinet, she cried and cried. In bed with me, she generally was quiet and would even nod off to sleep! But the guilties would creep into my thoughts . . . "What do I know? I've never done this before! Aren't they the nurses who have worked with hundreds of babies???"

(3) "Don't nurse more than 2-3 minutes on each side every two and a half to three hours—you'll get sore nipples if you do!"

I had read that in order for my milk to come in as quickly as possible, I must nurse my newborn as much and as often

Preparing for the Precious Arrival . . .

as she wanted and *needed* me to. I had also read that sore nipples are almost always a result of poor positioning, not from nursing too often or too much. But again, the guilties crept through my thoughts . . . . "What do *I* know? I've never done this before!"

(4) "Here, use this pacifier if your baby cries more often than you can feed her."

A nurse even made a pacifier for me to use, using a baby bottle nipple! Again, since I thought she was more in the know than I, I used it . . . for a few seconds . . . but something just didn't feel right! I then immediately brought my little one back into bed with me for nursing and cuddling! But the guilties that I experienced were a burden I didn't need and certainly didn't want!

Fortunately, I was quite determined to be successful because I was totally convinced that breastfeeding was the best for our baby. But difficulties did arise due to misinformation from the nurses at the hospital *and* misinformation from a pediatrician. Fortunately, too, my Lamaze class instructor had recommended that any mother having difficulty with breastfeeding should seek out Wellstart, an organization staffed by health professionals specializing in breastfeeding here in San Diego. Thanks to that advice and to Wellstart, my difficulties were quickly and simply corrected. Had our instructor not mentioned Wellstart, I would never have even guessed that such a service existed.

Wellstart trains health professionals in the management of breastfeeding. There are teams who have been trained for each of the public health regions in our country. Each team consists of a physician, nurse, and dietician. If you want to find health professionals in your area who specialize in breastfeeding, contact one of those on the team listed for your region for a referral. (See Regional Listings on pages 397-402.)

Mom to Mom...

> *Note:* Because of the growing interest in breastfeeding, the number of lactation consultants is also growing. To be sure that the guidance they give you will be accurate, be sure that they are both *certified* lactation consultants and *licensed* health professionals.

- *Attend a Lamaze Birthing Class at your delivery hospital or other birth facility to be totally familiar with the birth process and with your hospital or birthing center.*

- *Identify another mother/couple who will be having a baby at the same time or within a month of yours.*

   Good sources for such a contact are your Lamaze class, a couple in your neighborhood or circle of friends, or your church.

   > *No one else can relate to what a mother with a newborn is going through unless they are there at the same time. Time tempers one's memory and even a mother of a one-year-old or six-month-old forgets the pain, fatigue, frustration, and overwhelming responsibility of those first days and weeks. A mother of a new baby needs someone she can talk with (especially over the phone). As a couple, parents of a new baby need someone to meet, eat with, and "play" with to help them understand that they are not alone in their new adjustment.*
   >
   > Joanne Soukup
   > Holland, Michigan

- *Attend monthly La Leche League meetings before your baby arrives.*

   The meetings are very supportive and helpful. Women who are pregnant as well as women with babies, toddlers, and preschoolers attend. The meetings are run by a trained La Leche League

Preparing for the Precious Arrival...

leader and each meeting is dedicated to a specific topic. If any problems arise with breastfeeding once your baby arrives, you may call your leader immediately for assistance.

There are over 3,500 groups meeting every month all around the world. Consequently, the chances are excellent that there are one or more groups in your area. Meetings are generally publicized in the newspapers, and in the larger cities, La Leche League is listed in the white pages of the phone directory. If there is no listing, you can also try the maternity wards of larger hospitals.

If you have difficulty finding a La Leche League Leader in your area, write to La Leche League International, P.O. Box 1209, Franklin Park, IL 60131-8209 or call (718) 455-7730 between 9:00 AM and 3:00 PM, central time.

- *Find and join a mother's support group before your baby arrives.*

One mother suggests:

> *After having my first baby and deciding to be a "stay-at-home" mom, it was a very lonely and isolating experience. I was new to San Diego, all of my friends were working people, so I knew no one to socialize with during the day, as well as no one to share the joys, concerns, frustrations, etc., in being a new mom. It took me six months to find a wonderful parenting group and infant gym class which I joined. Both allowed me to meet other moms with kids the same age. I still have these wonderful friendships four years later. I met so many moms who have shared my feelings of isolation those first few months. I would love to tell everyone that there are so*

Mom to Mom . . .

> *many parenting groups out there and to join one for support and encouragement.*
>
> Lori Buschmann
> San Diego, California

- *Know exactly what you want and have your obstetrician write those wishes down in your record <u>before</u> your enter the hospital for your delivery.*

Is your obstetrician clear on your desires regarding medication and anesthesia?

Is he and the hospital staff well informed about your desires to breastfeed your baby *with no water given in the nursery?*

Will you be able to nurse your baby as soon as it's born, barring no significant birth difficulties?

Will you be able to keep your baby with you, even if you must go to a "recovery room" for an hour or two?

All the answers to the above questions should be "yes." If not, you may be very unhappy and unable to do anything about correcting the situation after you're at the hospital and in labor.

Consider these comments:

> *While I was pregnant, I made a special point of discussing with the obstetrician what type of anesthetic I wanted. I wanted as little anesthesia as possible, and I wanted to avoid any kind of spinal. I had the doctor <u>write down</u> my requests in my record, so that no matter who was in attendance during labor and delivery, my wishes would be honored. In both instances (two different babies, two different cities, two different doctors) the attending physician spoke of and honored my request in*

Preparing for the Precious Arrival . . .

> *the delivery room. I have heard many stories from mothers who have not discussed the issue and especially who did not ask to have their wishes written down, and the results were not so good! I feel this was really helpful—it's also important that your husband know what you'd like. Sometimes a steady mind is needed during labor and the mother isn't always the one who is the coolest!*
>
> Ann Gaines
Nevada City, California

> *You don't have to let the nurses take your baby to the nursery. You can arrange <u>ahead of time</u> for the baby to be weighed, bathed, examined, etc., right in your room.*
>
> Eileen Carroll
La Jolla, California

- *Enroll a big brother or sister-to-be in one of the excellent sibling classes that are now offered by many hospitals.*

One mother suggests:

> *Check with the hospital where you are delivering and see if they offer a "Sibling Class." It's well worth the time and money. I personally can recommend the class at Sharp Hospital here in San Diego. They make the new sister/brother feel so important and special!!*
>
> Lori Buschmann
San Diego, California

- *Arrange for a diaper service, at least for the first three to six months.*

See the explanation under diapers in the Clothing section below.

Mom to Mom . . .

Selecting a Pediatrician . . .

The pediatrician you select is a very important partner in caring for your little one. And the relationship you establish with him or her must be built on mutual respect and trust. You must believe that the advice you are receiving is the best available, and that he/she trusts you as a parent.

To ensure that you and your husband are the most comfortable and you receive the support that you need, consider following the process below:

- *Identify those things that are most important to you.*

    For example:

    * Are you committed to making a go of breastfeeding?

    * What kind of support do you foresee yourself needing? Will the doctor and/or his/her staff provide that kind of support? This includes the doctor's and staff's willingness to teach you as well as to tell you about what is needed.

    * How do you want your little one examined?

    I ask this question because the most gentle and most effective way for a pediatrician to examine a baby is with him on his parent's lap where he feels most secure. If he's placed on an examining table away from his parent and the closeness he needs and has become accustomed to, he may be very unhappy, which I guarantee will make you emotionally quite miserable. I learned this one the hard way.

    * How do you want to feel during the appointments?

    Do you want to feel that the doctor is unhurried, willing to answer any and every question? Do you want to feel that he/she is undistracted?

- *Create a list of at least five possible pediatricians.*

    To create such a list, use as many sources for recommendations as you can:

Preparing for the Precious Arrival . . .

(1) Your obstetrician
(2) Lactation consultants

   This is an especially good source because they are particularly aware of those doctors who are sensitive to the needs of infants, babies, and parents.

(3) Friends with young children
(4) Friends of friends who have small children
(5) Families at your church or synagogue
(6) Doctors and nurses whom you may know

It is *absolutely necessary* to select from a list rather than depend on only one recommendation such as from your obstetrician. Had my husband and I followed this advice rather than using our only recommendation from our obstetrician, we wouldn't have had the mismatch that we experienced.

- *Review the list and prioritize it—first, according to recommendations and then second, by location.*

- *Select the top three and call for an interview with each one.*

   Some pediatricians charge for such an interview, others don't. If those that you call *do* charge for the interview, just know that it's money well spent.

- *Interview each of the candidates carefully.*

   This is important for two reasons:

   (1) You will have an opportunity to see the office and get a feel for the atmosphere in which your child may be treated.

   Although you can't judge a doctor solely on the appearance of the office, you may find some important clues on how he/she cares about his/her patients. Is the waiting area pleasant? Are there books and toys that would appeal to various ages? Is the receptionist friendly? Are there separate waiting areas for well and sick children?

Mom to Mom . . .

(2) You will have an opportunity to personally meet the doctor.

Such a meeting is very important, because this doctor may be the person with whom you will share some of your greatest parenting concerns.

Don't be embarrassed to ask questions about anything that is important to you. Remember, a pediatrician is a *consultant* whom you hire and pay for his/her assistance and much needed advice. The doctor is as much a consultant as any other you would hire, such as an accountant, a lawyer, an interior decorator, a tax advisor. . . . If the "fit" isn't right, the relationship can be very uncomfortable.

When Tom and I went in for our first (and only) interview, we had no idea what to ask. After our having made the wrong selection of a pediatrician the first time around, here are some suggestions that may possibly stimulate some ideas for you:

Q: What are your office hours? When the office is closed, how are calls handled—for emergencies and non-emergencies?

If you are a parent who works or will be returning to work, do the office hours include some evenings and limited Saturday hours?

Q: How do you feel about breastfeeding and bottle feeding?

If breastfeeding is important to you and you have done some reading to prepare yourself, you may want to ask some very specific questions about how s/he would handle some difficulties if they should arise.

For example, what if your baby did not gain weight well in the first two or three weeks which might suggest a volume difficulty, how would s/he handle it? If the doctor says that s/he would have you supplement your

Preparing for the Precious Arrival...

breastfeeding, you may want to interview another doctor. If, however, s/he says that there are a variety of reasons for such a problem, such as whether or not a mother is consuming enough calories or whether or not the mother understands the needed frequency of feeding or whether or not the infant is sucking properly and that such a problem would be investigated, *then* you have a doctor who truly supports and believes in breastfeeding.

Q: *How do you examine an infant?*

Infants, babies, and toddlers are often much more calm when held in their parent's lap rather than when examined on a table.

Q: *How do you handle your call-backs? If I have a real concern but it only requires a phone conversation rather than an appointment, how do you handle such calls?*

Some physicians have routine calls answered by their quite knowledgeable nurses and physician's assistants, leaving the more serious matters to be responded to by themselves. If such is the case, then ask:

Q: *For those calls that are returned by you, when do you return them? Within the hour? Within three hours? Whenever you have a break? In the evening?*

Q: *What are your fees?*

Just as important, does the doctor ask you questions during the interview? Your interview should be a comfortable conversation—a time to get a feel for one another. Most important, the physician should draw out some of your feelings about becoming a parent.

After each interview, be sure to write some notes about how you felt specifically and in general . Otherwise, after you have completed all of your interviews and you begin to

Mom to Mom...

make your selection, your memories of those you interviewed may become a big blur.

- *Make your selection.*

    Now that the interviews are complete, how do you make that important selection? Review your notes and think about such things as:
    * Which one made you feel the most comfortable?
    * Which one seemed genuinely interested in you as a parent?
    * Which one made you feel confident?
    * Which one made you feel *secure?*

    A few words to the wise...

    After your baby is born and you have begun to use the selected doctor's services, do *not* feel obligated to stay with that doctor if the *chemistry* is not right. For example, if:
    * From the responses you receive to the questions you ask, you feel that your questions are "stupid," or...
    * You feel that your little one is not getting the doctor's full attention, or...
    * You feel hurried and unable to ask all of the questions you have on your list, or...
    * You have a myriad of other feelings about the developing relationship that aren't quite right...

    Remember: The doctor is a *consultant,* not a partner for life. Return to your list of those doctors you interviewed earlier and have your file transferred to the one who was your second choice! It's absolutely vital that you like, respect, and trust the doctor who is treating your child... and you!

Equipment Needed and Not Needed...

You're now on your last countdown toward that special due date. You have about two months to go and probably are beginning to feel comfortable and excited about buying baby furniture and other necessary equipment. But . . . what kind of crib is best? What equipment is "necessary"? What equipment is *not* necessary? Perhaps the suggestions below will give you the guidance you're looking for.

The Essentials and Some "Almost" Essentials . . .

Bassinet or Cradle and Accessories

Although I'm fudging a little bit since a cradle or a bassinet isn't really an "essential," it definitely is convenient. Like many parents, you will probably prefer to keep your baby close to you in your room for a few weeks or months at night and when you are resting. And, until she is a few months old, you may find it particularly convenient to have a bed that is easy to move from one area to another.

The main considerations are that it be simple, comfortable, and not expensive—it will only be used for three months or so because the baby will quickly grow out of it.

The needed accessories for a bassinet or a cradle are:

(1) Fitted sheets (2)

(2) Lap pads (3) to use in making up the "bed" and one to carry in the diaper bag

(3) Receiving blankets (You can never have too many of these!)

(4) Imitation lambskin mattress pads (2) to make the bed feel very soft and comfortable. They can also be

Mom to Mom . . .

used to cover the mattress in a buggy! These can be easily made, even if you've never dabbled in sewing:

Notions needed:

> Imitation lambskin fabric
> Thread
> Narrow (1/4" or 1/2") elastic

Directions:

These pads are also recommended for the crib, so the directions below include the crib mattress as well.

a. Measure your bassinet mattress and the crib mattress.
b. Buy enough imitation lambskin at a fabric store to make three mattress covers and two bassinet covers.

   Figure your yardage carefully. When at the fabric store, ask for the fabric's width and compute from there. If sewing is "Greek" to you, just ask the clerk to help you figure the needed yardage and to give you instructions on how to cut it into your desired pieces.

c. Cut the fabric into the desired pieces.

The pads for the bassinet/cradle are now complete. They don't require any elastic.

For the crib's mattress pads, continue as follows:

d. Using a tape measure, determine the elastic needed for each corner by

Preparing for the Precious Arrival...

measuring from the top of the mattress, 4" from the corner, down under the mattress to the opposite side:

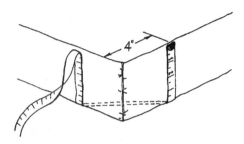

e. On the wrong side of the lamb skin, pin the ends of the elastic tape 4" from the corner on each side and sew:

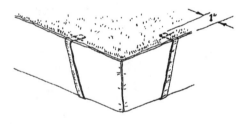

Voilá! Now you have lambskin mattress pads that will make the crib feel heavenly for your little cherub!

Crib and Accessories

There are cribs and then there are cribs! Some are quite functional and relatively inexpensive. Others come with all the bells and whistles of a limousine and are essentially a waste of money.

All that is needed is a simple, safe crib. The "bells and whistles" cribs are those that can be converted to a "junior" bed when the little one has outgrown the

Mom to Mom ...

crib. The slats, footboard, and side drawers (which, incidentally, are inconveniently deep) are simply removed. The chest of drawers can then be used separately. A spring and mattress extension are then added.

At first, this combo seems to save a lot of money in the long run, but it does have several annoying difficulties:

(1) The resulting junior bed is very narrow. Although the bed is lengthened, it remains the width of a crib.

Not only does this mean a very narrow bed, but you then are unable to use such delightful bed accessories as "sleepy" tents and sheets that have inserted inflated rollers as guard rails which are superior to the usual guard rails. And, fitted sheets, even if marked "Junior Bed," never really fit properly.

(2) The mattress extension means that there are two parts to the mattress. When making the bed, it is very difficult, even with a fitted sheet, to do it easily.

(3) The drawers, which are inconveniently deep as mentioned above, continue to be inconveniently deep and really difficult to use. In order to use the entire drawer, it must be pulled out quite a way before the back of the drawer can be reached. This can be a problem with a toddler who is learning to use drawers. There are usually no safety catches to keep them from falling out.

Preparing for the Precious Arrival . . .

When selecting a crib (to buy or to borrow), be sure that it is *safe*. A crib that is either borrowed or bought from a re-sale store is older and may not be as safe as those that are new. Whether you are considering a new, used, or borrowed crib, consider the following:

(1) The slats must be no more than 2 3/8" apart. Slats that are farther apart represent a real danger in that a baby's head could get caught between them.

(2) Decorative cutouts and "spindles" at each corner can be a hazard. Older babies have been known to get their heads caught between the spindle and the upper edge of the crib.

(3) Railings must be secure and made of non-toxic materials. Check the wood and metal hardware. Be sure that they are smooth with no splinters and no sharp or rough edges.

(4) The dropside must lock at the maximum height. The locking devices must be safe and secure and unable to be accidentally released by you or an older baby.

(5) The crib mattress must be the right size for the crib. To check, see if you can fit more than two fingers between the mattress and the crib side—at the top, foot, and sides of the crib. If you can, then the mattress is too small and should not be used.

In addition, look for a crib that offers adjustable mattress height. This feature allows you to lower the mattress as your baby grows and can possibly prevent your little one from falling or climbing out.

Mom to Mom . . .

The needed crib accessories are:

(1) Mattress

Believe it or not, a new crib does not come with a mattress. It must be bought separately.

When making your selection, be sure that the one you choose is firm. A baby, once he can stand, soon learns to jump and bounce on his mattress!

Also, make sure that it is waterproof (triple laminated is best), even though you will be putting a rubber protective pad over it.

(2) Sheets—3 or 4 fitted crib-size sheets

(3) Imitation lambskin mattress pads—3

See instructions on how to make them under Bassinet—Imitation Lambskin Mattress Pads above.

(4) Rubber Sheets—3

The best are the flannel backed rubber sheets. Although your crib mattress will probably be vinyl or otherwise moisture-proof, it's still a good idea to use these for protection.

I also found that if I made the bed in two or three layers (rubber sheet, lambskin pad, fitted sheet, rubber sheet, lambskin pad, fitted sheet, rubber sheet, lambskin pad, fitted sheet) it made changing the crib simple and quick. The crib will often have to be changed because of spit-ups or leaky diapers, so it's helpful to have a new set already on the bed, *especially during the night.*

Preparing for the Precious Arrival . . .

(5) Crib Bumper—1 set

A crib bumper provides a soft padding between the crib's slats, its head and footboards, and your baby. The bumper also protects your baby from drafts. As your baby begins to move around during his sleep, you'll find that he frequently will scoot toward the head or corner of the bed until his head bumps against it.

Although they come in both cloth and vinyl, the cloth type is more soft and comfortable and can easily be laundered and dried.

And, when selecting a set, be sure that the bumpers tie or snap securely to the crib slats in at least six places, top and bottom.

(6) Comforter or Thick Quilt

If you live in an area that is quite cool or very cold during the winter, you will want to have one of these on hand. Be sure that it is easy to launder and care for.

We found that the quilt we purchased for the crib was still quite useful when our daughter began using a bigger bed. So, although its primary use is for a couple of years in the crib, you will find that you will get an additional year or two's use from it.

Changing Table or Converter Kit

A changing table is so convenient! You won't have to bend over to change your baby and all of the materials you need are conveniently within reach. This quickly becomes a necessity when you find that diaper detail is a *very* frequent activity

Mom to Mom . . .

during your baby's first months! I can remember one marathon hour during the middle of the night during our daughter's first month when we changed her diapers five times! She would be quiet and satisfied for just moments before fussing again ... my husband and I kept thinking, "Surely not!" only to find that it was true, she'd done it again!

The changing table should have working safety straps to prevent falls, especially when your baby begins to gleefully roll and wiggle! Its drawers and/or shelves should be easily accessible so that your baby will not be left unattended. Even with a safety strap, accidents can happen.

If you choose not to purchase or borrow a changing table, you may want to consider the various converter kits that are available. Such a kit simply converts the top of an ordinary dresser into a changing table by providing attached safety rails around the top of the dresser, a soft pad, and safety belt.

Chest of Drawers

Three or four drawers will do.

A set of drawers not to consider is one that has a changing table on top of it that folds out toward you. At first, such a combination appears to be a great way to save on room and money. But, since a changing table must always be ready to use, it is always in the open position. Such an arrangement means that the first drawer under the changing table is virtually inaccessible. The lower drawers are also difficult

Preparing for the Precious Arrival . . .

to use because you'll find yourself crawling below the extended table above to reach things in those drawers. Even with the little one strapped in, you still will find that you must either try to access a drawer with one hand while the other is resting on your baby, or you'll find yourself quickly letting go of your baby to crawl under the table to find what you need in a lower drawer.

Transmitter Set

A transmitter set (a transmitter in the baby's room or wherever the baby is sleeping during the day and a receiver located wherever you are) is a must. There are two varieties available: one set requires that both parts be plugged in; the other set is essentially battery operated and can be moved easily anywhere in the home. The mobile unit can also be taken with you to a friend's home so you can easily hear your little one stirring even if you are downstairs or several rooms away.

Front Carrier or Sling

This is a must for keeping your little one close and contented. Many moms, including myself, have found it to be the greatest thing for calming a fussy baby. For the first several weeks, most infants need nearly constant holding, cuddling, and closeness. The easiest way to accomplish this while still being able to do a few things around the house and away from home is by using a front carrier or sling.

The carriers and slings come in a variety of fabrics and styles. To select one that is the most convenient and easy to use, first ask other mothers who have used them for

Mom to Mom . . .

their recommendations. What do they like or not like about the one(s) they use? Once you have a few recommended brand names in hand, try them on at the store. You might want to consider borrowing a little friend's baby-size doll to use while trying on the various styles.

You will want the one you select to be convenient and easy to use, of sturdy construction, with well padded leg-holes for your little one and well padded shoulder pads for you.

Both my husband and I found our front carrier to be indispensable. We're avid walkers, so we found the front carrier to be such a simple way to keep up our walking as well as our hikes to the grocery store and local shopping centers. We were able to carry our shopping bags and keep our little one close and contented simultaneously! No wonder women in many other cultures have used a similer convenience for centuries!

Baby Bathtub

A molded plastic baby bathtub with a textured or foam slanted base is inexpensive and a great way to get used to bathing an infant. If you have a double sink in your kitchen, you will find that the tub is molded to fit such an arrangement and is thus the most convenient. Not only is the tub at a comfortable, convenient height for you, but it easily accommodates two people (mommy and daddy!) helping with the bath!

Preparing for the Precious Arrival...

Baby Washcloths—3 and Hooded Baby Towels—3	Baby towels are not really a necessity, but they are very soft and absorbent. The hoods are especially helpful in that they keep your baby's head warm and help keep the towel in place.
	Baby washcloths are smaller and thinner than regular wash cloths and are much easier to use when bathing an infant and baby.
Lap Pads—3	These are similar to the rubber flannel-backed sheets described above for the crib but are much smaller and are used to protect your lap from leaky diapers when holding or feeding your baby. They are also useful to take along in the diaper bag for a changing pad.
Infant Seat	An infant seat keeps your little one involved in just about everything you do wherever you are. For example, you can set it on the kitchen counter or bathroom counter so your baby can watch what you're doing and you can set it on one of the dining room chairs (if it can fit securely enough) so she can see and watch you and your husband or the family while everyone is eating or playing games.

We also found that when our baby was three or four months old, she enjoyed sitting in her infant seat in the buggy. It was a great way to prop her up so that she could enjoy the passing scenery!

When buying one, be sure that it has:

- A wide, sturdy base for stability;
- Non-skid feet to prevent slipping;

Mom to Mom . . .

- Supporting devices that can be locked securely;
- Crotch and waist straps;
- Straps and buckle that are *easy to use;*
- A soft, quilted covering that is easy to remove for laundering.

Our patio table was large enough for us to set our infant seat right on it. Maryanna loved being in the midst of our activities and at eye level, and we were able to watch her and talk to her while we ate.

Convertible Buggy/Stroller

Although this type of carriage is more expensive, it allows you to continue using it until the child is three or four years of age.

Some considerations to keep in mind as you are shopping for one are:

(1) Height of handle bar

If you or your husband is tall, you will find that all stroller handle bars are not created equal! Push a few stroller/carriages around the store to see if they are truly comfortable to push for a distance. If the handle is too short, your feet will be constantly kicking into the axles and basket below.

(2) Safety features

- Are the brakes on the wheels tight?
- Are they easily applied and released?
- Are the wheels heavy and sturdy?

Preparing for the Precious Arrival...

- Are there secure locking devices to insure against accidental collapse?
- Is it stable and difficult to tip?

(3) Convenience features

Although you'll probably want to use a front carrier or sling at first and use a "backpack" carrier later, these features are important once your baby is 18 months or older. He is then either too big for the backpack or wanting to be out and about on his own!

- Is it relatively easy to collapse when wanting to put it in the trunk of the car?
- If you'll be using it for shopping, does it include a basket for the diaper bag, purchases, or toys?

Infant or Convertible Safety Seat

A top priority on your shopping list should be a safety seat for the car for your newborn. She should be buckled into a car seat during the drive home from the hospital or birthing center. Although she may cry, it is for her safety and it is the law. Cry as she might, you'll happily discover that soon after the car starts, your little one will most likely soon be asleep!

There are several types of safety seats on the market:

(1) Seats solely for infants that are only to be used in the rear-facing position;

We were able to use our infant car seat as a carry-around infant seat. Boy! Did we get a lot of use out of that! But, our car seat was vinyl—

73

Mom to Mom . . .

> *YUK! Contrary to my plans, car seat covers did not work with it very well!*
>
> Terri Ciosek
> Poway, California

(2) Seats that are convertible from rear-facing for infants to forward-facing for older babies, toddlers and pre-schoolers;

(3) Seats that are to be used only for toddlers and pre-schoolers.

What appears to be the most expensive option is to buy the convertible for both infants and toddlers/pre-schoolers. However, when you consider the cost of buying two separate safety seats, buying a convertible seat may be the least expensive option, because it will be the only one you will have to purchase.

Another option to consider is to check into short-term rentals of infant safety seats. Some hospitals, equipment rental companies, and public service organizations rent infant safety seats for the short period you will need it. Infant safety seats must be used from birth to around nine months or until the baby is 20 pounds.

Be sure that the seat that you plan to purchase (or rent) does, indeed, fit your car and belt system. And, if the seat the you purchase requires a tether to bolt it to the car, be sure that you are willing to go through the time and possible expense to have that done. If not, the safety seat will be ineffective because it will not be secured as it was created to be.

Preparing for the Precious Arrival . . .

To request free information on infant car seats, write or call the following:

American Academy of Pediatrics, 141 Northwest Point Road, Elk Grove Village, IL 60007, or (800) 433-9016.

Auto Safety Hotline, U.S. Department of Transportation, National Highway Traffic Safety Administration, Washington, D.C., 20590, or (800) 424-9394.

Car Window Shade

There are two varieties of window shades for the car that are wonderful in keeping the sun from shining on baby.

(1) A roller shade attached with suction cups

(2) Plastic shades that adhere to the window

Unless you are fortunate enough to *always* have someone sitting in the back seat who can shade your baby with an extra blanket, a shade will come in very handy and will make baby much happier!

Diaper Bag

Even if it costs a bit more than the cute ones, get one that is big and sturdy that can carry all that you need. Try to find one that isn't "babyish." If the bag shouts "baby," not only will you tire of using it after a couple of months, but it won't be able to "grow" with your little one. You'll find yourself spending more money to buy another bag that isn't so "infant-ish" and that can be used on through the toddler stage.

75

Mom to Mom . . .

Rocking Chair — There's nothing more peaceful than rocking your little miracle—for feedings, for calming, for story reading, and later for chats when she's older. We bought rocking chair at a resale store specializing in baby/toddler clothing and furniture. Resale stores usually have some good buys if you can take the time to search them out and hunt for the rocking chairs. If you aren't able to find one, but still have several weeks before your due date, many resale shops will take your name and number and will call you when one comes in that might interest you.

Plastic Baby Bottles — Although you may have decided to breastfeed your baby, you will still find that you will need plastic baby bottles just the same. For example, there will be times that you will need or want to hand express milk, and the best bottle to use for that is a plastic baby bottle—plastic because some of milk's special properties adhere to glass and are lost, but not so with plastic.

Also, there will be those times when you will want to leave a bottle for your baby so that your husband or a sitter can watch him for you while you step out for a bit of shopping or a break. Breastmilk can be stored in the refrigerator or freezer for just such an occasion. (See Breastfeeding, pages 127-128.)

Diaper Pail/Bucket — If you plan to use cloth diapers (excellent decision!) and you have decided to wash them yourself, you will need to purchase a diaper pail or bucket.

Preparing for the Precious Arrival...

But, if you plan to use a diaper service (another excellent decision!), the service will provide one.

The Non-Essentials . . . at this time . . .

Playpen	Don't buy this item until much later when you can decide whether or not you really need it. A better consideration would be a portable bed that can double as a playpen at a later time. Once the little one arrives, many parents, like us, opt for not using a playpen but instead childproof their home extremely well and use expanding gates for doorways, halls, and stairways.
High Chair	A high chair at this point is a needless expense. You will need one eventually, at around six months of age. (See pages 297-298 for guidance in the selection of one.)

Clothing Initially Needed and Not Needed...

There are a few necessities that infants need from the very beginning. But it's a good idea to invest *conservatively* at first just to be sure that you have only a few of all the necessities before buying any more. This is suggested simply because until your little one arrives, you won't know the appropriate size. For example, if you have a large baby, the "newborn" clothes may not fit or will last only a month or two at most. You'll also be receiving several things as gifts, and you won't know until your baby is here just which items you prefer using most often.

As for what size to buy, baby clothes are sized in a number of ways: by weight, by height, by age (number of months), or any combination of these three. The most inaccurate sizing is by age. Very often infants are wearing "6-months" outfits at three months, "twelve months" outfits at nine months or younger. The best gauges are height and weight.

Mom to Mom . . .

The Essentials

Undershirts *without* snaps at the crotch—4

> These will be used only until your baby's umbilical cord has fallen off. He will need an undershirt for extra warmth but one that isn't tight over that tender area.

Undershirts *with snaps at the crotch* —7 or more

> Undershirts that snap at the crotch are far superior to those that don't. Plain undershirts suggested above ride up so easily and therefore don't provide the warmth for which they are intended. The number that you'll need will depend largely on the season and area of the country. For example, in warmer climates, some babies will practically live in just these shirts and diapers.

Diaper Covers—4 or more

> This invention is marvelous! Safety pins are things of the past! You simply place a folded diaper in the cover and wrap it around your little one, fastening it with the velcro closures! They are water resistant and remain so if laundered properly.

> Vinyl covers are hot and don't "breathe." Consequently, their use can easily cause rashes and discomfort and really aren't recommended.

Cloth Diapers

> The arguments for using cloth diapers, especially during the first few months, are many. Not only are they soft and comfortable, but they "breathe," which disposable diapers do not. Disposables are also expensive, more so than using a diaper service (believe it or not!), and they definitely contribute to the ecological mess our world is now experiencing.

Preparing for the Precious Arrival . . .

Even if you do arrange for a diaper service, it's a good idea to purchase a dozen of your own cloth diapers to use for burp cloths, wiping, and cut-up for little clean-up wash-cloths. They are so much softer than anything else you can use!

If you choose to do your own laundry rather than use a diaper service, four dozen should be enough to get you started.

Sleepers with Feet (or Stretchies)—5-6

Your infant will be wearing these most of the time, day and night. The actual number you start out with will again depend on what you have been given as gifts (they are popular gift items) and the season.

Gowns—1-2

These sleeping gowns have either drawstrings or lose elastic on the bottom and are useful because they are easy to put on, are not tight over the tender umbilical cord area, and provide easy access for diaper changing. But most new mommies soon opt for the sleepers above once the cord has dropped off simply because the gowns do ride up, and when you are holding the little one, the gown tends to ride up and potentially make the baby quite uncomfortable.

Bonnet or Cap—1 or 2

Whenever you take your little one outside, even out into a warm summer evening, you will want to cover his head with a bonnet or cap. During the daytime, you will want to protect his head from the sun and drafts, and during the evening, you will want to protect his head from drafts.

Booties/Baby Socks (3-4 pairs)

Babies' feet become cold quite easily, so booties or socks are a must.

Winter Wear

Blanket sleepers—2 or 3
Knit Hat

Mom to Mom . . .

    Mittens

    Three-sided zippered blanket (of non-slippery material, e.g., not nylon) and a light blanket for the face when the baby is carried between house and car

        Note: Although these two items aren't "clothing," an expensive snowsuit for a baby just isn't necessary and is too quickly outgrown. The combination of these winter items should be sufficient.

The Non-Essentials

Rubber/plastic diaper covers

    They are hot, don't breathe, and can cause a rash.

Frilly dresses/cute little suits

"Dress" shoes

    You'll find that booties and baby socks are so much more convenient and flexible.

Jewelry

The Set-Up: Getting the Nursery Ready . . .

- *To prepare a complete main diaper changing area, include the following things:*

(1) Diapers

(2) Diaper Covers

(3) Water source (a small spray bottle or a small bowl for water)

(4) 1 baby wash cloth (terry or cut up cloth diaper)

(5) Bar of clear soap in a soap dish to wash bottom

(6) 1 cloth diaper used as a towel to dry a washed bottom

(7) Baby powder (talc/cornstarch combination)

(8) Baby oil

(9) Ointment (either A & D Ointment or Desitin)

Preparing for the Precious Arrival . . .

>   (10) Cotton swabs
>   (11) Cotton balls
>   (12) Box of tissues (A good brand that won't fall apart in the middle of the job!)

- *Establish an extra diaper changing area or two in your home* with just the bare necessities to save a lot of constant travel.

- *In addition to the furniture suggested in an earlier section, also consider including the following in your nursery, if your budget permits:*
    * Hanging musical mobile (to be used above the crib and bassinet)
    * Bookshelf (for books you begin to collect and toys that accumulate)
    * Lamp
    * Hamper or hamper substitute

A Potpourri of Ideas to Consider . . .

- *If you have a dog in the house, you will definitely want to read:*

    Your New Baby and the Family Dog by Mary Mueller

    > This is a booklet filled with information on how to help your dog handle the changes that will come about because of a new baby in the house. Pets can become jealous of a new arrival, just as older siblings can, but there are steps that you can follow to ensure safety and harmony in your home.

    > To order this helpful booklet, send $2.45 to MCS Marketing Division, 13520 West Lisbon Road, Brookfield, WI 53005.

- *A creative decorating idea:*

Mom to Mom . . .

> *While decorating our new son's nursery, we were low on money but wanted the room to look special. We decided to "handprint" the wall. We took red and blue paint and put our handprints around the wall near the ceiling. As our relatives come to visit, each puts up a yellow handprint. We have the prints of our son's uncles, aunts, grandmothers, grandfathers—even his great-grandma! Each print is labeled with its "owner's" name. This is an inexpensive, very personal, and special way to decorate a child's room.*
>
> (Christine Shebroe)
> ©198- Gruner + Jahr USA Publishing
> Reprinted from *Parents* Magazine
> by permission

- *Subscribe to <u>Growing Parent/Growing Child</u> and/or <u>Parents Magazine</u> and <u>Pediatrics for Parents</u>.*

Every month these three sources offer some of the best parenting guidance on a consistent, regular basis. I read each one from cover to cover within days of their arrival.

Growing Parent and *Growing Child* are co-subscriptions. Subscribing to one brings the other as well. A variety of parenting issues are covered each month in *Growing Parent*. *Growing Child* is specifically geared to the age of your child. When you subscribe, you give your baby's birthdate. The newsletters are then sent monthly according to your baby's age: six months, nine months, two years, etc., up through six years of age. Each newsletter explains the stage that your baby is in or will soon be entering and suggests excellent activities for development, generating curiosity, and delightful fun!

Pediatrics for Parents is also a monthly newsletter edited and published by Dr. Richard J. Sagall, a practicing pediatrician and the "Pediatricks" columnist for *Parents Magazine*. In his monthly

Preparing for the Precious Arrival . . .

newsletter, Dr. Sagall provides up-to-date pediatrics information, clearly explains medical terms and concepts that we as parents may hear about but may not understand, provides important information concerning your child's health, and includes articles that are written by health care professionals and medical writers.

To subscribe to *Parents Magazine,* pick up a copy at the newsstand and complete a subscription card, or write to *Parents Magazine,* P.O. Box 3055, Harlan, IA 51593-2119.

To subscribe to *Growing Parent/Growing Child,* write to: Dunn and Hargitt, P.O. Box 1100, Lafayette, IN 47902, or call (317) 423-2624.

To subscribe to *Pediatrics for Parents,* write to: *Pediatrics for Parents,* P.O. Box 1069, Bangor, ME 04401. (By sending $2.00 to the same address, you can receive a sample copy if you would rather see one before committing yourself to a full year's subscription at $15.00.)

- *You may want to consider making your own changing table on top of a chest of drawers or a dresser.*

    You can use a converter kit or do as Jane Martin of the Natural Baby Company did. She created her own by doing the following:

    1. *Place a cushioned pad on one side. Many stores sell these as "travel" changing pads.*

    2. *Fasten a plastic garbage bag by the edge of the dresser. We put the diaper bucket next to it and the clothes hamper next to that. This way everything goes right into its proper place without having to let go of the baby.*

        Note: Attaching a belt system for greater safety would be even better. Also, converter kits include a four- or five-inch rim that increases safety.

    3. *We use the drawers underneath for the baby's diapers, diaper covers, and clothes.*

Mom to Mom . . .

4. *A mirror right at the baby's level has always been a wonderful distraction for our baby. You can also try mobiles and pictures that you change from time to time.*

5. *We keep a box of tissues (not a bargain brand—they fall apart) on the dresser as well as a small plant spray bottle of water to clean his bottom.*

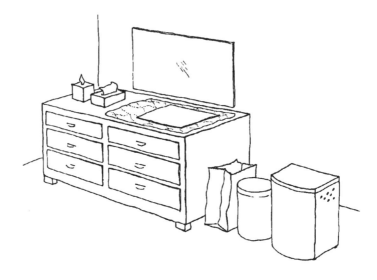

Jane Martin
The Natural Baby Company
Titusville, New Jersey

---

[1]Author unknown—words were copied into a personal journal from a card received in 1986 without noting card company.

Preparing for the Precious Arrival...

SHOPPING LIST

This checklist is provided to help you plan and organize your shopping. Review it and then adapt it to your needs. Once you have completed it, either photocopy it or remove it from this book and carry it with you whenever you are out shopping.

Needs	# Have	# Need	Borrow from or purchase	Done
Equipment:				
Bassinet or Cradle				
Crib				
Mattress				
Chest of Drawers				
Changing Table or Converter Kit				
Transmitter Set				
Front Carrier or Sling				
Baby Bathtub				
Infant Seat				
Buggy/Stroller				
Safety Seat (Infant or Convertible)				
Rocking Chair				
Diaper Bag				
Decorating Needs:				
Wallpaper				
Paint				
Curtains				
Lamp				
Wall Decorations:				

Mom to Mom . . .

Needs	# Have	# Need	Borrow from or purchase	Done
Linens:				
Bassinet/Cradle Sheets				
Receiving Blankets				
Crib Sheets				
Rubber Sheets (Crib)				
Lap Pads				
Imitation Lambskin				
Mattress Pads (Crib & Bassinet/Cradle)				
Imitation Lambskin				
Fabric				
Thread				
Narrow Elastic Tape				
Comforter/Thick Quilt				
Crib Bumper				
Baby Washcloths				
Baby Towels (Hooded)				
Clothing:				
Undershirts (no snaps)				
Undershirts (snaps at crotch)				
Diaper Covers				
Diapers (Cloth or Disposable)				
Sleepers with feet				
Gowns				
Bonnet or Cap				
Booties/Baby Socks				
Winter Clothing:				

Preparing for the Precious Arrival . . .

Needs	# Have	# Need	Borrow from or purchase	Done
Books: Your Baby and Child from Birth to Age Five (Leach)				
Changing Table/ Diaper Bag Needs:				
Small Spray Bottle or Bowl				
Bar of Clear Soap				
Baby Oil				
Ointment (A & D or Desitin)				
Cotton Swabs				
Cotton Balls				
Miscellaneous Needs:				
Plastic Baby Bottles (4) (more if you plan to bottle-feed your baby)				
Bottle Filler Bags				

87

Mom to Mom . . .

Clips and Notes

Preparing for the Precious Arrival . . .

Clips and Notes

Mom to Mom . . .

Clips and Notes

3

Your Little One's Coming!

*A baby—an armful of love
who sweeps you off your feet
and leaves you trying to remember
what life was like
before toothless grins, angelic smiles,
and wonderful sounds only a baby can make!*[1]

Only days or weeks are left before your rocking chair will be kept busy, lullabies will be sung, and a soft little bundle will be cuddleable and close! It's now time to focus on getting ready for your trip to the hospital or birthing center, your brief stay there, and your much welcomed trip home.

Recommended Reading...

Some of the books listed here have been recommended in the earlier chapters, but if you haven't had a chance to read them yet, try to squeeze them in during these last few days before your baby's arrival.

The Family Bed by Tine Thevenin

> This is a wonderful book with considerable food for thought! And, it's another one I wish I had read before Maryanna reached 15 months of age! It wasn't until then and I had experienced months of her waking many times a night and having difficulty returning to sleep that I finally, out of desperation, brought her to bed with me. What a revelation! She went to sleep immediately! I later ran across this book that validated what I had discovered on my own. Had I read it earlier, I wouldn't have experienced those months of nighttime frustration and exhaustion.

Mom to Mom . . .

> While sharing a family bed is a practice as old as the human race, it has become controversial in the 20th century. *The Family Bed* discusses the pros and cons and suggests that the family bed will help solve bedtime problems and create closer family bonds. Establishing an open-door policy to the parental bed can be a sensitive way of responding to the needs of a little one. The author of this book, Tine Thevenin, really speaks to your anxieties, reservations, *and* instincts.

Nighttime Parenting—How to Get Your Baby and Child to Sleep by William Sears, M.D.

> This book was invaluable to me, but what a help it would have been had I read it *before* our little one arrived! Unfortunately, I "bumped" into it when Maryanna was 15 months old, but it still was immensely helpful. In *Nighttime Parenting,* Dr. Sears explains how babies sleep differently than adults, how sharing sleep can help the whole family sleep better, and how to help little ones sleep more peacefully.

The Fussy Baby—How to Bring Out the Best in Your High Need Child by William Sears, M.D.

> Parents of a fussy baby will need this one within reach! Should you have a newborn who spends many of her waking hours crying, you will have a better idea of how to handle it rather than becoming frazzled and not knowing where to turn for advice. Dr. Sears provides a guide to interpreting a baby's cries and includes chapters on coping with colic, feeding, fathering, soothing, and avoiding maternal burnout. He includes plenty of support and reassurance as well as day-to-day survival tips.

Your Baby and Child from Birth to Age Five by Penelope Leach

> This is a wonderful book that covers the day-to-day care of a baby so you'll have some idea of what is involved as well as a great deal of information on infant/child development which will give you a feeling for what to expect and what will be needed for normal development. It was, and continues to be, one of our most frequently consulted books and it was often mentioned by many other parents who contributed to this resource.

Your Little One's Coming...

It is a comprehensive and outstandingly sensitive guide to child care. What I especially appreciated was its meeting my concern for both the physical and psychological well-being of our child. Its contents progress from birth through the newborn and settled baby, to the older baby, the toddler, and the pre-school child. Its index is an incredible A to Z reference in itself and concludes with an extremely helpful chart on playthings and play activities for the newborn on through preschool age.

To help prepare a sibling for the imminent arrival of the little one . . .

See How You Grow by Dr. Patricia Pearce and Edwina Riddell

This is a book I highly recommended in the first chapter. As I mentioned before, young children who are three years or older will be excited about the baby coming, but will also have some interesting questions. This is an excellent "lift the flap" book to share with them. It answers their questions in a clear, gentle way. It doesn't just stop with "where do babies come from," or "how does the baby live in there?" It also goes into questions such as, "What will I look like when I'm grown up?" and "What makes us grow?"

Becoming by Eleanora Faison

With line drawings and simple text, this book prepares small children for a new birth and answers their questions about their own beginnings. A transparent page makes it possible to "see" the unborn baby within the womb. Without too much detail, *Becoming* provides enough information to introduce the miracle of birth to children from as young as two.

I Love My Baby Sister (Most of the Time) by Elaine Edelman

Babies are both fun and trouble. Sometimes you have to jump around and holler, just to get a hug from mom. But baby sisters get nicer and can do more as they get older. The pictures in this reassuring book show a warm, very lived-in house full of love for everyone.

Mom to Mom . . .

Two to Four Weeks Before Your Little One's Expected Due Date . . .

- *Arrange for a diaper service . . . if you've decided to use one.*
- *Plan and prepare your birth announcements.*

   Once your baby arrives, there will be little time to do many of the necessary extras such as writing and preparing the birth announcements. Consequently, it's a good idea to do as much as you can now, before all extra time vanishes!

   First, if you plan to create your own announcement, do it now. Write it as you want it to read, leaving only the details to fill in when the baby arrives. If you plan to use one of the many delightful styles available at card stores, determine the number you will need and buy them now.

   Next, stamp and address all of the envelopes for the announcements. Presto! You're all ready!

   When the baby arrives, all you *or your helpers* will have to do is fill in the wonderful details, slip the announcements in the prepared envelopes, and off they go!

- *If you haven't already done so, find out **exactly** what your hospital's procedures are for handling your baby immediately after its birth.*

   For example, I had asked for full rooming-in, which I had interpreted to mean that our baby would be with me *from birth*. I knew that she would have to be weighed, bathed, and "tested," but I thought that would involve just a few minutes and certainly not two hours or more. I did know that I should make it clear when I arrived at the hospital that I wanted to nurse our baby as soon as she was born, but beyond that, I honestly believed that she would be with me from birth.

   I was wrong. Although my baby was quite healthy and I had had a relatively short labor and an unmedicated delivery, I was sent to a separate recovery room without her. I was able to nurse her after her birth, and Tom was able to be with us for about 20 minutes after her birth . . . just the three of us which was very

Your Little One's Coming . . .

special. But after that short interlude, our baby was taken to the nursery, I was wheeled off to the recovery room, and Tom was left looking at our baby through the nursery window!

There are several reasons why you need to be carefully monitored after delivery:

(1) Your vital signs—blood pressure and pulse—must return to normal.

(2) Excessive, abnormal bleeding, if it is to occur, will most likely happen within the first three to four hours after delivery.

(3) If any anesthetic was used at all during labor and delivery, its effects must completely disappear.

But, you should be able to have your baby with you during this careful observation period *if that is what you want*. Obviously, if you have had a very long and possibly difficult labor and delivery, or if you have had a C-section, you may very definitely need some time to rest and recover before attending to your little one. But, should you want you baby with you, without separation, you should be able to do so, unless, due to the medication and/or surgery, you are physically unable to attend to your little one at first.

I later learned that had I insisted on keeping our baby with me, I would have been allowed to do so. But, because I believed it to be "the rule" and, therefore, not to be broken, I unhappily accepted the situation.

At this point in your pregnancy, you may believe that you will want your baby with you, even during recovery immediately after birth. Then, if the following conditions are true:

(1) If your baby is quite healthy upon delivery and doesn't require immediate attention for some distress;

(2) If your labor and delivery went well without complication and you feel well after delivery;

Mom to Mom . . .

... be sure that sometime before entering the hospital, you make this wish clear to your obstetrician and have him write it into your record.

- *Find out **exactly** what is provided and not provided at the hospital or birthing center so that you can take a small suitcase with **only** the things that you will really need in it.*

    When packing my suitcase, I followed the lengthy list provided by the hospital. It included such things as sanitary pads and belt, nightgowns, toiletries, etc. But, once there, I used nothing that I had brought for myself other than my toiletries because everything else was, in fact, provided. The only other things I used from my suitcase were the little sleeper, diaper, diaper cover, and receiving blanket I had brought to take Maryanna home in.

- *Make out a contact list of people whom you want to immediately know about the birth, e.g., parents, other relatives, close friends, ...*

    If the list is quite long, consider creating a "phone tree" which is something that worked quite well for us. We listed all of the people whom we wanted to know about Maryanna's arrival ASAP, and then divided the long list into five shorter lists. We then called four friends and asked if they would be willing to call three or four others with the news when Tom called them. It worked beautifully!

    When Maryanna arrived, Tom had his list of family members plus the four friends on the "phone tree." He called them and they in turn called the names on their list! Voilá! Everyone was quickly informed!

- *Pack your birthing "goodie" bag.*

    The following list[2] of things to include in your birthing bag seems to be rather extensive, but it would be far better to have these things with you and not use them than to not have them and wish you did.

Your Little One's Coming...

Item	Purpose
Busy Work	Busy work includes cards, games, books, crafts, crosswords, etc. Such busy work will help pass the time between contractions if you need some distraction.
Paper and Pencil	You'll want to have these available to record experiences and other comments. For example, Tom wrote down a lot of the details that were special to include in Maryanna's journal, such as the weather (soft mist, cool, at 4 am in the morning, etc.), the funny things that happened on the way to the hospital, etc.
Focal Point	This can be a special picture or some other object that you may want to use to help you concentrate.
Chapstick or lip gloss	Lips can become dry during labor and one of these items will be most welcomed!
Mouthwash or spray	In order to avoid nausea and vomiting, you won't be able to drink anything, so it will be especially helpful to have one of these to cleanse and refresh your mouth.
Lotion	This will soote your skin when your partner or coach gives you a comforting massage.
Socks (thick) 3	Hospitals are kept cool and you'll find that your feet may get quite cold. If they do, you'll really appreciate the warmth of thick socks! The extra sock can be used to hold tennis balls. (See below.)
Tennis balls in a sock or rolling pin	One of these can be used to provide counter pressure along your spine when needed.
Fan (hand-held type)	You may need some cooling off during labor!

Mom to Mom . . .

Item	Purpose
Hairbrush and barrette	If you have long hair, you may want to tie it back and get it out of the way to be more comfortable.
Labor Guide	This is a list of reminders for your coach.
Paper Bag	This helps prevent hyperventilation, should you need it.
Glasses	If you wear contact lenses, you may want to wear your glasses instead, simply for comfort. Also, some hospitals do not allow contacts especially if you receive medication.
Coins and phone list	These are for your husband or coach to spread the news as soon as your little one has arrived!

Note: Be sure to keep this bag *separate* from your suitcase. Your suitcase may be taken from you and put into the room you will be in following your baby's delivery.

- *Include a camera (Polaroid or 35mm) and a tape recorder.*

  When Maryanna arrived, we shied away from taking a camera and recorder to the hospital. We had seen and heard of several couples who had taken pictures during labor and at the delivery and we just weren't interested in doing that.

  However, we later discovered that we should have thought it through more carefully! Although we were not wanting pictures of the labor and delivery experience, we have *so many times* regretted not having pictures of the three of us minutes after Maryanna was born! And . . . we have also regretted not having a recording of her first cries. Since her birth, we have regularly recorded her gurgles and babbles, first words and delightful conversation. But . . . how perfect the record would be if her first cries could have been included!

  So . . . the voice of experience is . . . take a camera and a recorder with you. You may choose not to use either of them, but if you decide that you want them, you'll have them.

Your Little One's Coming...

Incidentally, be sure that the camera has plenty of film in it, that the batteries and flash are in operating condition, and that the recorder has a fresh tape in it and has new batteries that won't disappoint you!

By the way, many women use a recorder to help them relax during their labor. There are so many wonderful soothing, relaxing tapes on the market today. So you may want to have the recorder serve double duty . . . relax you during your labor and then record those wonderful first cries when your baby is born.

- *Make several trial drives to your hospital or birthing center to determine which route is the fastest at various times of the day and night.*

- *As independent and as much in control as you may feel, be sure to plan for some help for the first few weeks after the baby's arrival.*

  Your responsibilities are to rest, to help your little one become accustomed to his new surroundings, to have an opportunity to become adjusted to being a mommy, if this is your first baby, or to become adjusted to be a mommy of two or more children.

  Accept help when it is offered and use all the help that comes along. But do *plan* for help. If your mother or some other relative is coming to stay for a couple of weeks, let her help with the meals and the laundry. If you are not accustomed to having guests do the work around the house, as I'm not, it's hard to do . . . but just know that they wouldn't be there if they didn't want to be, and they won't want to be there if they don't feel that they are being of any help. So . . . let them be all of the help that their big, wonderful hearts desire!

If You Have Other Children at Home . . .

- *When attending baby showers, be sure to have a gift or two for your older child(ren).*

  If your older child attends a baby shower with you, be sure to sneak in a present or two for him to open while you are opening

Mom to Mom . . .

all of yours. So much attention will be focused on you and gifts for the new baby, that the older child may feel left out, resentful, and unimportant. Gifts for "Big Brother _____" or "Big Sister _____" can make your child feel deservedly very important.

The same holds true if the child does not attend the shower with you. When you come home, you will have many gifts that are obviously for the baby. So be sure to have two or three little wrapped gifts that are just for him because he's the "Big Brother." How special that will make him feel!

- *Plan exactly how you are going to handle your absence from home.*

    (1) What have you told your child so she is *well aware of what will happen* when it is time for you to deliver your baby?

    (2) Will she be taken to someone's home? Will someone be coming to stay with her?

    - *Be sure to identify the friend or friends who are willing to come during the middle of the night at a moment's notice to stay with your child(ren) while you and your husband go to the hospital or birthing center.*

        You may not have to go during the middle of the night, but many babies certainly do seem to favor the wee hours of the morning to begin their trip into the world!

        But, even if you go during the middle of the *day,* it is still wise to have someone who is expecting your call. You will want someone to be with your other children during the day, early evening, and even into the night.

    (3) When will she be able to see you?

    (4) Is she well aware of the fact that even if you are going to the hospital, that you are *well,* not sick?

    (5) When will she be able to see the baby?

    (6) If all goes well, when do you expect to be back home with her?

Your Little One's Coming . . .

While at the Hospital . . .

- *Try to remember that:*
  - * *YOU are the mother of your baby and you will know by instinct what you and your baby need;*
  - * *The hospital staff is there to help and advise and NOT there to tell you what to do.*

  These are important points for you to remember. I wish I had underlined them in *my* mind when our baby arrived! It would have saved me many moments of feeling the "guilties" and a lot of frustration.

  For example, I had arranged for full rooming-in, so Maryanna was with me most of the time from my arrival in my room after leaving the recovery room to our departure the next day. She cried frequently, so I would pick her up and hold her, sometimes nurse her, all of which would calm her and sometimes put her to sleep. Yet, the nurses would frequently come into my room, see me lying there on the inclined bed with Maryanna lying there quietly and contentedly under my arm, and admonish me to put her back in her glass bassinet! "You need your rest—your body needs to recuperate from all of your exertion!" They would then pick her up, put her back in the bassinet, and leave the room. Moments after their departure, Maryanna would again begin to cry! I would again pick her up, cuddle her, and begin to nurse her, when a nurse would come in, "catch me" cuddling and nursing my baby, and admonish me again: "You're nursing her too frequently—you'll get sore nipples and then you will find nursing to be too painful. Don't feed her so often—use the glucose water instead." They would then proceed to put her back into her bassinet!

  Had I been more confident in my own instincts, I would have thanked them for their help, and then would have nicely but firmly explained how I wanted to care for *my* baby. Experience really is a great teacher!

- *Arrange for your older child(ren) to visit you and to see the baby*

101

Mom to Mom . . .

> *as soon as possible after the baby's birth.*

Joanne Soukup from Holland, Michigan, writes:

> *We always let our older children hold the new baby during their first visit to the hospital. During that first visit, they also received a gift from their new brother. I had picked out and wrapped a gift to tuck in the bottom of my take-along-to-the-hospital suitcase. A favorite and very useful gift was a book of lullabies. When the newborn was fussy, we'd all sit down and sing the lullabies to soothe <u>everyone</u>'s nerves!*
>
> *Another event for my hospital stay was to have the older sibling create a "welcome baby" card. The card was then taped inside the baby's hospital bed. The older child could then easily identify the crib (and baby) if it was in the nursery. The card became an addition to the baby's book.*

- *Have a pad of paper and a pencil next to your bed so you are able to keep track of friends who came by and what they brought.*

In all of the excitement and exhaustion that the birth can bring, if you're in the hospital for any longer than 24 hours, it will be very difficult to remember all who came by or what their thoughtful gifts were.

It's also fun to keep track of some of the things people say and some of the things that happen during your stay that you'll want to include in the journal you've been keeping for your little one!

- *If someone suggests over the phone that they bring a bottle of champagne to help you celebrate, tell them that it's a wonderful idea—but suggest they bring a bubbly apple cider instead, à la Martinelli's.*

Eileen Carroll of La Jolla, California, also suggests:

> *Don't let anyone talk you into giving your baby bottles "just until your milk comes*

Your Little One's Coming . . .

in." Instead, nurse, nurse, nurse your little one, right from the beginning. Colostrum (the first milk just after birth) is very good for your baby. Babies don't need formula or water—breast milk is perfect!

Returning to Home Sweet Home . . .

- *Be sure to securely strap your baby into his infant car seat.*

    Not only is it the law, but it could save his life should the accident that "never will happen," happen.

- *Sit on a pillow when riding in the car.*

    A dear friend of mine, Karen Johnson, gave me this piece of welcome advice before Maryanna arrived . . . and what a comfortable difference it made during the trip home! Sitting on an episiotomy on a hard seat can be quite painful, especially over bumps!

- *When you first get home, take a picture of Daddy holding the new baby at the front door.*

    Not only is this a wonderful first picture of a very special occasion, but it is a marvelous tradition to start with the child. Each year when Maryanna's birthday comes around, we take a picture of Daddy holding her in front of our home. He has tried to hold her in the same way each year in order to dramatically illustrate her growth for the last year. So far four birthdays have passed. It won't be long before she'll have to *stand* for the picture! What a delightful, very special record we have of her yearly growth.

Siblings and the Little One's Arrival at Home . . .

- *If there is just one, perhaps even two, older siblings at home waiting for your return and the arrival of the little one, you may want to consider having them come to the hospital to accompany you and the baby home.*

Mom to Mom . . .

Laurie Buschmann of San Diego suggests the following:

- *When you come home from the hospital or birthing center, have Daddy carry the baby into the home so that your arms will be be free to give all the hugs and kisses you can.*

- *Encourage all visiting family and friends to warmly greet the sibling(s) first so they will still feel important.*

- *Be sure to include the sibling(s) in the pictures taken.*

    Some pictures can be of the baby by herself, but some of the pictures should be of the siblings by themselves, too.

- *Let the siblings enjoy and get to know their new little brother or sister.*

    Joanne Soukup also suggests:

> *The most important thing we learned for helping our older children adjust to a new arrival was that babies don't break. Once home from the hospital, we laid the baby on the floor and sat while our older children poked, peeked, oohed, and aahed over the new wonder. If they tried to poke an eye or be harmful, we'd scoop up both children and show the older one how to be more careful, trying not to scold. A newborn cry can do wonders for "scaring" an older child away if he handles, pokes or tickles wrong. When the newborn does cry, we try to ask the older child, "What do you think your baby needs?" and then we try to follow the advice.*

- *Notify your child's teacher about the arrival of the new baby so that s/he can be sensitive to any behavior changes.*

- *Use a "Baby's First Year" calendar to involve your older children in marking the milestones of their baby's first year.*

> *I have always using the "Baby's First Year" calendars, especially the ones with stickers. The older children were always a part of*

Your Little One's Coming . . .

> *updating milestones (they put on "first smile" stickers, etc.) and, usually, helped to remind me to make an entry.*
>
> *This calendar has also been quite helpful for reminders on baby check-ups, immunization due dates, and the "vital statistics" from each check-up, e.g., height and weight.*
>
> Joanne Soukup
Holland, Michigan

And Wendy Davis of San Diego suggests:

- *Talk with the grandparents ahead of time and alert them to a big pitfall that they may experience—that is, paying nearly exclusive attention to the newborn grandchild and seriously neglecting the older grandchild who loves them soooo much.*

    A newborn is so exciting, so little, and so cuddleable. It's very difficult not to want to hold the baby at every opportunity. However, a grandparent *must* realize that as wonderful as the new baby is, the older grandchild is the one whose feelings can be hurt so easily, not the newborn's. For a grandchild who adores his grandparents, to be neglected and even consistently ignored by them can be devastating! Such an experience can lead to some difficult behavior problems that the parents will have to deal with in addition to handling the arrival of a new baby, and can also greatly contribute to some very angry feelings toward his new sibling.

Settling In During the First Few Weeks . . .

- *Follow your instincts and believe in them.*

    I can't stress this bit of advice strongly enough. You will be receiving a lot of advice, *especially* if you are a *new* mommy. The advice comes from a well meaning mother and mother-in-law, other relatives and friends, and even your pediatrician and his/her staff. But, *this* piece of advice comes heart to heart to you from every one of us who has experienced new motherhood...

Mom to Mom . . .

> Listen to the advice, smile and thank the person for sharing the advice with you, and then use it *or discard it* as you see fit.
>
> Don't let yourself become a victim of such confidence-destructing thoughts as, "I've never been a mother before . . . what do *I* know?!" *You* are the mother of your baby and you *do* know! You know a lot more than you may give yourself credit for! Instinct is a very strong influence and will guide you very well if you will simply remain calm, listen to what your instincts tell you, and know that you really do know best—*you are your baby's mother!*
>
> To give you just a couple of examples . . .
>
> . . . I was told that my baby was crying so much of the time because I was holding her too much! Yet, I really believed that she was what is called "a high need baby" and needed all the cuddling and TLC she could get . . . which turned out to be correct.
>
> . . . I was absolutely committed to breastfeeding our baby. Yet, one month after her birth, our baby still hadn't regained her birth weight! I was nearly frantic. Our pediatrician had had me supplement with formula "until my volume increased." That didn't sound right because of all the reading I had done prior to our daughter's birth. But . . . he was the doctor so he should know! After one month, our doctor said that I had a volume problem and would have to supplement my breastfeeding for the rest of her infancy—that there was nothing I could do about it. I couldn't believe it! I was a healthy woman . . . why couldn't I produce enough volume? Fortunately, I immediately sought out Wellstart, the San Diego Lactation Program, for their advice. After a thorough examination of both me and our baby, it was determined that our problem was quite simple: I wasn't eating enough calories to produce the amount of milk needed *and* I wasn't nursing her frequently enough (again, due to erroneous advice!). Those two things were immediately corrected, and after only three days of following Wellstart's guidance, Maryanna gained four ounces, and she continued to gain

Your Little One's Coming...

from then on at a record rate!

Joanne Soukup gives some additional valuable notes on this:

> *The most important thing I learned—on my own—is not to be fearful to hold, nurse, and play with our baby if that's what's needed. With our first baby, I was so concerned with putting the baby on a schedule and doing everything <u>right</u>. It took me six months to realize no one had written a book on how to care for <u>our</u> baby. Our son didn't fit the mold of the children described in baby manuals and I was always frustrated. I really didn't know what to do most of the time. Finally, I learned it was okay to feed, hold, etc., our child when <u>he</u> wanted—not when a book told me to. By the time our second and third babies were born, I was more relaxed and so were our babies. Sometimes, it meant nursing a baby every hour instead of every three or four hours. Sometimes, it meant waiting to start solids until six months of age—because that's when our baby was ready for the new step. Since a baby can't communicate very well, I learned to judge the child's needs by his body language—he is tense, calm, fidgety, etc. Then I found the best way to satisfy my baby and not the one described in a book.*

- *Expect the "hormonal ping pong"—the ups and downs of your emotions—and accept it, knowing that the hormones will calm down after a while.*

- *Accept all the help that is offered.*

    Although I'm at risk of becoming redundant, I'll again remind you to accept and use all the help you can during the first few weeks. It is an absolute must. You need all the time you can get for resting and recuperating, holding and caring for your baby, talking with and being close to your other children, and being

Mom to Mom...

with your husband.

Along these lines, Linda Brosio of Grass Valley, California, suggests:

When people ask how they can help, ask them to pick things up at the store for you or to bring frozen casseroles and groceries as baby gifts. You'll find that these are of enormous help!

Sandy Price of San Diego says:

Prepared frozen meals are an absolute godsend; an extra pair of hands in the shape of a mom or mom-in-law or husband on leave from work or a special friend is super, especially if you're a new mom or if there are siblings to be attended to.

Paid help at reasonable prices is also available. Consider hiring a college student for light housekeeping and giving some additional attention to your other children, if any. You might also consider having her do the grocery shopping and other errands that need to be done.

And, although more expensive, there is a service available in many states that promotes the idea of pampering and mothering the new mother. Those providing the service are called "doulas," a Greek word meaning "in service of." For $15 to $20 an hour, a doula will provide a variety of wonderful services: do some or all of the cooking, care for the other children, give advice on baby care and breastfeeding, and do whatever shopping may be necessary. The women who serve as doulas often have excellent credentials—they are usually either registered nurses or childbirth educators. For more information on such a service and to see if it's available in your area, contact the National Association of Postpartum Care Services at (201) 358-2703.

Your Little One's Coming . . .

- *Be sure to get as much rest as possible . . . a good way is to nap with your baby.*

   Don't make the very common mistake of thinking that now that the baby is down for a nap, you can "get a few things done." Take the advice of many, many moms . . . let those other things go—they'll wait—and get the rest that you need. If you don't, there are some real consequences, according to Linda Brosio:

   > *If you don't get enough rest, your milk supply will be low, you'll more likely get depressed and feel unbelievably fatigued, your body won't heal, and having a baby won't be as loving an experience by the time he's nine months old.*

   She also suggests:

   > *Tell your friends <u>ahead of time</u> who call about coming over for a visit that you look forward to seeing them and that you enjoy <u>short</u> one-half hour to one-hour visits.*
   >
   > *And, go ahead and wear your bathrobe to the door so that visitors can <u>see</u> that you're tired from being up all night.*

- *Tell yourself that it's OK to take three months to finish your thank you notes!*

   Wait for two or three weeks before trying to write your thank you notes. Then . . . do only two a day. Writing just one or two a day may seem like a turtle's pace, but you can be sure that you'll finish them . . . eventually . . . and everyone *will* understand! Spend most of whatever free time you may have on resting and relaxing!

Mom to Mom . . .

Potpourri of Other Great Ideas . . .

- *Tape record various stages of "talk" development from birth.*

    Conduct a delightful taping session periodically—at six weeks, three months, six months, etc. You will be so pleased with the results! You can begin each session with "Today is (date) and (name) is (age)." When they actually begin to respond to you, you can play with them, ask them questions, have them tell stories or talk about their adventure for the day, etc.

- *Also videotape their physical development.*

    Camcorders can be expensive but it is possible to borrow or even rent one for a short while from time to time. The great advantage of recording using video cassettes is that they can be viewed immediately and reused if the pictures didn't turn out as you had wanted. With movie cameras, the film must first be developed before you can screen it—at considerable expense—and if it isn't as you had hoped, it's too late. The day, the special occasion, or just that special moment has long passed. Most people today do have a VCR and a television, so it makes good sense to either invest in a camcorder or borrow one.

    We were fortunate enough to be given a camcorder as a gift from our family, but 13 months had passed since Maryanna's birth before we had one. Although we have hundreds (thousands?!) of wonderful pictures of her infancy and babyhood, we do not have a "moving" record of her beginning to crawl or of her standing up holding onto the couch or coffee table or of her taking her first steps . . . . So we highly recommend finding a way to use one occasionally to record those special, never-to-be-repeated times.

A couple of other delightful suggestions from other moms . . .

Cut out big, colorful, happy faces from magazines or use photos of family members. Punch a hole at the top of each one and pin the pictures around the inside of your baby's

Your Little One's Coming...

bassinet with safety pins. Babies love to look at these!

Sue Brandes
Des Plaines, Illinois

In order to cope better with your day, be up and dressed with make-up on before the baby and/or other children wake up each morning.

Sandy Price
San Diego, California

Note: But beware... don't bury yourself in "the guilties" in the first few weeks if you find yourself still in your bathrobe at three in the afternoon! *Every* new mom, including myself, has found herself in the very same situation! Sometimes it would be two or three days before I'd find myself in anything else but a bathrobe!

Just consider the day after we brought Maryanna home as an example! We had breakfast at 2 in the afternoon, lunch around 5, and dinner at 8:30 or so!

To give you an idea of what to expect, I overheard my husband say on the phone a few days after we had brought Maryanna home, "Maryanna just sleeps and eats and yet we don't seem to do anything else!"

Remember, it really does get easier every month that goes by and ... you can't spoil your baby, even if you hold him all day.

Linda Brosio
Grass Valley, California

---

[1] Author and source unknown
[2] Adapted from the handout, "Lamaze Goodie Bag," from the Prepared Childbirth Education Program at Mercy Hospital and Medical Center in San Diego, California.

Mom to Mom . . .

Clips and Notes

Your Little One's Coming . . .

Clips and Notes

Mom to Mom . . .

Clips and Notes

4

Feeding Time!

I often feel a spiritual communion with all the other mothers who are feeding their babies in the still of the night. Having a baby makes me feel a general closeness with humanity.[1]

When our first baby was born, I was convinced that **breastfeeding** was the way to go. But I had some real difficulties in the first month, and had I not known of some important resources to turn to for help, encouragement, *and solutions,* I might have quit. It's because of that experience that my coverage of feeding predominantly concerns breastfeeding. The coverage includes a review of some of the *common* problems that can be encountered by some women so that if you, too, have difficulties at first, you may less likely become discouraged. By having the information, I hope you'll feel more knowledgeable and therefore more willing to seek out guidance, even beyond your pediatrician if that's necessary.

Whether to breastfeed or bottle feed your baby is a big decision and one that only you can make. The decision depends on many things—your temperment, the kind of life you plan to lead or need to follow, e.g., will you have to return to work soon after the baby is born or will you be able or wanting to spend the first several months caring for your baby yourself? The answers to these and other questions will determine which method of feeding you will ultimately choose. Although breastfeeding is best for your baby *physically,* if it's something you're just not comfortable with, then bottle feeding will be the best choice. But, if you're not really sure, you might consider trying breastfeeding first, since you can always easily switch to the bottle if that turns out to be best for you. Unfortunately, the

Mom to Mom . . .

reverse isn't true—you can't easily begin with the bottle, and several days or weeks later decide to try breastfeeding.

Regardless of whether you have decided to breastfeed or bottle feed your baby, there two little books that I highly recommend you have from the very beginning:

Good Nutrition for Your Baby by Elizabeth Jones, Ph.D, R.D.

> This *excellent* booklet not only concisely gives the basics of sound breastfeeding and bottle feeding methods, but it guides you from the first month on through 12 months and beyond in what to feed your baby and how. It briefly explains by month the developmental stage of your baby and guides you in when, how, and in what amounts to start solids. It was written by the pediatric nutritionist for Wellstart, the San Diego Lactation Program, and I used it faithfully until my baby was completely on solids, with nursing remaining as just a supplement.
>
> You can order this booklet ($6.95) by calling the publisher: Slawson Communications, 1-800-SLAWSON, 8 to 5 Pacific Time. Or, you can write to them at 165 Vallecitos de Oro, San Marcos, CA 92069.

Another excellent guide that I found to be quite helpful is:

First Foods by Elisabeth Morse (one of the *Mothercare Nursery Guides*)

> This little book is loaded with information and guidance that covers the first two years of a baby's life. It's illustrated with helpful charts and beautiful full-color photographs. It includes guidance in breastfeeding and even covers what you'll probably experience for the first 14 days after birth. You'll also find complete information on bottle feeding, the introduction of solid foods, problem eaters, eating utensils for all stages of messiness and poor coordination, common weaning problems, etc. It's well worth having on your bookshelf!

Feeding Time!

BREASTFEEDING

Recommended Reading . . .

Here are two books on breastfeeding that will give you much of the information you'll need when you need it. The La Leche League is a good source of information, and a League Leader is usually available by phone to give you assistance. But you may occasionally have some important questions in the middle of the night—not a real popular time to be calling anyone!

Why two resources instead of just one? As excellent as each of these books is, I found that there were times when one didn't give me the answer that I was looking for, but the other did.

The Womanly Art of Breastfeeding, Fourth Edition-Revised 1987 by La Leche League International

> I found this book to be the most helpful in preparing for as well as in managing breastfeeding. This latest edition is especially encouraging and helpful. It has a new easy-to-access format that makes reading and quick reference quite simple! It is filled with the latest information on positioning your baby at the breast, avoiding sore nipples, breastfeeding and working, and breastfeeding when your baby is jaundiced. Two chapters are devoted to breastfeeding in special situations, such as breastfeeding twins, a premature baby or, as in my case, a baby with slow initial weight gain. It also discusses such important topics as child-led weaning and mother-led weaning and how to accomplish it in a loving, gentle way.

Successful Breastfeeding by Nancy Dana and Anne Price

> This is a great reference and also very easy to use. The chapters are laid out and sub-headed so well, making them easy to skim, allowing you to find the answers to your questions easily. It's very well written and includes many pictures and other helpful illustrations.

In addition to the above, if you also have Penelope Leach's book, *Your Baby and Child from Birth to Age Five,* you'll have practically a

Mom to Mom...

complete set of information at your fingertips! Her section on feeding during the infant's first days is very thorough and gives some valuable advice and guidance for the breastfeeding mother.

Breast is Best...

Experts in infant nutrition and feeding, including The American Academy of Pediatrics, agree—breast is best when feeding an infant. These experts believe that the *best* infant nutrition can be obtained from *exclusive* breastfeeding for the first four to six months of life.[1] Breast milk supplies the optimal ratio of fat, protein, and carbohydrates as well as the correct amount of calories to provide the very best nutrition a mom can give her infant. Although formula also provides each of the elements above, the *composition* of each just can't be artificially duplicated. In addition, all the other elements in breast milk—vitamins, minerals, enzymes, and water—are in the exact amounts that an infant needs and can best utilize.

Most experts in breastfeeding also agree that unnecessary supplementing with formula or with early introduction of solids "compromises and diminishes the maximum benefits of breastfeeding."[2]

Here are some of the wonderful benefits breastfeeding provides:

1. First and foremost, your baby receives the *best nutrition* available for his early growth and development.

2. Your baby can't be allergic to your breast milk—but he *could* possibly be allergic to any of the various formulas on the market.

   Although it's possible that your baby could react to certain foods in your diet, those culprits are generally commonly known and can be easily eliminated from your diet.

3. Your baby can't be overfed, as is possible with formula, which is a big plus for his health.

4. Your baby receives a whole army of immunological benefits from breast milk which is *impossible* for formulas to duplicate.

Feeding Time!

Such a benefit means that your baby will experience fewer incidences of ear infections, diarrhea, respiratory infections (e.g., pneumonia), and will often be able to resist many illnesses to which you are exposed.

For us, we were amazed at how healthy our baby was and continued to be! Her first hint of illness came at *16 months* old—and that was simply an unsightly reccurring rash due to a minor virus. Until then, she only experienced runny noses due to teething! She was even exposed to chicken pox at three months—I was horrified! But, probably thanks to exclusive breastfeeding, she remained free of the disease! And as for diarrhea, her *first* short bout of that occurred when she was *three years* old!

According to the La Leche League International:

> *It has only recently been discovered that the mother of a nursing six-month-old has even more immunities in her milk than in her colostrum* [when her baby was born], *and at one year the level of immunities is higher still. Therefore, in addition to comforting the older baby, you are also helping to provide him with protection from illness as long as you nurse.*
>
> "La Leche League discusses The Joys of Breastfeeding"
> *Baby Talk,* November 1985

This again has proved to be true from our experience. I followed child-led weaning, and consequently nursed our daughter until she was three and a half. Although nursings were only at bedtime by the time she was weaned, her first three years were relatively illness-free with the exception of the common cold.

5. Breastfeeding promotes proper tooth, gum, and jaw development which can be a problem with bottle fed infants.

   A study done by Miriam H. Labbok, M.D., of the Johns Hopkins School of Hygiene and Public Heralth, and Gerry E.

Mom to Mom . . .

Hendershot of the National Center for Health Statistics suggested that breast fed babies have straighter teeth. The dental histories of over 10,000 children were reviewed by these two researchers and it was found that those who had been bottle fed or had been breast fed for three months or less had a much higher incidence of irregular teeth. The theory seems to be that babies who are breast fed use their tongues differently than those who are bottle fed, and they use their mouth muscles more vigorously during breastfeeding, all of which seem to influence bone growth and tooth alignment.[3]

6. Your baby's stool will not have nearly the disagreeable odor that the stool of formula-fed babies has.

7. When your baby spits up, which is inevitable, it too will not have the disagreeable odor that formula can produce.

8. Breastfeeding enhances the bonding process.

    Breastfeeding requires some quiet cuddling time that both you and your baby will thoroughly look forward to! In addition, due to the hormones released during breastfeeding, you will find that if you're feeling harried and worn, you will soon relax and completely enjoy the cuddling moments with your little one.

    When Maryanna was a few months old and into her big toothless grins, she would often pull away from my breast for a moment, look at me intently for a second and then give me the biggest, most wonderful toothless grin! She'd then enthusiastically return to her nursing! What a joy!

9. Breast milk is the most convenient and portable food you can have for your baby!

    Wherever you go with your baby, your milk is always ready—it never needs mixing, it's always the right temperature, and its "containers" are always sterile. There are no dirty bottles to mess with and no equipment to carry around with you in your diaper bag. It's perfect and sooooo convenient!

Feeding Time!

10. Breast milk is inexpensive—its only cost is that of keeping your diet well balanced and full of nutrition.

11. In producing breast milk, your body uses up calories and works on the fat stores that were created during your pregnancy.

You CAN be Successful with Breastfeeding . . .

Breastfeeding, as you can see, is the best choice for feeding your baby when personal preference and circumstances allow. But unfortunately, many women discontinue their breastfeeding within the first month because they erroneously believe that they aren't and can't be successful at breastfeeding their babies. They come to this conclusion because of inadequate information, or pressure from "well-meaning" family members, or because of erroneous advice from their inadequately informed pediatricians. (Yes, there really *are* inadequately informed pediatricians!)

If you choose to breastfeed your baby, that's *wonderful!* But be prepared. You may have no difficulties at all—and then again, you may. *But the vast majority of difficulties experienced can be easily solved and eliminated.* Your breastfeeding *can* be successful and *will be* successful if you're *committed enough* to finding the solutions.

According to Dr. Margaret C. Neville, failures in breastfeeding are most often because of "improper interaction between mother and infant, either due to inadequate feeding routines or inadequate suckling for some other reason."[4]

Below are just some of the reasons I have heard women give for discontinuing breastfeeding:

1. "I was losing weight too fast, so my doctor told me I had to quit breastfeeding."

2. "My doctor said that my baby wasn't regaining her birth weight because I couldn't produce enough volume, so I had to quit."

Mom to Mom ...

3. "My mother-in-law said that my baby was crying all of the time because I didn't have enough milk, and my husband agreed."

4. "My nipples were always sore—I just couldn't breastfeed. It hurt too much. I just wasn't made for breastfeeding."

5. "I had to take a really strong medication, so I was told I couldn't breastfeed my baby any more."

Although these are reasons given by women who discontinued their breastfeeding, there are simple ways to correct at least the first four of the above problems without having to discontinue breastfeeding. The mothers simply didn't have the correct guidance and probably were unaware of other sources to go to for help and guidance. As for number 5, there are often similar medications that are safe that can be substituted for the one that is contraindicated for breastfeeding.

If you should experience some difficulties with breastfeeding your baby, do not stop your breastfeeding before you consider the following:

1. There are medical practitioners who *specialize* in the evaluation of breastfeeding problems and the successful management of breastfeeding. Contact a member of the team listed for your region for a referral to a specialist in your area. (See Appendix B: Indispensible Resources, Lactation Consultants—Regional Listings on pages 397-402.)

2. There are several *correctable* reasons why there may be difficulties with breastfeeding. Some concern the mother—some concern the infant.

    (The following is a compilation and condensation of the reasons for poor infant weight gain found in Dr. Neville's book, *Lactation: Physiology, Nutrition, and Breast Feeding*[5] and in Dr. Ruth A. Lawrence's book, *Breastfeeding—Third Edition, A Guide for the Medical Profession*[6])

    Concerning the mother ...

    (a) Poor Milk Production Due to Inappropriate Feeding Techniques

Feeding Time!

This occurs primarily because of inadequate knowledge and inexperience on the part of the mother and is the leading cause of poor weight gain in newborns. Examples of this are:

(1) Feeding intervals may be stretched to four hours or more when, for breastfed newborns, the intervals should be no more than two to three hours.

(2) Feedings may be restricted due to sore nipples, resulting in insufficient breast stimulation to generate a sufficient milk supply.

(3) The baby may be put to one breast for too short a period of time and thus won't stimulate a good milk supply.

(4) The mother may incorrectly expect her newborn to sleep through the night.

(5) The mother may be away from her infant for extensive periods of time during the day.

(6) The infant may be given a pacifier too frequently, making him too tired to suck adequately when feeding.

(7) The mother may give water after breastfeeding which provides no calories but fills a baby up, causing him to subsequently nurse less often.[7]

(b) Poor Production Due to Other Causes

   (1) Fatigue

   This is the most common and may be a result of the demands of the mother's infant (and other children) during the night, pressures by the family for meals and other needs, or demands she places on herself concerning career, job, and/or social commitments.

   (2) Inadequate diet

   (3) Illness

Mom to Mom . . .

    (c) Interference with Milk Let-Down

    This situation may be caused by:

        (1) Severe or chronic sore nipples

            (which in turn may be caused by incorrect positioning at the breast)

        (2) Substance abuse

            (Excessive smoking and alcohol intake)

        (3) Some medications

        (4) Psychological inhibitors

            [a] Anxiety

            [b] Stress

    (d) Failure of the Breast to Respond to Appropriate Nursing Stimulation

    This may be due to:

        (1) Some drugs (legitimate and otherwise)

        (2) Another pregnancy

        (3) Supplementing the daily diet with 25-200 mg. of B_6 daily

            The RDA for a lactating mother is 2.5 mg./daily. However, some nutrition-conscious mothers take far more than the recommended dosage without realizing that large doses of B_6 can suppress lactation.[8]

        (4) Prior breast surgery (diagnostic and cosmetic)

    (e) Abnormalities in Milk Composition

    This is a rare situation, but it is commonly overdiagnosed. In order to correctly determine the composition of a mother's breast milk, the breast must be completely emptied and analyzed under research conditions. Normally, in an office visit, just a sample is taken. Consequently, all that is collected is the foremilk—that which

Feeding Time!

contains little fat—and does not include the hind milk which is loaded with fat.

If there is inadequate vitamin content, it's due to the mother's deficient diet.

Concerning the infant . . .

(a) Insufficient Suckling Stimulation

This refers to the infant who simply does not nurse vigorously and does not demand to be fed as often as he should.

(b) Physical Abnormalities which Hinder Feeding

Such abnormalities include cleft palate, micrognathia, high arched palate, cept of the tongue, or other malformation.

(c) Possible Organic Illness in the Infant

If you believe you're having difficulty with your breastfeeding, be sure that your difficulty is being *thoroughly* investigated by your pediatrician. A pediatrician who is trying to identify the reasons for an infant's poor weight gain should be asking *a lot of questions*. These questions should touch on such things as your feeding schedule, the pattern of those feedings (e.g., are you supplementing at all?), the presence of any physical or emotional stresses (e.g., attitudes of your husband and other relatives), whether your periods have begun (which indicates insufficient nursing), etc. If your pediatrician is not asking questions like these, don't hesitate a minute to contact a medical practitioner who is a *specialist* in breastfeeding.

Our pediatrician asked none of these questions and apparently assumed, when my baby was four weeks old and was *still* five ounces shy of her birthweight, that I was unable to produce the necessary volume and would therefore have to supplement her feedings until she was weaned. Fortunately I knew of Wellstart—the San Diego Lactation Program co-directed by Dr. Audrey Naylor, a pediatrician, and Ruth Wester, R.N., who, along with their staff of pediatric nutritionists and nurse practitioners, are specialists in breastfeeding. After just the first visit to their

Mom to Mom . . .

office, our baby began to gain very quickly—four ounces in just three days! Their solutions were quite simple: Eat more calories and feed her more frequently. Our pediatrician had me feeding her every three to four hours, with four hours being the preferred of the two according to him, so my breasts "could fill up"!

Some Helpful Tips Concerning Successful Breastfeeding . . .

- *If you need to supplement initially because your milk is delayed in coming in after birth, seek out the help of a lactation consultant, for there are methods of supplementing that do not require using a bottle.*
- *To increase your volume:*

    (1) Watch your diet carefully—be sure to eat a sufficient number of calories.

    A lactating mother requires approximately *500 extra calories a day,* over and beyond the number of calories she needs to maintain her own body. Milk production requires approximately 900+ calories a day. The additional calories needed over and above your intake of 500 comes from your stores of fat accumulated during pregnancy.

    Your weight loss should not exceed one or two pounds a month after the initial loss of fluids following birth. If you are at or below your prepregnancy weight, you may need to increase the number of additional calories from 500 to possibly 900 or 1,000.

    (2) Drink plenty of fluids (water, juices, milk).

    Drink to satisfy your thirst each time you feed your baby, at least eight to ten times a day.

    (3) Nurse your baby every two hours—or more often if your baby is hungry— for 15 minutes at each breast.

    Dr. Nancy Powers of Wellstart in San Diego suggests that it's better to watch your baby than to watch the clock. "I usually advise watching the baby instead of the clock. Feed

Feeding Time!

your baby until your baby is no longer actively swallowing, then change sides. You can return to the first side again."

Remember, every two hours means two hours from the time you *began* the last feeding, *not* from the time you stopped the last feeding.

(4) Express any remaining milk from each breast.

This is easier if you use a warm compress on your breasts first, then express either by hand or pump.

- *Refrigerate or freeze expressed breast milk to be prepared for those times when you may have to be away at feeding time.*

There are good reasons for having some breast milk stored in the refrigerator or freezer:

(1) You may have to be away from your baby at a feeding time because of an appointment where it would not be the most convenient to have your baby with you.

(2) You may want to give your husband an opportunity to feed the baby.

(3) Or, as in a situation I experienced, you may be given a very strong drug to rid yourself of an extremely severe headache or some other brief circumstance, and thus not be able to nurse your baby for 24 hours.

When Maryanna began sleeping for six and seven hours straight at night and my breasts would get uncomfortably full, I would hand express some of my milk to store in the freezer for use at another time. The stored milk came in handy many times, especially when I started preparing cereals for her at six months.

Mom to Mom ...

Breast Milk Storage Regulations[10]	
Fresh Breast Milk	If not to be used within 30 minutes, it must be refrigerated.
Refrigerated Breast Milk	24 hours in 40 degrees F. refrigerator
Thawing Breast Milk	40 hours in 40 degrees F. refrigerator
Frozen Breast Milk	6 months in 0 degrees freezer

- *To express breast milk, either express it by hand or use one of several breast pumps on the market.*

    Some of the better pumps are:

    (1) Kaneson (sometimes called the Marshall-Kaneson) Breast Pump (approx. $30)

    This is the only pump that Wellstart, the San Diego Lactation Program recommends because it is "consistently effective."

    (2) Egnell Hand-Operated Breast Pump (approx. $13.95)

    (3) Lloyd-B Breast Pump (approx. $49.95)

    These pumps are available at many baby stores and some large department stores with baby departments.

    It's important to remember that a breast pump is helpful but *it does take practice.* Don't become discouraged if the amount of milk you are able to collect isn't much at first. Just remind yourself that using a pump—or even hand expressing—is a skill and it takes practice to collect several ounces.

- *To hand express breast milk that you plan to store:*

    Materials needed:
    (a) Sterile plastic baby bottle
    (b) Or, Hand Expression funnel by Medela

Feeding Time!

(1) Use a warm compress on each breast. (Wring out a wash cloth in very warm water) and hold it on each breast for a minute or two.

(2) Holding your breast with the palm of one hand, gently massage the breast by stroking down toward the areola—the nipple area.

(3) Continue the massage all the way around the breast.

(4) With the right hand for the right breast and the left for the left, support your breast with the palm.

(5) With the opposite hand, hold the container in which the milk is to be collected.

(5) Now, place your thumb about half-way up your breast and then firmly move it down the breast.

(6) When your thumb comes to the edge of the areola, press in and up, without touching the nipple. Your milk will squirt from your nipple into the waiting container.

- *To refrigerate or freeze breast milk for future use:*

    Materials needed:

    (a) Sterile disposable bottle liners (e.g., Evenflo's box of 100)

    (b) Wire twist strips

    (c) Masking tape for labeling (date and number of ounces)

    (1) Empty the collected breast milk into sterile disposable bottle liners—one and two ounces to a liner.

    Storing the breast milk in such small amounts is the most convenient because:

    (a) When frozen, it thaws faster when placed in warm water.

    (b) A large portion of breast milk isn't spoiled when only a small amount is needed.

Mom to Mom...

For example, when your baby is ready for solids, you can use a one- or two-ounce bag of breast milk from the freezer to prepare her cereals without much waste.

(2) Squeeze as much of the air out of the liner as possible and twist shut, securing it with a wire twist strip.

(3) Prepare a label with masking tape for each of the liners filled, writing *the date and the number of ounces* that the liner contains.

(4) Place the liner standing up in the coldest part of the freezer.

(5) When the milk is frozen, you may want to consider putting the liners into a large zip lock bag.

Collecting the numerous little bags into one big bag is far more convenient than having several little bags loose in the freezer. If you have many little bags, you may want to label the large zip lock bag with the running dates it contains.

- *To thaw frozen breast milk:*

(1) Place the bag of frozen milk in a bowl of tap water about body temperature.

(2) *Do not use a microwave oven to defrost the milk* as it may alter the milk.

- *If a nursing strike occurs ...*

When your baby refuses to nurse for one or several days, your baby may be "on strike." A mom may think that child-led weaning is occurring, but that's almost never the case, since child-led weaning doesn't often occur before a baby is at least a year old and it doesn't occur suddenly.

Dr. Ruth A. Lawrence suggests some of the common causes of a nursing strike and some ways for bringing the strike to an end:[9]

Causes for nursing strikes:

(1) The beginning of the mother's periods

Feeding Time!

(2) A mother's dietary slip

(3) A mother's change in soap, perfume, or deodorant

(4) Stress in the mother

(5) Earache or nasal obstruction in the infant

(6) Teething

(7) An episode of biting that startled the mother or caused her obvious pain

Suggestions to help end the strike:

(1) Make feedings special and quiet with no distractions and no other people around.

(2) Increase the amount of cuddling, stroking, and soothing given to the infant.

(3) Offer the breast when the infant is very sleepy.

(4) Don't withhold feedings in order to make your baby so hungry he'll eat.

(5) If simple steps such as those outlined above do not result in a return to nursing, see the baby's physician to rule out illness or infection.

- *If you have any problems with plugged ducts . . .*

I found that a baby's hot water bottle was the perfect solution for me!

If the plugged duct(s) is on the outside of the breast—it usually feels like a hard lump—fill the little hot water bottle with hot tap water and lay on it for several minutes. If it's in another location of your breast, simply hold the water bottle firmly against the affected area for several minutes—ten, if possible. Then nurse your baby starting with the affected side first.

Mom to Mom...

Some Additional Thoughts on Breastfeeding from Other Moms...

I am a firm believer in nursing a baby on demand, especially the first several weeks. Think of what the little one has been through! It's a real shock for their little systems, I'm sure! Give them as much T.L.C. as they want and need.

I also felt that it was very important that I keep the girls in my room at night. If they awakened during the night, I would nurse them and both of us could get back to sleep easily. I never saw anything wrong with bringing little ones into bed with us. They always felt comforted lying either on my chest or Harry's. They loved the warmth and comfort!

Jan Sundblad
San Diego, California

Both of our babies were breast fed, and I would never do it any other way. We weren't rigid about a schedule, but we did try to keep fairly regular hours. That seemed to help everyone—we knew just about when to be in a good spot for lunch, and we could predict when "the crabbies" might set in. After they were well established, I encouraged them toward about four hours between nursings. A walk or other activity sometimes helped us stretch the time a bit.

Ann Gaines
Nevada City, California

If your doctor prescribes medication for you and tells you you'll have to stop nursing because of it, call the La Leche League or the Drug Hot Line at UCSD (University of California at San Diego)—(619) 294-6084—or a similar drug information line in your local area to check it out. Many medications are

Feeding Time!

safe for nursing mothers and doctors are often unaware of this.

Eileen Carroll
La Jolla, California

Breastfeeding and the Working Mom...

Recommended Reading...

Practical Hints for Working and Breastfeeding, a pamphlet by the La Leche League International, publication #83

> This illustrated, handy reference for working breastfeeding mothers contains guidelines on pumping, storing, and transporting breast milk, with feeding instructions for substitute caregivers. Also included are tips for the working mother on how to get the most from her experience.

The Working Woman's Guide to Breastfeeding by Nancy Dana and Anne Price

> This book offers practical advice for mothers who want to continue to breastfeed in situations that involve separation. It tells of the benefits to the mother, the baby, and the employer, as well as how to pump and store milk, select a breast pump, and work with day care. It also gives tips on how to dress and which types of supplies you'll need. Includes personal experiences of many employed, nursing mothers.

An Important Tip...

- *If at all possible, delay your return to work for 16 weeks following the birth of your baby.*

> There are two very important influences on whether or not a mother can maintain a long nursing relationship after she returns to work: the timing of her return and whether she works full-time or part-time.

Mom to Mom...

> If a mother returns to work before 16 weeks, her milk supply most likely is not firmly established and she may experience frequent bouts of engorgement and breast infections. According to a study done by Kathleen G. Auerback, Ph.D., and Elizabeth Guss, in their article, "Maternal Employment and Breastfeeding," in the *American Journal of Diseases of Children* (October, 1984), they found that those women who returned to work after 16 weeks had firmly established their nursing relationship and experienced relatively few difficulties compared with those mothers who returned to work sooner.[10]

BOTTLE FEEDING

Recommended Reading...

> *First Foods* by Elisabeth Morse (one of the *Mothercare Nursery Guides*)
>
> Highly recommended! The description of its contents appears on page 116 at the beginning of this chapter.
>
> *Your Baby and Child from Birth to Age Five* by Penelope Leach
>
> This reference provides ample guidance in bottle feeding your baby. Excellent discussion is given in choosing formulas, preparing the bottle-feedings, hygiene, and following a "supply and demand" schedule for the bottle-fed baby. Needed equipment is outlined and illustrations clearly depict the steps to take in sterilizing bottles, preparing various formulas, and feeding your baby. As I've said before, it should be on every mother's bookshelf!

Equipment...

For bottle feeding your baby, you will need to have the following equipment on hand:

    (1) 8 8-ounce plastic or glass bottles with nipples and lids

    (2) 6 4-ounce bottles with nipples and lids

Feeding Time!

(3) 4 extra nipples and nipple covers

(4) Tongs

(5) Covered jar to store sterile nipples

(6) Bottle brush

(7) Nipple brush

(8) Strainer

(9) Funnel

(10) Measuring cups

(11) Bottle warmer (optional)

Notice that sterilizing equipment is no longer included on a list for the equipment needed for bottlefeeding. Most pediatricians in the U.S. no longer feel it's necessary. Instead, they recommend using hot soapy water and a bottle brush for the nipples, bottles, and caps. In many other countries, sterilization remains a necessity.

An Important Caution . . .

- *Be sure to prepare the formula <u>exactly</u> as the instructions read on the label.*

    Over diluting or under diluting the formula or packing the formula in the measuring spoon can eventually be harmful for your baby.

Keys to Successful Bottle Feeding . . .

- *Every morning, prepare at one time all the formula that you will use during the next 24-hour period and leave it in the refrigerator.*

- *Keep all the equipment you need in one place, cleaned, and ready for use.*

- *Warm the formula when it's feeding time by standing the bottle*

Mom to Mom . . .

> *taken from the refrigerator in a bowl of hot water or in a bottle warmer.*
>
> - *Cut down on the interruptions during a feeding by collecting the things you will need during the feeding, e.g., tissues, a diaper (for spit-ups and spills), etc.*
> - *Sit in a comfortable chair (a rocker?), and try to prop your feet up.*
> - *Be sure to keep the nipple filled with milk to try to avoid air bubbles.*
> - *Burp your baby half-way through the feeding.*
> - *Throw away any leftover formula.*

MINIMIZING SPIT-UPS . . .

Spitting up is normal—all babies do it. But here are a few suggestions by Peggy Eastman to help keep them to a minimum:[11]

> *(1) Time your feedings so your baby isn't overly hungry, because when she's very hungry she'll tend to gulp food and swallow air, which can trigger throwing up.*
>
> *(2) Try short, frequent feedings of smaller amounts of milk.*
>
> *(3) Burp her before a feeding, especially if she was crying.*
>
> *(4) If you're breastfeeding, burp your baby when you switch breasts and after each feeding.*
>
> *(5) If your baby is bottle-fed, burp her about halfway through the feeding and at the end.*
>
> *(6) After feeding and burping, put your baby at a 35-to 45-degree angle in a baby seat for half an hour.*
>
> *(7) Place your baby on her right side to go to sleep—the milk is less likely to come back up in this position.*

Feeding Time!

INTRODUCING SOLIDS . . .

Some will tell you that giving your baby solids at three months or even sooner will "give him more food" and will "help her sleep through the night," both of which are false. Your breast milk is providing all the nourishment that your baby needs for the first four to six months of life and whenever your baby "needs more food," your baby simply increases his demand. Your body then produces more or, if you're bottle feeding, you provide more formula. It's miraculous and it's wonderful! Once you begin to introduce solids, your baby will begin to take in less breast milk—or formula.

When you and your baby are ready to begin solids, there are some excellent books to give you some needed guidance on what to prepare and how.

Good Nutrition for Your Baby by Jones, Elizabeth G., R.D.

> This excellent book was recommended at the beginning of this chapter. If you haven't already ordered a copy, you may want to consider it now. It's extremely helpful in getting you through the introductory stages of solids. (Ordering information is listed with its description on page 116.)

Baby's First Helpings by Chris Casson Madden

> This isn't just a great cook book full of nutritious snack and meal items for your little one, but it's full of excellent information of additives, preservatives, salt and sugar. Her style is delightful, the recipes delicious for little ones, and the guidance outstanding!

First Foods by Elisabeth Morse (a *Mothercare Nursery Guide*)

> This book has been recommended before under breastfeeding and bottle feeding. Here again, it is highly recommended, for it gives thorough guidance in the introduction of solids and specifically how to prepare your own baby foods. The illustrations are helpful and the steps are very easy to follow and understand.

Mom to Mom...

Instant Baby Food by Linda McDonald

> This is a great book! It gave me, as a new mother, that much needed guidance on "when, how, how much, and how to prepare." Linda McDonald shows her readers how to make foods palatable and how to retain food values, and she provides a list of what foods to avoid. She then continues with several chapters of recipes for wonderful, nutritious ways to prepare solids for little ones.

To Begin Introducing Solids...

- *Follow your pediatrician's guidelines.*

But, be sure that your pediatrician does give you the guidance that you want and need. We had the experience of our pediatrician simply giving my husband the list of foods to introduce and in what order, but that was it. There was no caution expressed about how rapidly to introduce them or in what amounts. Either he assumed that we were well read in this area or that we had guidance from other parents of small children.

Generally, pediatricians recommend the following:

(1) Introduce one food at a time at weekly intervals, in the following suggested order.

   In this way, you can easily identify any likes and dislikes, and, more importantly, any problem foods that seem to cause digestive difficulties or allergic reactions.

(2) As a first food, introduce iron-fortified rice cereal.

   Begin with very small amounts—1 teaspoon of dry cereal mixed with 2 teaspoons of breast milk or formula.

(3) Follow the rice cereal with other iron-fortified baby cereals or alternate with #4 below, the introduction of various fruit.

(4) Next, introduce fruit or vegetables.

   Mashed banana as a first fruit is a real favorite with babies. They *love* it! Other fruit to introduce are apples, pears,

Feeding Time!

peaches, melons, and apricots. These should be stewed, to make them soft and easy to handle. However, an alternative is to use a grapefruit spoon (the type with a jagged edge at the end of the spoon) and scrape the apple or pear—it works beautifully, and the fruit in its skin serves as its own bowl!

If, for some reason, your baby is one who doesn't care for mashed banana, you might try a sweet potato or yam that has been baked in its shell (to preserve its nutrients).

There are just a few cautions to keep in mind with fruit:

(a) Fruit that has little seeds should be introduced after a baby is six months old.

(b) Citrus fruits should be avoided until after 12 months of age because of possible allergic reactions.

(c) Canned fruit, unless packed in water, is loaded with sugar.

(d) Dried fruit such as dates, raisins, and figs, are nutritious but should be given toward the end of the first year and in small quantities. They are very sweet and tend to stick between the teeth promoting tooth decay.

(5) Meats

(6) Whole-Grain Breads and Cereals

Finger-sized pieces of dried or toasted whole wheat bread are great for chewing and teething on.

Good snacks are also Oat Rings (in the baby food section of the grocery store) and Cheerios (the unsugared variety).

- *The mess that may be created after a feeding session won't be nearly as difficult to clean up if you use an old shower curtain or newspapers under the high chair!*

- *Due to its link with causing botulism in babies, do not give honey to your baby in any form until after he is a year old.*

Mom to Mom . . .

Making Your Own Foods . . .

Although there is greater convenience in giving your baby commercially prepared foods, there are a number of advantages to preparing your own:

(1) You can be certain of each item's contents (ensuring that salt, filler, and sugar haven't been added);

(2) Home-prepared foods are very adaptable to your baby's appetite, taste, and digestion;

(3) Home-prepared foods can be served in different ways, changing their appearance and texture;

(4) Home-prepared foods can be adapted to finger foods as your little one gets older.

(5) You can control the amount of food prepared for any one meal and avoid a lot of waste.

All of this is not to say that you should never consider using commercially prepared baby food. On the contrary . . . it is much easier to put jars of fruit, meat, and vegetables in your diaper bag if you are planning to be away from home at meal time, because you don't have to be concerned about refrigeration.

An additional advantage of home-prepared food is that it serves as an excellent preparation for family meals. Your baby will become familiar with the various tastes, aromas, and textures of what your family normally eats, and he will delight in the fact that he is eating what everyone else is!

- *The following items will be helpful in preparing your little one's early solids:*

    (1) Baby grinder (food mill)

    (2) Blender

    If your baby is six months or older when he begins solids, he will not not need his food to be liquefied or pureed—just mashed. He'll need and want some texture to his food.

    (3) Steamer or steaming basket for a pot

Feeding Time!

- (4) Extra ice cube trays
- (5) Small zip-type plastic bags or small plastic bags with wire twists
- (6) Large zip bags or large plastic bags with wire twists
- (7) Masking tape for labels

• *When thawing or reheating food previously prepared, place it in a cup and put the cup in boiling water to heat through.*

• *When feeding your little one solids, have these materials available:*

- (1) High chair

    (See pages 297-298 for suggestions in shopping for one.)

- (2) Plastic bibs (preferably with velcro closures)

    Terry cloth bibs are soft and feel nice but they must be rinsed out or washed after every use. Plastic bibs, on the other hand, can be easily wiped off and presto! They're ready for the next meal!

- (3) Grapefruit spoon (to finely grate apples or other fruit)
- (4) Teflon-coated spoons
- (5) Cups with lids with a spout
- (6) Plastic plates with dividers, straight sides, and a suction cup on the bottom (the suction cup prevents the plate from sliding around on the table or high chair)
- (7) Baby spoon and fork for baby to play with (when your baby is over six months)
- (8) And, equally important, a big apron for you or whomever feeds your little one!

Additional Suggestions from Other Moms . . .

Joanna was positively bored with nursing at six months; the cup was much more exciting to her. Unfortunately, both of our babies were allergic to cow's milk. After

Mom to Mom . . .

reading the label on a can of soy formula ("Nothing real added") I began to look for a better way. Goat's milk was the answer. It can be bought canned (evaporated) and reconstituted 1:1 with water, or in cartons, both whole and 2%. It proved to be a perfect solution. Both children were able to tolerate cultured milk products like cheese and yogurt, and later, cow's milk.

When they began eating solids, I integrated their diet with ours as quickly as possible. I set aside small amounts of whatever we ate, pureed it in the blender, and froze it in ice cube trays. Then I packaged it in the freezer containers. Shortly before mealtime I took out "cubes" of whatever I needed, put them in a dish (china or stoneware) and set the dish in a small amount of water in a saucepan. Then I covered the saucepan and brought the water to a simmer until the cube was defrosted and just the right temperature. The dish stayed warm while the baby ate.

Ann Gaines
Nevada City, California

I bought a portable grinder and would carry it in my diaper bag. Whenever we'd stop at a restaurant, I was able to let our baby eat what we were eating.

Jan Sundblad
San Diego, California

Preparing for Sitters

Regardless of whether a sitter comes to your home or you take your little one to her home for care, you may want to prepare your little one's "meals" ahead of time, not only to ensure that he will be fed adequately but will also be fed according to your requirements.

Feeding Time!

For Breastfed Babies...

- *If you have bags of expressed milk stored in the freezer, remove the number that will be needed for the time you will be away and place them in the refrigerator.*

- *Write out the instructions on how to prepare it and be sure to include the precaution: "Do not warm in the microwave oven."*

    Be sure that:

    (1) Your instructions are absolutely clear—go over each one verbally with the sitter before leaving.

    Include instructions on when to feed your baby—at a certain time? When he becomes especially fussy? Also include where to find more milk (in the freezer?) should the sitter need it.

    (2) All the sitter will need is out on the kitchen counter and ready to use, e.g., bowl for warming the milk, plastic bottle(s) and nipple(s), burping cloth, bibs, washcloth, etc.

For Bottlefed Babies...

- *Collect everything that the sitter will need and write out your instructions.*

    Be sure that:

    (1) Your instructions are absolutely clear—review each one with the sitter before leaving.

    Be sure to include instructions on the number of ounces of formula, how it is to be mixed, how to warm it, when your baby should be fed—at a certain time or when fussy? Where can she find more?

    (2) All the sitter will need is out on the kitchen counter and ready to use, e.g., bottle(s), nipple(s), bibs, burping cloth, washcloth, etc.

Mom to Mom...

For Babies on Solids...

- *Set out everything that the sitter will need to feed your baby.*

    If you make your own baby foods and they must remain refrigerated or frozen until needed, put the amounts you want given to your baby in little 2 oz. plastic containers or, if they are already frozen in one to two ounce amounts, collect the various "cubes" of food that you want given and have them ready for the sitter to remove and prepare.

    If you use commercially prepared baby foods, simply set out the jar(s) that you want used.

    Be sure to set out all the necessary implements as well, e.g., teflon-coated spoons, bibs, washcloth, cup or "teacher-beaker," bowl or sectioned-plate, etc.

For All the Above Categories...

- *Write out a standard list of instructions and either place it in a plastic sheet holder or laminate it with clear contact paper.*

    Each of the categories above included the suggestion, "Write out your instructions." This can be rather tedious, whether you leave your baby with someone frequently or even just occasionally. Also, the feeding routine may become so familiar to you that you will eventually leave an instruction or two out. When you have a spare minute and you aren't preparing to leave your baby with a sitter, take a few minutes to draft your instructions and review them. Once you are convinced that everything you would want a sitter to know has been included, slip the sheet of paper into a plastic holder or cover it using clear contact paper.

---

[1] Simone Bloom as quoted in *A Mother's Journal,* Running Press Book Publishers, Philadelphia, PA, 1985.
[2] Marianne Neifert, M.D., *Dr. Mom,* (New York, 1987), p. 173.
[3] *Ibid,* p. 174.

Feeding Time!

[5] Dr. Margaret C. Neville, *Lactation: Physiology, Nutrition, and Breastfeeding,* New York, 1989.
[6] *Ibid.*
[7] Dr. Ruth A. Lawrence, *Breastfeeding—Third Edition, A Guide for the Medical Profession,* C. V. Mosby Company, St. Louis, 1989.
[8] Comment added by Dr. Nancy Powers, pediatrician and breastfeeding specialist with Wellstart, the San Diego Lactation Program, San Diego, California.
[9] Nancy Dana and Anne Price, *Successful Breastfeeding—A Practical Guide for Nursing Mothers,* New York, 1985.
[10] Doris Haire and J. Haire, *Implementing Family Centered Maternity Care,* Seattle, 1974.
[11] Lawrence, p. 251.
[12] Karen Levine, "Breastfeeding and Work," *Parents Magazine,* November 1987, p. 67.
[13] Eastman, p. 93.

Mom to Mom . . .

Clips and Notes

Feeding Time!

Clips and Notes

Mom to Mom . . .

Clips and Notes

5

Daily Care

*Oh, cleaning and scrubbing will wait till tomorrow,
But children grow up, as I've learned to my sorrow.
So, quiet down cobwebs, dust, go to sleep.
I'm rocking my baby. Babies don't keep!*

Ruth Hulburt Hamilton[1]

Daily care—it can seem like such an enormous, overwhelming task once the reality sets in—and reality, you'll find, takes only a day or two to set in! There is so much to do, so much to become accustomed to. Not only are you getting used to breastfeeding and its demands—or bottle feeding and *its* demands—but you're changing diapers *frequently,* you're blurry-eyed because your little one hasn't the foggiest notion that you desperately need some sleep, rest, and recuperation... especially at night! And then, beyond the many diaper changings and the many clothes changings and the many feedings, you've probably discovered that your little one's crying frequently doesn't seem to be calmed by changings and feedings and routine checking for other discomforts. Now what?

The Best Advice...

The best advice for responding to inconsolable crying and to other perplexing circumstances is to *listen.* Listen to your little one... listen to your *instincts... listen.* By simultaneously listening to your little one and to your instincts, you'll know what to do, most of the time.

This wonderful advice which I try to put to constant use with our child came from Tine Thevenin, in her book, *The Family Bed.* She wrote a true story entitled "The Silver Bell" about herself and her little one, a

Mom to Mom...

story which is the best illustration of really *listening* to your baby—your child—that I've ever read. It had a profound influence on me. With her kind permission, I share it with you here:

> *Listen! Above the dresser in my bedroom hangs a little bell. A silver bell. It's a family birthbell which, with joyful ringing, first announced the birth of my mother, then myself, and then rang for the birth of the first grandchild—my daughter, Yvonne.*
>
> *One day I took it off the wall and, giving it a little shake, smiled at its clear, distinct sound. "Listen," it seemed to ring. "Remember to listen."*
>
> *It was twelve years ago when, full of confidence, I gently placed my newborn infant in her bassinet. I was proud and self-assured at the awesome responsibility of mothering. After all, I had read all the books and all I needed was a little cooperation and I would have the solution to any problem.*
>
> *I shook that silver bell then. But little did I realize what painful, frightening, confusing sounds, what utter cacophony I would experience before I truly heard with clarity the meaning of that ring. "Listen. Remember to listen."*
>
> *Oh, we had the usual moments of wavering, when things did not go as planned. Like any mother, I found some things perplexing. But, I figured, "She will learn."*
>
> *One day, for instance, I decided it was time for her to eat her first spoonful of mashed banana. I placed her in her high chair and coaxed, "Open up. Here comes the airplane." But just as the airplane landed she stuck out her tongue. What a stubborn child, I thought. Why doesn't she listen to me? She should eat it.*
>
> *When she was a year-and-a-half old, she began to protest at naptime. She would stand up in her crib and cry. For a fleeting moment I thought perhaps I should lie down with her until she was asleep, and then carefully climb out. But I decided against it because I was afraid the crib would collapse.*

So I put her in her bed, told her to go to sleep and walked away. As before she began to cry and this time she begged, "Mama, stay." But I did not really hear her plea. I only got frustrated because she did not cooperate with my scheme. I became angry at her crying because it made me feel powerless. So I ran away to the basement and waited, confused and very alone. And in the distance I heard her call me, "Mama."

At last it was quiet. I crept upstairs, and as I carefully approached the crib I saw my little baby child asleep. Yet even in her liberating sleep she was still sobbing. The words of Elizabeth Browning warned: "A child's sob in the silence curses deeper than a strong man in his wrath."

The daily agony continued, the battleground growing more fierce. With stubborn selfishness I listened only to myself, my own reasoning, and never once gave her a chance. I did not listen to her. I did not understand her. I did not know how. Instead I cried, "What is wrong with her?"

Then one evening while I was rocking her before bedtime, she began to weep. "Mama, stay." The crying intensified. Louder and louder she sobbed. She trembled. And I rocked and rocked. I rocked and rocked, rocked and rocked, back and forth, back and forth. And she cried and cried, and I rocked and rocked until at last I could not stand it any longer. I did not want to hear her anymore and I screamed, "Stop it!"

In shocked silence the world stood still and Yvonne lay her tear-drenched face upon my shoulder and whimpered.

Then it was as if God reached down and touched that silver bell.... I began to hear the meaning of that ring, "Listen. Remember to listen." And so, instead of putting her in her bed, I stayed.

Slowly I began to rock and softly, with a trembling voice, I began to hum a cradle song. When she was asleep, I carefully put her down and looked into the face of a little angel. I whispered, "I'll begin to listen now."

Mom to Mom . . .

> *Then a miracle happened. The brick wall of the tower, in which I had so securely placed myself, crumbled. As I began to listen I heard her fear, her needs, and her joys. One day she called, "Mama, look at the butterfly!" I turned and looked and then we both ran down the street chasing butterflies. I felt closer to my children than I had ever felt before. I had discovered the joy of listening....*
>
> *And so... I shake this silver bell again, because my life has been enriched when I remember to listen.*
>
> *And that, dear reader, is what this book* [The Family Bed] *has been all about; listening to the needs of your child and trusting in their innate goodness. Are things always going to go smoothly? No. Will it be rewarding? Yes.*[2]

It's a special story that makes a remarkable impression, isn't it? I read it when Maryanna was 15 months old and how I had wished I had read it much, much earlier. Like many new mothers-to-be, I had read "all the books" and felt prepared for most anything. But Maryanna's desperate wish for me to stay with her until she fell asleep just didn't follow the books. "The books" generally said to be firm, let her know it was time to sleep, and leave the room, returning only every five minutes or so to reassure her. The system apparently works for many children, but it didn't with Maryanna. Her crying just intensified and her desperate pleas for me to stay increased. She and I were *miserable*.

And then I read the above story. Since then, I and sometimes her daddy have happily rocked her to sleep, something my instincts had been prodding me to do for months. It's a very special time for us. Today she is four and will someday outgrow her need for us to be with her when she falls asleep, but until then we're happy and so is she. We finally listened.

About this chapter . . .

Several excellent books are on the market about the physical day-to-day care of your baby, some of which you may already have on your bookshelf, such as Penelope Leach's *Your Baby and Child from Birth to Age Five*. Consequently, this chapter is a supplement and suggests the little tricks and hints that have worked for other moms and me that the specialty books don't mention.

Daily Care . . .

Baths and Washing Hair . . .

Equipment

- Tub or basin
- Soft baby washcloth and hooded towel
- Very mild baby soap (bar or liquid)

(Shampoo isn't needed until your little one really has some hair. The mild baby soap will do.)

- *Remember that your infant's little body should not be submerged in water for a full bath until her umbilical cord has fallen off.*

- *Infants don't get very dirty, so a "full bath" really isn't a daily necessity.*

Their little bottoms, faces, and necks do need to be washed well daily, but not the full body. Full baths can be as often as once a day or as infrequent as once or twice a week.

- *When you do give a full bath, fill the baby tub or basin with just a small amount of water—that's all you will need and you'll feel more reassured and comfortable.*

- *If you're first-time parents, make bathing your infant a twosome activity!*

It is much easier to learn how to bathe an infant when there is an extra set a hands available to help! Just having the moral support of someone else is a tremendous help! Most newborns are not real excited about this bath idea and exercise their lungs and voices to let their displeasure be known!

Because of Maryanna's *extreme* displeasure with baths when she was a newborn, I would often wait to give her a full bath until Tom had returned from out of town. Instead, I would thoroughly wash her bottom and her face and neck and skip the full bath routine until he came home. I initially felt guilty but I found that it really was okay. Newborns just don't get very dirty except in the bottom department!

Mom to Mom . . .

- *Choose a "bathtub" that is most comfortable for you and your husband to use.*

  If you are a first-time parent, you may find that purchasing a molded infant tub that fits over the divider in your kitchen sink is the best bet for bathing your infant. These molded tubs are inexpensive and come with a foam covered, slanted bottom that makes it much easier to handle a wet baby. The baby is tilted which keeps his head away from any water and the foam covering keeps him from sliding down toward the bottom. Because it's molded to fit over the divider, the other side of the baby tub is a container for bath items that you'll find quite convenient. It keeps everything within easy reach when you need it.

  For experienced parents, you may find that such a tub is no longer necessary. If you still have one from your first baby, great! But if not, you'll probably find that using the kitchen sink or bathroom basin is just as simple, although you may at first believe that being an octopus would be more advantageous!

  If you use the sink or basin routine, be sure to:

  (1) Cover the kitchen sink's depressed drain cover with a commercial rubber circle for that purpose (using a regular washrag doesn't work—it floats to the top or constantly shifts due to the movement of the water).

  (2) Move or cover the faucet so that if your baby's head accidentally hits it, the "bonk" won't be too serious, or, if the faucet is quite warm, your baby's skin won't be burned should his arm or shoulder or back or . . . bump against it.

- *Be sure the room you use is warm and draft-free.*

- *Tie the baby towel around your neck (or pin it to your shirt, robe, or dress with clothes pins) so that you'll remain dry and you'll have the baby's towel readily available to wrap around him.*

  If you use the hooded variety, simply put the hood facing out at the bottom right when you pin it to yourself. Then it will be ready for you to bring up and put over your baby's head.

Daily Care...

- *Suggested bath routine:*
    (1) Use a soft washcloth or your hand to wash your baby.
    (2) Wash your baby's face with water only—even mild soap can cause irritation.
    (3) Give extra attention to such areas as the back of the ears and places where milk and spit-up can hide (e.g., chin crease and neck folds).
    (4) Talk to your baby—tell her what you're doing and what she's feeling.
- *Consider bathing your little one in the regular bathtub with you.*

    Stevie Wooten from Seattle, Washington, writes:

    > *I never had any trouble bathing or washing the hair of either Sean or Ryan when they were infants. After the first two weeks with Sean balanced in the little baby bath, squirming and whimpering, I bagged it and took him into the bathtub with me. It was easier to handle him. Plus I was so close and in the water with him that he thought it was a real ball! Bath time was his very favorite time and he liked having his hair washed. I followed suit with Ryan when he was a newborn and had the same results. A word of caution, though. I got in the tub first, and Ed handed the baby to me and later took him out. I didn't want to slip and have a bad accident.*

- *For just washing bottoms, see diapering suggestions below.*

Clothing and Dressing...

- *Be sure that your infant (and child as he grows) always sleeps in flame retardant clothing.*

    If you enjoy sewing and enjoy making your little one's sleepers, be sure that the fabric you use says "flame retardant" on the bolt. If it doesn't, it's not.

Mom to Mom...

- *Dress your newborn in soft, loose-fitting nightgowns at first.*

    Until his umbilical cord falls off, he will be much more comfortable if nothing stretches tightly over his navel area.

- *Dress your baby properly for the out-of-doors.*

    Babies can be taken out-of-doors at anytime after birth, but must be dressed *appropriately*. What's "appropriate" will depend on the weather. A good rule: Dress your little one in the same number of layers that *you* will need to be appropriately dressed.

    In the winter, a hat is a necessity because much of a baby's body heat (as well as an adult's) is lost through his head.

    Be sure to "glove" an infant's hands. Remember that frostbite targets are ears, fingers, toes, and chin.

    You can easily check to see if your baby is warm enough by slipping your fingers behind his neck. If he feels warm and comfortable, he is. An infant's hands and feet are often cool and therefore not accurate "thermometers" of his comfort.

Winter-time...

The following suggestions from the *Growing Parent* newsletter are quite helpful in dressing little ones during the winter:

Handy Tips for Winter Wear[3]

1. *Use several layers, i.e., thermal undershirt, long-sleeved cotton knit shirt, sweater, jacket.*
2. *Temperatures and chill factors should dictate the number of layers.*
3. *If temperatures are above 0 degrees, the outside layer should be water proof or repellent.*
4. *Below zero layering should be material that breathes: leather, cotton, down, fur.*
5. *Fit layers loosely into each other. Stuffing or packing a kid into clothes negates the layering effect. Check frequently for size changes.*

Daily Care . . .

6. Keep clothes clean and dry. Dampness and dirt clog insulating air spaces.

7. Warm heads mean warm feet. Seventy percent of one's body heat escapes out of the head.

8. For a baby, use blanket-weight sleepers, a size larger than usual, rather than an expensive snowsuit [and then securely wrap in blankets].

Making clothes last when little ones grow soooo fast . . .

- *Buy clothes a size or two larger than your baby's actual size.*

    Cuffs—at the ankles and at the wrists—can be rolled. Or, better yet, you can use colorful "cuff holders," either the commercial type especially for baby, or elastic sweat bands wrapped around snugly but not too tightly.

- *Add length to clothes by sewing extra length onto the pants and add a matching patch.*

    > *Little legs tend to grow more quickly than the rest of the body sometimes! Consequently the cute overalls and other wonderful little clothes that they can wiggle and crawl around in become short before they become small. I've solved this problem by getting some cute fabric like callico, checks, plaids, and other cute little prints, and sewn bottoms onto the legs. I then sew on one patch or more of the same fabric in the shape of a heart elsewhere on the outfit so it looks like its supposed to be like that! It works beautifully!*
    >
    > Janine Schooley
    > San Diego, California

Crying . . .

Perhaps the most difficult part of caring for your infant is learning to deal with her crying. There are many reasons for a little one to cry. Pain, hunger, over-stimulation, loneliness, and anger are just a few of those

Mom to Mom . . .

reasons. It helps to remember that crying is your infant's only means of communicating with you for several months to come, and you'll find that after a while, you'll miraculously be able to distinguish one cry from another most of the time! It may seem impossible to you now, but you'll be surprised how well your little one communicates with you, once you learn to "decode" her cries!

Sometimes, however, the crying is for no reason—it's just fussiness. Newborns especially are prone to this. Unfortunately, their fussy period will probably occur in the late afternoon and on into the evening, just when you and your husband are the most tired and worn out.

But you may find some comfort in knowing that, according to a study conducted several years ago by the famous pediatrician, Dr. T. Berry Brazelton, most healthy babies will cry simply out of fussiness for periods of two to three hours a day for the first few months of life. Even a daily total of four hours was not abnormal! He also found that the fussy periods became longer until an infant became six weeks old, and then began to slowly decrease in duration after that "magic" age.[4] Through my own informal discussions with so many parents, six weeks really does seem to be a "magic age," as does three months. After three months of age, little ones simply are more settled, more content, more in tune with absorbing the world and its adventures and excitement.

So, take heart. If your infant is crying . . . and crying . . . and crying . . . the seemingly incessant crying really will end before too long. But until then, perhaps the following tips and hints will be helpful:

- *Respond to your baby as soon as he cries—do not let him "cry it out."*

  Considerable research has been done on the advantages of immediately responding to a baby's cries. By your immediate response, your little one learns quickly that his needs, whatever they may be—physical or emotional, will be attended to. His feelings of trust develop early, and this leads to "a better quality of attachment between caretaker and baby, and is to be preferred to either deliberate or inadvertent ignoring of crying."[5]

Daily Care . . .

- *Consider one or more of the following:*

  (1) Are his diapers wet or soiled?

  (2) Has he been fed within the last two hours (breast-fed) or within the last three to four hours (bottle-fed)?

  (3) Is he in a draft which is making him cool or cold?

  (4) Is he overdressed and consequently too warm? Is he sweating?

  (5) Was there or are there loud noises or sounds?

  (6) Was he startled by something?

  (7) Is he burping or passing gas?

  Trapped air in his system could be causing pain. Does he need to be burped? Perhaps he has been fed recently and the needed routine burping was forgotten.

  Or, try moving his little legs in a bicycle motion. This is an excellent way to help him eliminate gas, if that's his problem.

  (8) Is he being subjected to something "new," like a bath?

  (9) Is he being undressed?

  Babies generally don't like to have their skin exposed to the air, regardless of whether that air is comfortably warm or not.

  (10) Is he jerking as he falls asleep, thus awakening himself?

  (11) Is he being held and rocked or walked?

  Most babies love physical contact and feel the most content and secure when they are. Most cultures, in fact, know this, and many mothers will "wear" their babies most of the time during the day.

  Consider a front carrier or a sling to "wear" your baby. This will give him the rocking and the close contact that he needs, wants, and appreciates!

  Or, try dancing to some soothing music with your baby cuddled close.

Mom to Mom . . .

(12) Have you provided any rhythmical sounds?

Examples: Mellow music (combined with dance?), whirring fans, humming clothes dryers, car engines, singing lullabies . . . .

You might consider doing the vacuuming with your little one in a front or back carrier. The steady sound and the motion may just put him to sleep.

Two mothers made these suggestions:

Here's a crazy cure for a crying baby (less than six months or so) that doesn't respond to the usual comforting methods—running water! It worked for us with Katie when she was three or four months old. I'd take her over to the bathroom or kitchen sink and run the water. She would stop crying and just stare at the water, mesmerized! Not very smart ecologically, but it gave us a few minutes of silence when we were desperate!

Terri Ciosek
Poway, California

Running the shower always seemed to calm our babies!

Karen Johnson
Satellite Beach, Florida

(13) Does he need extra warmth?

Many newborns want very warm temperatures. In fact, it's best to keep your newborn in a warm environment of at least 75°F. Try not to subject him to any drastic changes for a while, such as a walk outdoors on a chilly day or a ride in a cold car.

Daily Care ...

(14) Has he laid on Mommy's or Daddy's chest?

   This worked wonders for us, especially at night. One of us would put Maryanna on our chest and hum the "Merry Widow Waltz" to her. Not only would the humming put her to sleep, but I'm sure the sound of our heartbeat and just the close contact made it quite cozy and cuddly.

(15) Is he running a temperature?

(16) Is he beginning to teethe?

   Generally this isn't a problem with a newborn, but babies as young as two months have been known to have their first teeth come in.

- *"Wear" your baby.*

   According to Dr. William Sears, "research has shown that carrying babies is not just a fashionable trend; it actually benefits infant behavior and infant development. Carried babies cry 50% less and show enhanced visual alertness."[6]

- *Play a music box!*

   The tune of a music box really seems to catch the attention of an infant and older baby. Incidentally, this is a good item to pack away in your diaper bag for short or long journeys away from home!

- *If all else fails, try "wrapping" your little one.*

   Infants find being snuggly wrapped a very soothing experience. The suggestion below is from a mother who used "wrapping" successfully. Just keep in mind that you should keep your baby's arms and legs in their natural bent position and don't try to straighten them out before wrapping him.

   > *An elderly lady who babysat for us gave me some advice to comfort little ones who were crying. She snuggly wrapped the baby in a blanket so the baby would feel secure.*

Mom to Mom . . .

Example:

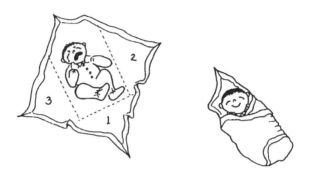

Keeping the baby's limbs in their natural position, fold up the bottom corner, then bring a second corner across the baby, tucking the corner in lightly. Finally, bring the third corner across the baby, tucking it under him. In this way, the only thing keeping the wrap from unwrapping is the baby's own weight.

I did this frequently and it would quiet our babies very quickly.

Jan Sundblad
San Diego, California

- *If your crying baby (or child) is unable to catch his breath, blow into his face.*

    Believe it or not, blowing air into a little one's face triggers a reflex reaction that causes the little one to take a breath!

Diapering . . .

As with many areas of daily care, books such as Penelope Leach's *Your Baby and Child* can give you excellent guidance in diapering your baby. What's provided below are some extra hints and tips that you may not otherwise come across.

- *Whenever possible, use cloth diapers and cloth diaper wraps.*

    Cloth diapers and cloth diaper wraps are softer and "breathe" so much better than the disposables and plastic pants. The big

Daily Care . . .

advantage of using cloth is in a lower incidence of irritating diaper rash.

Cloth diaper wraps use velcro for closure, eliminating the need for safety pins. They're more expensive, and you will have to buy larger sizes as your little one grows, but they are by far more comfortable and better for your baby than plastic covers.

Our little one never experienced any diaper rash, thanks to the almost constant use of cloth diapers, cloth diaper wraps, and frequent diaper changing. I say "almost constant use" because by the time she was five months old and we started taking her on frequent trips, I began to use disposables for traveling, but would take a supply of cloth diapers for nighttime. It meant rinsing out the diapers every morning, hanging them over the shower rod to dry, and taking them home in a plastic bag in our suitcase, but she always slept well because she was *comfortable*.

- *Use a spray bottle, tissues, and baby oil to clean your baby's bottom instead of baby wipes.*

    A newborn's skin is very sensitive and can react to the various chemicals found in regular soaps and commercial baby wipes. To clean your little one's soiled bottom effectively without subjecting it to any unnecessary chemicals:

    (1) Use tissues to clean off the main mess.

    Keep a box of tissues there at your changing table, but be sure that the brand isn't an obscure one! Those brands tend to fall apart before the job is done!

    (2) Using a small spray bottle, spray his bottom with water and wipe off the rest of the mess with another tissue.

    For those stubborn spots, use some baby oil on some tissue, and whatever remains will come right off.

    An alternative to using a spray bottle (the water could be cold if the bottle hasn't been recently refilled), is to use cut-up diapers as washcloths. Simply wet the diaper-cloth with warm water and, after the "tissue procedure" above, wipe off his bottom.

Mom to Mom . . .

    (3) Rub a little baby soap on your hand and wash his bottom.

    (4) Rinse his bottom thoroughly with a warm, wet diaper-cloth.

    (5) Dry his bottom completely and dress him in a clean diaper and cover.

- *Try not to use baby powder.*

   Now, that's a surprise, isn't it?! We've all grown up to believe that babies' bottoms are supposed to be powdered to keep them dry and hopefully rash-free. But the truth of the matter is, the only way a baby can be kept dry is to change his diapers frequently and dry him completely after washing his bottom.

   The powder really serves no purpose and the talc that it contains can be very harmful to your baby if he should inhale it.

   But, if it's really ingrained in you to use baby powder, then rather than shaking some powder on his bottom, put just a small amount in your hand and rub it on your baby. In that way, it will keep the talc from becoming "air-borne" from shaking and patting.

- *To increase the absorbancy of cloth diapers for nighttime and naptime, use two diapers at once.*

   For an older baby, increasing the absorbancy by "double-diapering" may help him sleep for a longer period of time.

When washing cloth diapers (if you're not using a diaper service) . . .

- *Be sure to run the diapers through a second rinse to ensure that all the soap has been completely removed—this will help avoid diaper rash.*

- *Avoid using commercial fabric softener on your cloth diapers.*

   Baby skin is quite sensitive to commercial softeners. Using them may result in a very uncomfortable rash for your baby.

Daily Care . . .

Instead, use some wonderful common household softeners:

(1) Vinegar

This is a great "fabric softener" and it helps whiten the diapers as well. Just add one cup of vinegar to the second rinse water.

(2) Baking Soda

Baking soda makes diapers feel softer and makes them smell fresh, too. Add about a half-cup to the second rinse.

Equipment . . .

Most of the equipment you need you've already acquired before your baby arrived. There are two other items that we found absolutely indispensable from the beginning.

The first is a front carrier—other moms have reported the same positive results from using a sling. Tom and I were parents who believed in "wearing our baby" and did so, practically from the beginning. Some pediatricians believe that the front carrier shouldn't be used until after the first four weeks, others believe it can be used from the very beginning. Check with your own pediatrician for his advice.

Being carried and held are two activities that the newborn loves most. In order to accomplish it and still get one or two other things done during the day (don't count on accomplishing any more than that in a day's time for a few months!), you'll find the front carrier or sling to be ideal! It keeps your little one close, she can hear your heartbeat, and she continues to enjoy the motion that she so enjoyed when she was in the womb!

At about five months or so, though, the front carrier ceases to be as loved as it was in the beginning—from your little one's point of view! That's when she can graduate to a backpack or back carrier. It's another remarkable device, and our daughter (and many other little ones we know) have thrived in one! Whenever we would go anywhere, we took the backpack with us so that Maryanna could have a bird's eye view—or at least an adult's eye view. She *loved* every minute in the backpack!

Mom to Mom . . .

Whether we walked to the grocery store or drove in the car, we took the backpack. She would then see everything that we saw, and we would talk to her over our shoulder, telling her what this was and that. She may not have understood at first, but she would often shriek and giggle and coo and have the most delightful time.

Nice to have but . . .

An automatic swing is an item many new parents either buy or receive as a gift. This device slowly and gently swings your little one while you are able to do something else for a few moments, e.g., begin dinner, clean up the kitchen, make the bed, write a few thank you notes. If your infant can see you while he's swinging, and if he's there for a few minutes at a time, you'll find such a device rather helpful. But it *can* become a "mommy substitute," which isn't in your baby's best interest.

Not necessary . . .

Those items that new parents often rush out to buy are walkers and playpens. When your little one can sit up with support, the bouncy chairs or walkers can seem to be fun for him and good exercise. But they can be especially dangerous if not supervised well. See the discussion on walkers in Chapter 8, pages 225-226.

For us and other parents we've talked to as well, playpens tend to be a big waste of money. I used ours two or three times, at most, and only for a few minutes each time. Instead, I found that I felt better securing the rest of the house through the use of hallway and stairway gates and appropriate child-proofing, and then letting her wiggle and later roll and then later crawl wherever she wanted within those limits.

Another mother who contributed to this book shared the same thoughts:

> *Playpens and walkers are a waste of money and will interfere with your baby's development. Walkers are also very dangerous, especially around stairs.*
>
> Eileen Carroll
> La Jolla, California

Daily Care...

Playtime...

You may be wondering, "How do I play with this baby?" "What do I *do* with this baby?" I was worried with the same thoughts, and yet, miraculously, I found that instinct really does take over. You'll find that you'll do all the things that your little one loves. Especially as your baby begins to smile and outwardly show his pleasure, you will see that just playing with his hands and feet and rocking him and gently bouncing him and all the other things people do naturally with their little ones are *exactly* the things that please them most!

But, if you are like me, you'll want some guidance anyway. Three excellent resources that will give you some outstanding ideas are:

Your Baby and Child by Penelope Leach

> By now you'll understand why I suggest this book should be on every new mother's bookshelf. It covers absolutely everything in wonderful detail.
>
> The section especially helpful to you is toward the end in the extremely useful index that ingeniously doubles as an encyclopedia. Under "Playthings," pages 498 to 505, you'll find a multitude of ideas and background for play. For example, the initial chart has four sections: "First weeks," "From about five weeks," "From about three months," and "From about six months." Each of these sections has three areas: "What he (baby) needs," "Why he needs it," and "Suitable toys."
>
> The ideas and the information given are exceptional.

First Fun (A Mothercare Nursery Guide) by Shelia Gregory and Diane Melvin

> This little book is packed with wonderful ideas! If you have ever had any doubts about what to do with an infant, baby, and toddler in terms of play, this book will guide the way! The authors include developmental charts which help you look for the exciting progress that your baby is making in becoming a child. Each chapter, devoted to a certain developmental stage, lists toys to buy and toys to make that are appropriate for that

Mom to Mom . . .

stage. Each chapter also includes highlights on safety for each developmental stage. This book is little . . . but it's mighty, and well worth having on your bookshelf!

Rainy Day Activities for Preschoolers published by the mothers and professionals of the Mercer Island Preschool Association

This is full of great ideas for games and activities for little ones. To get a copy, send $13.95 to MIPA, Book Distribution, Box 464, Mercer Island, WA 98040.

And, if you choose to subscribe to the monthly newsletter combo recommended earlier—*Growing Child/Growing Parent,* you'll receive wonderful ideas every month on what to do with your baby.

For example, here are some suggestions that have appeared in past *Growing Parent* newsletters, quoted here thanks to the editors' kind permission. (Please be sure that when you do these and other activities, don't leave long strings, small pieces, or sharp objects where little ones can reach them.)

(1) *Cut or draw simple, colorful pictures or patterns. Look for faces, bold geometric patterns, or black and white designs. Glue each picture on a piece of cardboard and fasten it to the bars of the playpen or crib, low enough so the baby can see them. Change the pictures often.*

To do the above, you'll need: magazines, cardboard, scissors, glue, markers, yarn, paper punch, and tape.

Growing Parent
November, 1987

Sue Brandes of Des Plaines, Illinois, gave us a similar suggestion when Maryanna was born. We cut out large pictures of faces from magazines and pinned them to the inside of Maryanna's bassinet. Eyes apparently fascinate infants, and Maryanna found those pictures fascinating from the first weeks! She would stare and stare at them and turn her head from side to side to see as many as she could. It's a *great* idea!

Daily Care ...

(2) *Attach a bell to each of baby's booties. Each time he kicks, he'll be rewarded with sound.*

To do the above, you'll need jingle bells.

Growing Parent
June, 1988

(3) *Fill a 2-liter soda bottle 2/3 full with water and tint it with food coloring. Replace the cap securely and put tape around it. Put the bottle on the floor. When baby pushes it, the water will slosh and bubble. This is a great toy for crawlers and creepers.*

To do the above, you'll need an empty 2-liter soda bottle, food coloring, water, plastic tape.

Growing Parent
March, 1988

(4) *Put some beans or pebbles into an empty egg-shaped container* [L'Eggs stocking container is ideal] *and tape securely closed. As baby pushes it along the floor, it will roll and rattle.*

Growing Parent
December, 1987

(5) *Create a Jingle Bell Cradle Gym. Poke a hole in the bottom of five or six paper cups. Thread a piece of string through a jingle bell and through the bottom of each cup. attach the cups to a line strung across the crib or playpen. Baby's movements will be rewarded with ringing!* <u>*Be sure to remove once the baby is able to touch the mobile with his hands or feet*</u>.

To do the above, you'll need paper cups, jingle bells, and a string or ribbon.

Growing Parent
January, 1988

As for selecting toys for an infant, here's a general guide:

First three months:	Infants have very little control of their arms, hands, and legs, so the appropriate items are mobiles (with the objects facing down toward them rather than hanging up and down for others to see!)

Mom to Mom . . .

                            and bright patterns and pictures, as was mentioned earlier. Soft crib toys like teddy bears and other soft animals are great little interest-sparkers!

Three to six months: Infants are in the early stages of learning to use their hands and discover their toes. Rattles and squeeze toys for the bath are perfect for this age. Also consider toys like balls or soft spongy blocks made out of different fabric. Little ones love to feel things and enjoy the different sensations.

As for suggestions beyond what you'll find in the resources mentioned above, here are some that we found to be delightful—for us and for our little one!

- *Bubbles delight anyone of any age, but especially babies, toddlers, and pre-schoolers!*

Take your little one outside on a warm day, prop her up either in her buggy or stroller or in an infant seat, and blow bubbles for her. She'll become mesmerized!

- *Lie your baby on his back on a blanket or quilt under some trees on a warm, breezy day.*

Your little one will become completely absorbed in the moving branches and leaves. If he's like ours, he'll begin to kick and wave his arms and squeal with delight!

- *Find a bright plastic colored "roll doll" for your little one to push or bat at.*

One of the best baby gifts we received was a plastic Japanese doll that had a round bottom and clanging bells inside. The doll was bright orange, had big round eyes, and would roll from one side to the next with each "bat" and push that Maryanna could manage. She *loved* it! It clanged with even a slight nudge, so she

Daily Care...

was always "rewarded" with every attempt to push or hit it. We had it beside her on the floor whenever she was lying there on her back or tummy—it became a favorite toy for many, many months!

- *Enjoy doing the "usuals"—the games we all play by instinct: cuddling, water play in the bath, clapping hands, playing with the feet and toes, playing "peek-a-boo" and "pat-a-cake."*

- *And—TALK to your baby!*

Dealing with the "Not Accomplishing a Thing" Syndrome...

All mothers at one time or another find themselves surrounded by things left undone... the laundry, the dishes, thank you notes that are four months overdue, magazines and newspapers left unread, the incredibly untidy house, the dying house plants, the junky cupboards, the unmade beds... the list is endless! Caring for an infant—a child—*does* take a lot of time. But take heart! There are ways to cope with these feelings of frustration that you are experiencing!

(1) Take some credit for the things that are going well in your life.

E.g., your baby is thriving!.

(2) Put some structure in your days.

Plan something specific to do or somewhere to go every single day. Make lists of what you want to accomplish and enjoy the satisfaction of crossing off the items as they are completed.

(3) Schedule errands at the time of day when your baby is least likely to be fussy and don't try to do them all in one afternoon.

(4) Start something that you can finish.

Now is not the time to take on big projects that will only sit there and remind you that they're not getting done. Quick, easy

Mom to Mom...

projects will give you a sense of accomplishment because you can finish them in the time allotment that you have.

(5) Break big jobs down into little pieces.

(6) Get help for those bigger projects.

(7) Save the jobs and pleasures that require intense concentration for naptime.

(8) Take full advantage of breastfeeding.

It gives you several times every day to relax. Use the time to boost your spirits.

Your baby is a baby for such a short time .... Two years from now he'll be drawing pictures for you. When you're in a position to look back, these few years will seem like what they are—only a tiny part of your lifetime. The things you didn't get done—the curtains that didn't get made, the committees that did without your services, the career that went on hold—won't be the things you remember from these months. You will remember the feeling of holding your baby in your arms, rubbing your cheek against his head, snuggling up and nursing him in the middle of the night. Building memories such as these takes a lot of time out of every day, but it's time well spent. Memories last a lifetime.

"La Leche League—A Question of Time"
by Gwen Gotsch
Baby Talk
August, 1988

Daily Care . . .

---

[1]"Song for a Fifth Child" by Ruth Hulburt Hamilton, © 1958, Meredith Corporation. All Rights Reserved. Reprinted from *Ladies Home Journal* magazine with permission of the author.

[2]Tine Thevenin, *The Family Bed,* Avery Publishing Group: Wayne, New Jersey, 1987, pages 149-151.

[3]Corrie Player, "Sensible Tips for Children's Winter Wear," *Growing Parent*, November 1988, Vol. 16, No. 11, p. 3.

[4]Robert H. Pantell, M.D. et al, *Taking Care of Your Child, Revised Edition,* Addison-Wesley Publishing Co., Reading, Massachusetts, 1984, page 66.

[5]Burton L. White, *The First Three Years of Life,* Avon, New York, 1984, page 30.

[6]William Sears, M.D., "The Growing Family, Part Two: Your Baby's Early Weeks," *Baby Talk,* February 1987, p. 23.

Mom to Mom . . .

Clips and Notes . . .

Daily Care . . .

Clips and Notes . . .

Mom to Mom . . .

Clips and Notes . . .

6

Sleepy Time . . .

Sleep, baby, sleep!
Thy father watches the sheep.
Thy mother is shaking the dreamland tree,
And down falls a little dream on thee.
Sleep, baby, sleep.

Sleep, baby, sleep!
The large stars are the sheep.
The little stars are the lambs, I guess.
The big round moon is the shepherdess.
Sleep, baby, sleep!

Kay Chorao
The Baby's Bedtime Book

Sleepy time . . . just the thought of it evokes yawns and stretches for us, especially if we have one of the "wakeful" babies. If you *do* have a wakeful baby, you should find comfort in knowing that wakeful babies are much more common than the familiar myth we've all heard—that most babies "sleep through the night" after so many weeks or months— would have us believe!

Recommended Reading . . .

Some of the books recommended below have been recommended before. If you haven't read them yet, you may find them especially helpful now.

Mom to Mom . . .

Nighttime Parenting—How to Get Your Baby and Child to Sleep by William Sears, M.D.

This book was invaluable to me, but what a help it would have been had I read it before our little one arrived! Unfortunately, I "bumped" into it when Maryanna was 15 months old, but it still was immensely helpful. In *Nighttime Parenting,* Dr. Sears explains how babies sleep differently than adults, how sharing sleep can help the whole family sleep better, and how to help little ones sleep more peacefully.

The Family Bed by Tine Thevenin

This is a wonderful book with considerable food for thought! And, it's another one I wish I had read before Maryanna reached 15 months of age! It wasn't until then and I had experienced months of her waking many times a night and her having difficulty returning to sleep that I finally, out of desperation, brought her to bed with me. What a revelation! She went to sleep immediately! I later ran across this book that validated what I had discovered on my own. Had I read it earlier, I wouldn't have experienced those months of nighttime frustration and exhaustion.

While sharing a family bed is a practice as old as the human race, it has become controversial in the 20th century. *The Family Bed* discusses the pros and cons and suggests that the family bed will help solve bedtime problems and create closer family bonds. Establishing an open-door policy to the parental bed can be a sensitive way of responding to the needs of a little one. The author of this book, Tine Thevenin, really speaks to your anxieties, reservations, *and* instincts.

Your Baby & Child from Birth to Age Five by Penelope Leach

The chapters of this book reflect the various stages of growth: the newborn, the settled baby, the older baby, etc. Each chapter includes a section on sleeping which is quite helpful and will give you the guidance you may be seeking.

Sleepy Time . . .

Some Sleepy Time Hints for the Newborn . . .

- *Pick a favorite waltz or other soothing song or lullaby and use it as a ritual sleepy time song.*

    When Maryanna was just a three days old, she started the usual mix-up of days and nights. Tom would take her and lie down with her on his chest (she'd be screaming!) and he would begin to softly hum *The Merry Widow Waltz,* one of our favorites. After many minutes of his soothing humming, she would drop off to sleep.

    It started a ritual and we have been using that as her sleepy time song ever since. We have added some words to it such as, "Mommy loves her baby and Daddy does, too; Grandma loves our baby and Grandpa does, too," etc.

    The usual baby lullabies such as Brahms' Lullaby are wonderful, too, and so is *Edelweiss* from *The Sound of Music!*

- *Don't bother buying the various stuffed toys that have the sound of a mother's heartbeat in them.*

    Although it *might* work for several weeks or months, it probably won't. A little lamb was given to us and I was delighted for I had read all of the advertising that had said that "most babies will settle quickly at the sound of it for months"! The lamb had this effect on Maryanna exactly once! Since then I have heard several other mothers mention the same thing. If one is given to you . . . try it, it may work for a while. But don't waste your money—your infant will know whether you're close by or not!

- *Be sure to continue making the normal, usual sounds during the day and evening while your infant sleeps.*

    If you tiptoe and try to muffle all normal, day-to-day sounds, you'll find that your little one will soon not be able to sleep at all unless the house is absolutely, totally quiet. Such total, unnatural quiet might be easy to accomplish for a while, but keeping the house *that* quiet whenever your little one is sleeping

Mom to Mom...

is very difficult to continue, especially if you have an older sibling or two at home!

- *Install a dimmer switch in the baby's room.*

    For late night feedings and diaper changings, the dim light will be enough for you to see what you're doing, yet low enough that it won't signal daytime wake-up time for your baby!

- *Nurse and/or rock your baby to sleep if this is comfortable for you.*

    Too often advice is given that is contrary to our own feelings and instincts. A good case in point is that of nursing and/or rocking a baby to sleep. Some respected sources will tell you that it is a mistake... that your child will never learn to fall asleep on her own if you insist on nursing and/or rocking her to sleep.

    I can't imagine why a little one or any young child *must* go to sleep by herself. There simply can't be any better, more soothing, more comfortable way to go to sleep than being rocked in a parent's arms! Ours is a family of rockers... I was rocked to sleep, my cousins were rocked to sleep until they were five or so, my husband fondly remembers being rocked to sleep, and all of us find it very easy to fall asleep on our own as adults. When Maryanna was a baby and was with a sitter, our sitter would rock her to sleep, whether it was naptime or bedtime. Now that Maryanna is four, our sitter just sits with her in the dark and they "girl-talk" until Maryanna falls asleep.

    Rocking a little one *does* take time. There were times when Maryanna was switching from one nap a day to no naps when it would take me an hour or so to get her to sleep. Yet the time we take to cuddle and be close to her each night is our real connection time. The day can be busy (when aren't they?), the day can have its hassles, and the day can sometimes be one of disagreements where we were on an unusual collision course. But the rocker and our rocking time gives us our connection, our closeness, and the busy-ness of the day and any frustrations between us that we may have experienced simply melt away and

Sleepy Time . . .

we're *happy*. As I said before, what a beautiful way for a little one to go to sleep.

Many respected sources may say it's foolish . . . but experience tells me that its the stuff that memories and love are made of!

The rocking doesn't last "forever." Soon after Maryanna's fourth birthday, she decided she only wanted to be rocked for one or two of her favorite "sleepy-time songs" and then wanted to go to bed—and to sleep—on her own! She now crawls in bed and says, "Tell me a little story." Once the "little story" has been told, we have lots of hugs and kisses, and it's "good-night"! She has had *no* trouble falling asleep herself.

- *Don't be afraid to bring the little one into bed with you during the night—the experience adds to the bond you're building and it contributes to a lot more sleep!*

    Although *The Family Bed* suggests letting your baby/child sleep in your bed from the very beginning of the night, I disagree. As much of a believer as I am in letting children sleep with their parents when they want to, even if it's a portion of *every* night until they're older, I do believe that babies and young children should be put down in their own beds at first. In this way the little ones know that they have their own room with their own bed. At some point, when they are ready to spend the whole night there, they will. Putting them in their own bed also gives you your initial privacy which you and your husband both need. But letting your little ones join you during the night allows you to also meet their needs of security, comfort, and warmth.

- *Follow the sleepy time routine that best suits you, your baby, and your instincts.*

    There are a variety of suggestions on how to put a baby to sleep that one can find in baby care books, from the family's pediatrician, and from other family members and friends. But the important thing to remember is—the *best* method or the best routine is *the one that suits you best and makes you feel the most comfortable.*

Mom to Mom . . .

It took me a long time to recognize that fact, but once I did, I wondered why I had sent myself through the agony and guilt of trying to follow all the "expert" advice when all along I knew "deep down inside" what was right for me and our baby.

A neighbor who is a former pediatric nurse practitioner had told me that once I put our six-week-old child down in her bassinet in our darkened room, I should leave, even if she cried and cried. She assured me that she would stop crying "after 20 minutes or so" and that, if I did this consistently "for a few nights," she would learn to fall off to sleep. Well, she didn't, and I felt miserable.

When that failed, I followed my instincts of rocking her and staying with her until she was asleep. When she was a few months older, I read "the books" which suggested laying her down and going back every five minutes or so to reassure her that I hadn't abandoned her. That, too, made us both miserable. So, again, I returned to my instincts, and we both were much happier.

It simply depends on you, your baby, and the needs you both have. When you juggle those three, you can then decide on what the best method for sleepy time is for you and your little one. If your little one is having trouble sleeping at night, remember that every baby is different. Some will easily follow the good advice you'll find in some books, and some will not. Again, you just have to listen to your baby . . . and to yourself . . . and find what works for you.

Terri Ciosek of San Diego, California, further stresses this point:

Katie was sixteen months old and still not sleeping through the night. I know now that isn't so unusual for a toddler, but sometimes she would call me and want to nurse several times a night. I began to resent that and the fact that we never knew when her bedtime would be. (I would nurse her to sleep

Sleepy Time . . .

then pray that I wouldn't wake her when I tried to put her in her crib.) As I talked to other parents, including our pediatrician, I kept hearing the same name—Dr. Richard Ferber. His book, <u>Solve Your Child's Sleep Problems</u>, gave us the courage and the method to end those nighttime hassles. It took some time and some crying but it worked. Now we all get a good night's sleep. What's more, Katie doesn't hate us for it, as I had feared. Instead, she enjoys our new bedtime rituals and goes to bed like an angel!

Some Tips from Some of the Experts that May Help . . .

- *Try to put your baby down in his crib or bassinet when drowsy but not asleep.*

    Some experts believe that if you feed and rock your baby before naptime or nighttime, that you should put him down when he's drowsy rather than asleep. The reason? He will learn to organize himself for sleep—suck on a finger, watch a mobile above him, whatever—and then, when he reawakens during the night, he will be able to go through the same "routine" to put himself back to sleep.

- *Use a pacifier as a sleep inducer only occasionally.*

    Pacifiers can be especially helpful for a colicky baby and for a bottlefed baby who has finished his formula but still needs some sucking comfort.

    But, a baby who always needs to have a pacifier to fall asleep will become an older baby who will need to have several in his crib so that one will always be within reach when he needs to fall asleep again during the night.

- *Begin to eliminate night feedings after six months of age.*

    Dr. Richard Ferber is a pediatrician who has spent many years working with babies, toddlers, and children with "sleep prob-

Mom to Mom . . .

lems" in his Center for Pediatric Sleep Disorders at Boston Children's Hospital.

He believes that a little one experiencing a case of the hungries during the night after six months of age simply has become accustomed to being fed at night. He suggests:

For the bottlefed baby: Decrease the number of ounces of formula in the bottle or water down the formula for the night feedings.

For the breastfed baby: Try not to be too hasty in rushing to the little one with the first whimper or two. Wait to see if he will fall asleep by himself.

He believes that the routines of rocking, using pacifiers, and feedings at night are simply that—routines, and the baby becomes dependent on those routines. The only way to change such routines is to implement a *new* routine.[1]

- *Understand that most babies won't be sleeping through the night even by three months of age, but that their longest periods of wakefulness will probably be during the daytime by that age.*

If your baby at three months is still having long periods of wakefulness during the night at three months, you can begin to help him change that habit. If he sleeps for a long period during the day, you can begin to wake him earlier and earlier. He will then begin to pick up the "missed" sleep at other naptimes, eventually making the longest sleep period at night.

---

[1] Dr. Richard Ferber, "Sleep Problems Every Parent Faces," *Baby Talk,* September 1988, pp. 14-17.

Sleepy Time . . .

Clips and Notes . . .

Mom to Mom . . .

Clips and Notes . . .

7

Health...

When you are a mother, you are never really alone in your thoughts. You are connected to your child and to all those who touch your lives. A mother always has to think twice—once for herself and once for her child.

Sophia Loren[1]

One of your biggest concerns as a new mother is how to care for your infant's health. "What if he gets sick?" "What do I do?" "How will I know—he can't talk!" "When do I call the doctor?" "Will my doctor think I'm a pest?"

These questions sound quite familiar, don't they! *All* new mothers—and even many experienced mothers—are plagued by these same thoughts and questions.

The purpose of this chapter is to provide you with a collection of tips and hints that will guide you through those many questions that I know are buzzing through your mind.

An Important Basic...

- *Put a list of emergency telephone numbers at each phone in your home.*

    The first two numbers should be:

Mom to Mom . . .

(1) Your *Poison Control Center's* telephone number

You may never have to use this number—but should you ever need it, you'll be very grateful that you don't have to waste valuable moments thumbing through the telephone book or getting the information operator.

(2) Your pediatrician's telephone number

Visiting the Doctor . . .

REGULAR CHECK-UPS . . .

- *Keep a pad of paper in a convenient location to collect questions that you want to ask your pediatrician when you next see him.*

  The best location for us was on the refrigerator door.

- *Take some paper and a pen or pencil with you to your appointment so you can write down your doctor's instructions, answers to your questions, etc.*

- *Make appointments as far in advance as possible so that they will be convenient for you.*

  You may want to keep in mind when scheduling your appointments:

  (1) Your doctor is more likely to be on time in the early morning, when his office first opens, and right after lunch, since you would be the first or close to the first being seen.

  (2) It's best to avoid those times when your baby normally naps or has a feeding.

  (3) After school hours are probably the worst time to take your baby to the doctor.

  Older children with communicable diseases often flood doctors' offices after school. The only exception to this is when you are scheduling an appointment for an immunization. See the tip suggested by Janine Schooley in the upcoming section, "Preparation for Immunizations."

Health...

- *Request that your infant be examined with him in your lap.*

  Many pediatricians do this as a matter of practice, although some do not. It's the most gentle and most effective way for a pediatrician to examine a baby because the baby feels most secure with his parent. If he's placed on an examining table away from his parent and the closeness he needs and has become accustomed to, he may be very unhappy, which I guarantee will make *you* emotionally quite miserable too.

WHEN SICK . . .

- *Call the doctor if:*

  (1) Your infant exhibits some significant changes such as lethargy, listlessness, and unresponsiveness, or gives some indication of severe pain.

  (2) Your infant has a fever.

  (3) Your infant has continuous diarrhea, blood in his stool, decreased urination, or an inability to take in fluids.[2]

  Don't *ever* hesitate to call your pediatrician if you're concerned about anything regarding your infant's health.

- *When visiting the doctor's office, be sure to remind the receptionist that your little one is ill.*

  Many doctors' offices are now equipped to separate sick and well children. If your doctor's office is not, then his staff is more able to take measures to separate your little one from the well children, as a consideration for you as well as the other children in the waiting area.

PREPARATION FOR IMMUNIZATIONS . . .

> *To help with those DPT shots, bring a dropper bottle of acetaminophen with you to the doctor's office. As soon as the nurse gives the shot, give your baby the recommended dose. Don't wait until you get home and your*

Mom to Mom . . .

> *baby becomes fussy and feverish. It takes a while for the medicine to take affect, so start it as soon as the shot is given. I learned this one the hard way after several bad fussiness experiences following DPT shots!*
>
> Lori Buschmann
> San Diego, California
>
> *Try to schedule your baby's shots for late afternoon. Because of the shot and because of the acetaminophen given afterwards, a baby will be very sleepy. By having the shots given in the afternoon, it better fits in with the sleep schedule and will more likely not alter the sleep patterns that have been established.*
>
> Janine Schooley
> San Diego, California

Caring for the Sick Infant . . .

- *Some important things to keep in mind about fever . . .*

  (1) Remember to "treat the child, not the fever."

  This means that if your baby is not acting ill, leave the fever alone. It is the body's mechanism for fighting off disease. Often toddlers will feel quite well even with a temperature of 103 degrees! A sleeping baby also will not feel any discomfort. These little ones require no fever medication—only those who behave ill need some relief.

  (2) Dress your baby lightly—your little one doesn't need a blanket sleeper.

  (3) Cover your baby with a sheet or a light summer blanket.

  (4) Offer small feedings of cool, clear liquids—if your baby is breastfed, nurse him often.

  (5) Give your baby acetaminophen *(not aspirin)* only if he acts and feels ill.

Health ...

(6) If the temperature hasn't dropped within an hour and your baby continues to act sick, bathe him for 20 minutes in tepid water.

(7) Call your doctor if:

* The temperature is over 100.5 degrees in an infant two months or younger.

* The temperature is over 104 degrees at any age.

* The temperature is over 101 degrees for more than 24 hours.

* The temperature is over 100.5 degrees for three or more days.

* The fever is accompanied by rash, constant crying, unusual listlessness, cough, persistent vomiting, rubbing and/or pulling at the ears, or convulsion.

(8) "Abnormal behavior is a better indication of serious illness than is high fever, and a thermometer will never replace a watchful parent."

Adapted from:
Patient Information Flyer on Fever, 1986
by Frederick A. Frye, M.D.
San Diego, California

- *The biggest danger of diarrhea is dehydration. The signs of dehydration are:*
  (1) Weight and water loss
  (2) Drowsy and lethargic behavior
  (3) Dry mouth
  (4) Dry eyes
  (5) Dry skin
  (6) Diminishing urine output
  (7) Fever

- *If your baby has diarrhea and you are breastfeeding, it is important that you continue to do so.*

  Breastmilk is more easily tolerated by the intestines than cow's

Mom to Mom . . .

milk. If your baby has gastroenteritis, a main cause of diarrhea, continue to nurse him. Bottlefed infants will often refuse their formula when they have diarrhea, but the breastfeeding infant will often want to nurse more often.[3]

- *For a young baby who is having diarrhea . . .*

  As always, it's best to check with your pediatrician. Normally, a breastfed baby should continue to be nursed; a bottlefed baby may be given diluted soy formula since that formula has no lactose. Your pediatrician will guide you in how much to dilute the formula.

  Babies over four or five months who have begun solids, should stop solids and formula for the first 12 to 24 hours and be given clear liquids and an oral electrolyte solution like Pedialyte.[4]

  Especially in cases of severe diarrhea, the electrolyte solution is very important because juice and water alone cannot prevent dehydration and electrolyte depletion.

  The clear liquid diet shouldn't continue for more than 36 hours because nutrition and sources of energy are needed. To begin foods again, Leah Yarrow suggests starting "with half-strength formula or half-strength whole or 2-percent milk, bananas, applesauce, Jell-O or Jell-0 water, rice, hard toast, hard cheese (like cheddar, which contains very little lactose), and yogurts. . . . Homemade soups can also be added to the diet."[5]

- *When your baby (or child) is being treated by a doctor for some distress, be sure to:*

  (1) Learn all you can about the illness;

  (2) Question the doctor extensively as to the reasons your baby is being given certain medications, what to expect from the illness and the medication, how long to keep him on the medication(s), etc.

  This advice comes from Donna Jean Strauss of Honolulu as she describes in detail an experience that taught her and her husband a very important lesson:

Neither my husband nor I has ever been asthmatic, and consequently we knew nothing at all about the illness or how to care for an asthmatic child. In retrospect, I think Kris suffered needlessly at first because of our ignorance.

Kris had his first severe asthma attack at the age of five. I rushed him from our home in Kaneohe to Children's Hospital where he was given a series of three treatments. I was casually told by the E.R. physician to "keep him on his medication." It was late at night when we returned home and because of the adrenalin that Kris was given, it took him a long time to get to sleep. He was exhausted. I thought it was more important for him to get his rest than awaken him at 4 AM to give him his medication.

By 6 AM, he was back in the ER with his second asthma attack. I didn't know how vitally important it was to keep his blood chemistry at a certain level and that he should have had his 4 AM dose, no matter what.

Paul and I learned a very important lesson that day, at Kris' expense. From that moment on, we were determined to learn everything we could about asthma (and teach Kris, too). We repeated every instruction his doctors ever gave us and drilled them endlessly as to the reasons he was being given certain medications, what to expect, how long to keep him on them, etc. At one point, we even switched doctors because we wanted a more "pro-active" physician involved in his treatment—more intense involvement on both sides.

My advice to parents of a sick baby (child) is to learn as much about the illness as possible and QUESTION, QUESTION, QUESTION, if you're not sure. If your child is old enough to understand, educate him or her

Mom to Mom . . .

> *about what's happening. Kris was so good at "listening to his body" that he would tell me when it was time to take him to the E.R. for treatment of an asthma attack. The more educated he was, the less he was scared (his parents, too!). In fact, isn't that the whole principle of Lamaze?*
>
> *At age ten, Kris had completely outgrown his asthma, but he remembers positively the times we all went through. He has very little, if any, negative thoughts of the experience.*

Administering Medication . . .

- *Use an oral medication syringe to be sure you are administering the correct amount of medication.*

  Measuring spoons used for cooking and flatware teaspoons actually vary and are therefore not appropriate for measuring medications for infants *or* for adults. Consequently, the oral medication syringe is a much better measuring device, plus it has the added advantage of making it easier to give the medication to your baby.

  To be sure that most (and hopefully all) of the medication is swallowed by your little one, insert the syringe to the side and back of your baby's mouth and then gently squeeze the syringe until the syringe is completely empty. By placing the syringe at the side and then back of your baby's mouth, he won't gag from the sudden splash of medication nor will it startle him or be easy for him to push it back out of his mouth.

- *Another ingenious method of giving medication to a young baby is by using a bottle nipple without the bottle!*

  As was suggested in the December 15, 1989, issue of *Emergency Medicine:*

  > *Getting your nursing child to take medicine can be a real problem. If she is using a bottle, there's a temptation to put the medicine*

> *in with the formula or water. But what do you do if she doesn't take all of the liquid?*
>
> *An alternate is to give your child a nipple without the bottle attached. Once she is sucking on it, pour the medicine into the nipple. After she has sucked in the medicine, fill the nipple a couple of times with a water chaser. Although not a foolproof method, it works much of the time.*
>
> <div align="right">As quoted in <i>Pediatrics for Parents</i>
January 1990, page 8
Edited by Dr. Richard J. Sagall</div>

- *For each medication that is prescribed for your baby, ask your doctor about guidelines for what to do if not all of the medication is swallowed.*

Even as simple as the procedures suggested above may sound, sometimes some of the medication will still end up on his sleepers or your blouse or some other creative location! It's a good idea, then, to ask your doctor what leeway you have with the medication and what you should do if your baby doesn't receive the full amount.

Normally, with antibiotics and acetaminophen, there is a considerable safety margin and you can guess how much additional must be given to make up the difference. However, there are drugs that are potentially toxic if over-administered, such as cold and cough medications and anti-wheezing drugs.

So ask your doctor for guidance *in advance* for *any* medication, whether it is an antibiotic or acetaminophen or an over-the-counter cold medication.

If your baby is being treated for an illness that causes him to vomit, it is also a good idea to ask when it would be appropriate to re-administer the medication due to vomiting. Most medications are colored so that they can be seen should your

Mom to Mom...

little one vomit. Normally, medications are absorbed by the system within 30 minutes and there will be no evidence in the vomitus of the medication. In that situation, it would not have to be re-administered until the next scheduled time. However, be prepared in advance by asking your doctor what to do if your child vomits and there *is* evidence that the medication has not been completely absorbed.

- *Know which medications can be given to your baby just during waking hours and which must be given at specific intervals, requiring wake-up.*

   Many medications are labeled "give three times a day," or "give four times a day." This usually does not mean that you must wake your sleeping baby in order to give the medication at specific intervals. However, directions of "three times a day" also do not mean giving the medication at breakfast, lunch, and dinner, but rather it means giving the medication early in the morning upon waking, mid-day, and later in the evening just before bedtime. Doing so would ensure that the medication is being given approximately eight hours apart. If, instead, the medication were given at breakfast, lunch, and dinner, the number of hours between the last half-teaspoon (or whatever) one day and the first half-teaspoon the next day may make the medication ineffective in dealing with the infection it's supposed to treat.

- *When using a dropper to administer medication, whether into the mouth, eyes, or nose, the dropper should be thoroughly washed before being replaced in the bottle of medication.*

   Medications should never be shared. As an added precaution, if there is more than one child in the family, each child should have his own bottle of medication such as acetaminophen, eye drops and nose drops or sprays.

- *Be aware of the differences in same-name medications and the dosages recommended for each.*

   Over-dosing or under-dosing your infant can occur if you're not aware of the differences in medications such as acetaminophen. Liquid acetaminophen drops are much more potent than is the acetaminophen elixir for children. For example, the drops are 500 mg per teaspoon and the elixir is 160 mg per teaspoon, so be careful not to use such medications interchangeably. As always, it's best to read the labels carefully. But, according to Gary Holt, Ph.D., R.Ph., "for best results, dose your children according to their weight, not age. If the instructions do not provide this information, ask your pharmacist."[6]

- *To prevent insects biting your infant, use netting over the stroller, buggy, or playpen placed outside and a "net tent" over an infant seat or over a blanket where he is lying.*

   Insect repellents contain the active ingredient, DET (diethyltouamide), which "can cause unsteadiness, slurred speech, and even seizures in young kids."[7] Consequently, it's best to use netting for children under two years of age.

Some Helpful Suggestions...

- *Give your sick little one lots of TLC.*

    Hold your little ones—let them know their security is still there. Even though I always held my girls a lot when they were not sick, I held them even more when they were sick.

    When their heads needed to be elevated, I would adjust the crib so that one end would be higher than the other.

    Jan Sundblad
San Diego, California

    Note: A baby's head can also be elevated by:

    (1) Placing a pillow under the crib's mattress at the head-end to slightly raise it.

    (2) Purchasing a foam "sleeping wedge" which is placed under the crib sheet to elevate the baby's head.

Mom to Mom . . .

- *To take your infant's temperature . . .*

   To take your infant's temperature, use a rectal thermometer—the type that has a rounded bulb at the end.

   (1) Lay your infant belly down across your lap or on the changing table.

   (2) Dip the bulb of the thermometer into petroleum jelly or a water soluble lubricant.

   (3) Spread his buttocks until the anal opening is visible.

   (4) Carefully insert the thermometer only about an inch into the rectum.

   (5) Keep your infant from moving around by tightly holding the thermometer between your fingers while pressing your hand firmly against the buttocks.

   (6) After two minutes, remove the thermometer and read the temperature.

   A *normal* rectal temperature is *99.6* degrees Fahrenheit (one degree higher than an oral temperature of 98.6 degrees).

- *To aspirate your infant's nose . . .*

   This is never a pleasant task for your infant or for you, for it's very uncomfortable for your baby and she lets you know it with every bit of strength she has!

   Sometimes this procedure is a necessity though, since infants don't know how to breathe out of their mouths. So, keep in mind as you force yourself to do this that you are helping your little one to be much more comfortable in the long run!

   To aspirate her nose, you'll need a nasal aspirator and sterile saline solution. Then:

   (1) Lay your little one on her back across your lap so that her head hangs back.

Health...

(2) Place two drops of sterile saline solution in each nostril.

(3) Sit her up.

(4) Depress the nasal aspirator's bulb, put its nozzle in one nostril, and release the bulb. (This procedure should pull some of the mucus out of her nostril.)

(5) Repeat two or three times if necessary.

(6) Repeat the procedure for the other nostril.

Treating Rashes...

- *To treat a little one's bottom that is red from diarrhea...*

  Frequently soak your infant's bottom in a baking soda bath (one tbsp. of baking soda to two inches of water) and apply a zinc-oxide barrier cream.

  William Sears, M.D.
  "Summer Ailments"
  Baby Talk, August 1988
  Page 37

  Also try using Maalox (plain) with cornstarch. Make a paste and apply.

  Frederick Frye, M.D.
  Pediatrician
  San Diego, California

Another suggestion to care for rashes...

  Rashes can occur in a baby's neck folds and underarms. Rub some Desitin in those areas to alleviate it or on hot days, to avoid it altogether.

  Also, if a baby has a skin problem—rash, chicken pox, etc.—put some oatmeal in a sock

Mom to Mom . . .

> *and soak the sock in the baby's bath water.
> Doing so will will relieve the itching.*
>
> Janine Schooley
> San Diego, California

Dealing with Hospitalization . . .

Unbelievably, nearly half of hospitalized children are infants and toddlers.[8] We never want to even consider that our infant may have to be hospitalized, but should this happen, here is a list of excellent ideas suggested by Christine Palm in an article written several years ago:[9]

(1) *Accept that it's real and carry on.*

(2) *Learn everything you can* (about your baby's illness, situation, etc.)

(3) *Make your baby's environment more like home.*

> Ms. Palm suggests bringing some sleepers from home if the hospital can and will use them, a small toy, perhaps, and a picture of you taped sideways in the isolette. "No one is sure whether the baby can focus on it, but, in all likelihood, many babies can. This will be a comfort to you as you realize that a constant reminder of you is there with the child when you can't be."

(4) *Get to know the staff and make sure they know you.*

(5) *Talk to your baby.*

(6) *Breastfeed your baby whenever possible.*

(7) *Allow yourself the right to grieve.*

(8) *Be direct with family and friends.*

> Ms. Palm suggests here that friends and other family members may try to minimize the situation or talk about other things to help you keep your mind off of the situation. So be firm with them if you feel you *want* to talk with them about it or, the

reverse is also true, tell them you don't feel like talking, if you don't.

(9) *Try to stay fairly cheerful.*

Your little one *needs* your good cheer. Try not to show your anxiety around her and "be calmed by any efforts the child is making and be grateful for any improvements however small they may be."

(10) *Be hopeful.*

(11) *Don't run yourself ragged.*

(12) *Don't exclude siblings from the ICU (intensive care unit) experience.*

Your other child or children will want to be included in the "family crisis" and will feel resentful if they are not. They may also believe that the baby has died and that you aren't being truthful with them. So do include them. Be sure, however, to prepare them for the shock of the unit. Explain what their little sibling will look like so they'll be prepared in advance.

(13) *Don't be intimidated* (by the baby's condition and situation).

In addition, try to participate in your baby's care as much as possible. This would include doing such nonmedical routines such as feeding your baby, bathing and dressing your baby, and settling him in for the night.

The Association for the Care of Children's Health offer two excellent pamphlets which are quite helpful:

(1) *Caring for Your Hospitalized Baby*

(2) *Preparing Your Child for the Hospital*

Although your little one may not need hospitalization now or even in the future, you may want to order these publications to have on hand just in case. To order them, write a check out to ACCH for $2.00 and send it to the Association for the Care of Children's Health, 3615 Wisconsin

Mom to Mom...

Avenue NW, Washington, D.C. 20016. You may also give the association a call at (202) 244-1801 if you should have any questions.

Teeth and Teething...

Your little one's first teeth are so important. Many parents think of them as "temporary," but the front teeth may remain until your child is seven years of age, and the back teeth aren't replaced by permanent teeth until they are around twelve years of age! So they have a job to do for several years and need to be well taken care of. Also, the first teeth perform several valuable functions:

(1) They aid in chewing, important for getting proper nutrition.

(2) They aid in proper speech development.

(3) They help the permanent teeth come in properly.

(4) And, they certainly provide proper appearance.

Practicing preventive dental activities from the very beginning will help ensure that your child will grow up having healthy teeth and gums, something we would all want to ensure. These preventative activities include: daily cleaning of the new teeth, the use of fluorides when necessary, and careful watching of the daily diet.

Recommended Reading...

"Breastfeeding and Dental Caries," Publication #31 by Mary White of the La Leche League International

> This little pamphlet is packed with some very important information. More and more mothers in our society are leaning toward child-led weaning, a practice which consequently allows nighttime nursing long after a child's baby teeth have come in. "Bottle mouth," dental caries caused by nighttime bottlefeeding which tends to leave formula in the mouth after a child has fallen to sleep, is a great concern to dentists and parents. It is often suggested in other sources that nighttime nursing will also cause "bottle mouth" or "nursing caries," as some refer to it. This pamphlet presents the research that proves otherwise, and I suggest that if the possibility of your little one

Health ...

developing bottle mouth due to nighttime nursing is a concern of yours, please write for a copy of this pamphlet. It put my concerns to rest and I'm sure it will do the same for you.

As a footnote to the above, our daughter Maryanna continued to have an occasional nighttime "snack" up until she was three years old. She is now four and has yet to develop her first dental caries! As the pamphlet suggests, early tooth decay in babies and small children has much more to do with poor eating habits than with nighttime nursing.

- *Be sure that if your baby is using a bottle for feedings that you not allow him to fall asleep with a bottle at naptime or during the night.*

    When teeth begin to appear, bacteria are there ready and waiting. Formula and milk both contain sugar—the greatest cause of tooth decay. Allowing your little one to use a bottle for a pacifier at naptime or at night will allow the formula or milk to remain around his little teeth long after he has fallen asleep.

    However, if your little one is being nursed at night, the mechanics are quite different. The human nipple stretches and goes deeper into the baby's mouth. The milk, therefore, is not around the teeth but goes directly down the throat. For this reason, there is not the danger of tooth decay from nighttime nursing as there is from allowing a little one to fall asleep with a bottle, which would allow his teeth to be coated with formula or milk.

- *Do not allow the bottle filled with formula or juices to become a frequent handy pacifier.*

    Doing so will mean that your baby's teeth and those under the gums are continually bathed with sugary liquids.

- *Begin cleaning your infant's teeth as soon as they begin to erupt.*

    Some experts feel that the beginning of good oral hygien? should begin even before the eruption of the first teeth. B? not then, the practice of caring for your baby's teeth s? begin no later than with the eruption of the first tooth.

Om to Mom...

To clean the new little teeth, moisten a clean gauze pad or a small, soft infant toothbrush with water and rub or brush the teeth. Don't use any toothpaste for the first year, as a baby will tend to swallow some of the toothpaste and make it difficult to ensure that your little one is taking only the amount of fluoride necessary. More daily fluoride than necessary can cause mottling of the teeth—white spots or splotches that will appear on the permanent teeth later on.

For a young baby, the best position for cleaning his teeth is to have his head resting on his parent's lap.

- *To provide some relief from teething discomfort . . .*

    (1) Clean your baby's gums two or three times a day with a clean, moistened piece of gauze. Just gently wipe all exposed surfaces. Apparently the pressure from the gauze rubbing against the gums can provide some real comfort and relief to your infant.

    This procedure will also help eliminate some bacteria which not only cause dental caries but also cause teething discomfort.[10]

    (2) Rub cold smooth objects against the gums.

    (3) Use a teething medication that your pediatrician recommends.

- *Be able to distinguish the signs of teething from the signs of illness.*

    Many parents mistakenly believe that fever, diarrhea, vomiting and rash around the expected teething period are simply signs of "cutting teeth." Instead of being signs of cutting teeth, those are symptoms of illness and should be reported to your pediatrician.

    Signs of teething are:

    (1) Red, puffy, irritated-looking gums
    (2) Increased irritability
    (3) Excess drooling
    (4) Possibly a loss of appetite for a day or so

Health...

Equipment	Have	Need to Buy
(3) Gauze squares and bandages		
Alcohol (70% Rubbing)		
This is especially good in keeping the healing umbilical cord area clean and for cleaning utensils such as thermometers.		
Hydrogen Peroxide		
This is preferable to alcohol since it doesn't sting as much.		
Tweezers and Sharp Needle		
These are needed for removing splinters and insect stingers.		
Medications		
Fever Reducing Medication (child strength)		
A brand of acetaminophen is the best choice. *NOTE: Aspirin is now not recommended for children under 10, and not recommended for children under 15 in certain circumstances.*		
Acetaminophen comes in drops and *infant* suppositories. Your pediatrician should recommend the dosages for each of these.		
Decongestant (child strength)		
Cough Syrup (child strength)		
Anti-Poison Medication		
Syrup of Ipecac: This is given to a baby or child who has eaten a poison that **can** be vomited immediately.		
But give this medication only under the direction of your pediatrician or your local Poison Control Center. This medication can be toxic itself if inappropriately administered.		
Note: Activated Granulated Charcoal is no longer recommended as an anti-poison medication for the home medicine cabinet. According to the local Poison Control Center, "If		

207

Mom to Mom . . .

Equipment	Have	Need to Buy
the child is in enough trouble to need the activated charcoal, the child should be in t hospital."		
Topical Teething Medication Be sure it is alcohol free and aspirin free.		
Diaper Rash Cream A protective zinc-oxide base cream is best, e.g., Desitin or Diaperene.		
Calamine-base Lotion For bug-bites—it relieves itching.		
Saline Solution This is used to help clear a baby's nasal passages. It's used in conjunction with a nasal aspirator. It comes in nose drops and nasal spray for pediatric use.		
Sunscreen Lotion Be sure that it's paba-free and that its SPF is 15 but *no higher*. The chemicals in lotions that have an SPF greater than 15 can actually be harmful to your baby's skin. Also, select one that is made for pediatric use because it is made to be gentle and non-irritating, e.g., Coppertone's Water Babies, PreSun for Kids, or Johnson's Baby Sunblock.		
Suggested Reference Books		
A Sigh of Relief: The First Aid Handbook for Childhood Emergencies by Martin I. Green		
Safety Is No Accident by Jay M. Arena, M.D.		

Health...

- *Additional tips concerning the medicine cabinet...*
  (1) Toss out all over-the-counter medications that have expired and all prescription drugs no longer being used for treatment.
  (2) Be sure that childproof caps are on all those medications that remain in the cabinet after doing the above.
  (3) Be sure that the medicine cabinet and first aid box are out of the reach of all children.
- *Room vaporizers and humidifiers must be cleaned every day that they are being used because they give mold an ideal haven.*
- *Keep the following guidelines[12] in mind when going for an outing in the sun with your little one:*
  (1) Babies under the age of six months should be kept *completely* out of the sun. Sunblock, even with SPF 15 and paba-free, is not recommended for babies under six months because of the sensitivity of their skin.
  (2) For those over six months, a waterproof sunscreen with an SPF of 15 should be applied every two hours and after any exposure to the water.

  Also be aware that little ones always need sunscreen when outdoors, even if they are under beach umbrellas or big, expansive tree.. Reflected sunlight can also cause severe burns. And, cloudy, overcast days aren't "safe"—sunscreen needs to be lathered on for these days, too. The sun's harmful rays can burn right through the clouds! (As a 10-year-old, I had the worst burn of my life—ouch! to the touch and many, *many* blisters—on a very cloudy day... so be careful!)
  (3) Be sure to use sunscreen *even under your baby's clothes.* The sun will filter through lightweight, light-colored clothing.
  (4) Always use a hat with a brim or ruffle to protect your baby's head and give added protection to his neck and ears.
  (5) Infants should never be out in the midday sun.
  (6) For yourself as well as your older baby, avoid being out in the sun between 10 in the morning and 3 in the afternoon.

Mom to Mom...

(7) Be sure that *anyone* who cares for your baby knows that your baby should be protected with sunblock.

- *Help your infant develop his visual skills.*

  Here are some ideas to help you develop your baby's visual skills:

  (1) Hang a mobile or other dangly objects above the crib for your infant to focus on.

  (2) Place interesting little toys within eight to twelve inches of your little one so she can focus on them and eventually to reach for them.

  (3) Change your baby's position in the crib from time to time so he isn't always looking in the same direction and at the same things.

  (4) Change his location occasionally during his waking hours so that he has different things to look at and focus on.

  (5) Pin magazine pictures of faces or other bold pictures around the inside of his bassinet to give him additional visual pleasure!

  (6) And, if you're bottle feeding your baby, alternate sides just as a breastfeeding mother does naturally.

- *Be sure that you are prepared for an emergency by taking a course in CPR (cardiopulmonary resuscitation) and the Heimlich maneuver.*

  Most local Red Cross offices offer excellent instruction in CPR and the Heimlich maneuver, as do many YMCA's and YWCA's. Your own pediatrician can also give you some initial guidance in choking prevention and emergency procedures.

  There is an excellent free brochure entitled, "Choking Prevention and First Aid for Infants and Children," prepared and distributed by the American Academy of Pediatrics. You can get a copy by sending your request and a self-addressed, stamped, business-size envelope to:

Health...

Choking Brochure
American Academy of Pediatrics
Department C
P.O. Box 927
Elk Grove Village, IL 60009-0927

- *Prepare a medical release form to have on hand for any caregiver to use in an emergency should emergency personnel not be able to reach you for consent to treat your baby.*

Doctors are able to administer treatment without consent of a parent or guardian only if the situation is life-threatening or delay in treatment would result in the loss of a limb. Consequently, it is a good idea to have a medical release form prepared and ready for use in the unlikely event that such a situation would occur. To prepare one of these forms, you have two options:

1. *Create your own.*

    To create your own, type the following on a sheet of paper:

    (a) The current date

    (b) Your baby's name

    (c) A statement that as the parent(s) you are authorizing any licensed physician, dentist, or hospital to give emergency medical treatment upon request of the person presenting the release form.

    (d) Three blank lines

    Under the first blank line, type your name; under the second blank line, type your husband's name, and under the third, type "witness."

Then sign it, have your husband and a witness sign it. Once you have completed it, call the hospital emergency room that your family or caretaker would most likely use and discuss the contents of the release to be sure that it meets their requirements.

Mom to Mom...

> 2. *Use a blank "consent" form that you can order.*
>
> An excellent "consent-to-treat" form that has space to include your child's detailed medical history, can be obtained free by sending a postcard request to:
>
> > Communications Department
> > McNeil Consumer Products Company
> > Camp Hill Road
> > Fort Washington, PA 19034
>
> The American College of Emergency Physicians was involved in developing this form. It's a good one, and I recommend that you get a copy, complete it, and keep it with the information you regularly provide your baby's caregiver.

- *When talking with your pediatrician, make the distinction between medical advice and parenting advice:*

  > *When you visit your pediatrician, be sure to make the distinction between <u>medical</u> advice and <u>parenting</u> advice. Most pediatricians also give a lot of parenting advice (e.g., let your baby cry it out, baby should be sleeping through the night by six weeks, baby should be weaned at one year, etc.) in the guise of medical advice.*
  >
  > Eileen Carroll
La Jolla, California

Health . . .

[1] *A Mother's Journal*, Running Press Book Publishers, Philadelphia, PA, 1985.
[2] Leah Yarrow, "Pediatricians Answer 20 Nagging Questions," *Parents Magazine*, January 1989, pp. 83-84.
[3] William Sears, M.D., "Summer Ailments," *Baby Talk,* August 1988, p .36.
[4] Leah Yarrow, "Pediatricians Answer 20 Nagging Questions," *Parents Magazine*, January 1989, p. 88.
[5] *Ibid.*
[6] Gary Holt, Ph.D., R.Ph., "Medicine Chest," *Family Circle*, July 25, 1989, p. 50.
[7] *Ibid.*
[8] Peggy Eastman, "Diaper Set," Working Woman, March 1990, p. 90.
[9] Christine Palm, "When Your Newborn is in the Intensive Care Unit," *Baby Talk,* November 1986, pp. 11-12.
[10] Steven J. Moss, D.D.S., "Teeth and Teething," *Baby Talk,* November 1987, p. 38.
[11] Katherine Karlsrud, "Here Come the Teeth," *Parents Magazine,* October 1988, p. 206.
[12] Adapted from a list suggested by Christine Loomis in "Sun Safety for Baby," *Parents Magazine*, July 1988.

Mom to Mom . . .

Notes and Clips

Health . . .

Notes and Clips

Mom to Mom...

Notes and Clips

8

Safety for Little Ones . . .

Definition of a baby . . .
That which makes the home happier, love stronger, patience greater, hands busier, nights longer, days shorter, purses lighter, clothes shabbier, the past forgotten, the future brighter.

Marion Lawrence[1]

One of the things that you, like all new parents, are concerned about from the very beginning is keeping your baby safe from serious injury. But once you bring your baby home, you may find yourselves lulled into thinking that it'll be months before you'll have to worry about exposed outlets in the living room and glass double boilers in your bottom cabinet in the kitchen and the cleaning agents under the sink. You'll think that you have all the time in the world to identify all of the other seemingly zillions of things you'll have to be mindful of when your innocent little one begins rummaging about with his boundless curiosity.

Perhaps one of the best pieces of advice concerning childproofing that we received was, "begin childproofing the day you bring your infant home!" At first it seems rather ridiculous . . . what mischief can an infant get into? Obviously, none, but the reason for the advice is that the days and months begin to fly and suddenly, overnight, your little one who wasn't able to open cabinet doors *suddenly* can! Your little one who couldn't crawl *suddenly* can! Your little one who couldn't pick up anything in his hands *suddenly* can! The list of his "sudden" new behaviors is endless. And it's because of this sudden blossoming that it's

Mom to Mom . . .

best to begin your safety consciousness immediately and to begin preparing for the inevitable day when you hear sounds you haven't heard before . . . like the pots and pans being *not-so-gingerly* removed from the kitchen cabinet!

As we begin this chapter . . .

- *Keep in mind the ABC's of safety:*[2]

    *Your **A**wareness and that of any caretakers of your child's environment*

    *The **B**ehavior of your child and yourselves and any caretakers when using nursery equipment*

    *Using **C**aution when selecting and maintaining nursery equipment or other children's products*

    *'**S**afety—the sum total of the ABC's*

BATH SAFETY . . .

- *Avoid phone calls and doorbells when you have your infant in the tub or basin.*
- *Never leave water in the tub.*
- *Be sure that the thermostat on the hot water heater is set to 125 degrees Fahrenheit or lower so scalding water cannot be inadvertently put into the tub or basin.*
- *Use a non-skid mat in the tub and on the floor.*
- *When washing your little one, hold him with one hand as you wash with the other.*

CAR SAFETY . . .

- *Use your infant car seat correctly.*

    This tip seems rather obvious, doesn't it?! But in reality, 73% of parents in two different studies used car seats incorrectly.[3]

Safety for Little Ones ...

The most common mistakes were:[4]

(1) Not using the car's seat belt to anchor the safety seat.

(2) Failing to fasten the tether strap at the top of some models.

(3) Leaving harness straps unfastened.

(4) Not using the padded shields that protect the child's midsection in some models.

(5) Failing to position infant seats so that babies under 20 pounds and shorter than 26 inches faced the rear of the car.

CHILDPROOFING ...

GENERAL ...

- *Get down to the infant and crawler's point of view to determine what might be "attractive" hazards.*

- *Prevent burns from scalding tap water by lowering your hot water heater's thermostat to below 125 degrees Fahrenheit.*

  A baby's skin is extremely sensitive compared with an adult's. It would take a young child's skin only six seconds to develop a third degree burn from water at 140 degrees Fahrenheit.[5]

- *Cover unused electrical outlets with safety plugs and ensure that electrical cords and plugs are in good repair.*

- *Tuck exposed electrical wires under rugs and behind furniture.*

- *Install protective shields in front of fireplaces, radiators, and heat pipes.*

- *Unplug the iron when not in use and place it and its cord back on a counter to cool, as far from the edge as possible.*

- *Install smoke detectors on each floor near sleeping areas and periodically check their batteries.*

- *Keep chemical fire extinguishers wherever fires may start and have them checked periodically to ensure that they are in working order.*

Mom to Mom . . .

> We keep fire extinguishers in the kitchen, in our upstairs office and in our downstairs bedroom closet. We have one upstairs because of our computer system in the office and because our home's gas heater is in a closet in the upstairs hallway. And, midway between our bedroom and our daughter's is the laundry room where the gas water heater is located. In the unlikely event of a fire there, we have a fire extinguisher readily available in our closet!

- *Cover or remove sharp-cornered furniture.*
- *Gate stairs as soon as your little one begins to crawl.*

    The following advice on selecting and using a gate is provided by the U.S. Consumer Product Safety Commission:

    (1) Choose a style of gate other than the accordion-type. Gates with a straight top edge and rigid mesh screen instead of V-shaped or diamond-shaped openings do not present the entrapment/strangulation hazard.

    (2) Be sure the baby gate is securely anchored in the doorway or stairway it is blocking. Children have pushed gates over and fallen down stairs.

    (3) Gates which are retained by means of an expanding pressure bar should be installed with this bar on the side away from the child. A pressure bar may be used as a toehold and enable a child to climb over a gate.

- *Use gates at both the top and the bottom of the stairs.*

    Normally, parents use just one gate at the top of the stairs. We found that Maryanna enjoyed the stairs soooo much that she tended to climb them whenever the opportunity presented itself. We wanted her to climb the stairs—she enjoyed it and we enjoyed watching her, but there were times when we just weren't able to watch her every minute, so we used an expanding gate with a pressure bar at the bottom of the stairs (as well as the top) whenever we weren't able to be with her every minute.

Safety for Little Ones...

- *Remove poisonous house plants from the home until your child is well beyond the mouthing stage.*

    House plants are very special and make such a delightful, warm, inviting environment. But... many house plants are quite toxic and represent a real danger. As hard as it is, either give away your lovely house plants or lend them to a special friend for a few years. This includes hanging plants. Hanging plants can drop their leaves, tempting little crawlers to munch the crunchy, mysterious items he finds on the floor!

    What plants are poisonous? I'll mention a few here, but call your local Poison Control Center and ask if they publish a list of poisonous house and garden plants. Many centers do, highlighting those plants that are plentiful in their local areas.

    Some examples of poisonous plants are:

    > Azalea, Caladium, Castor Bean, Daffodil, Daphne, Deffenbachea, Dumb Cane, English Ivy, Foxglove, Holly, Hyacinth, Hydrangea, Iris, Japanese Yew, Jerusalem Cherry, Lantana, Lily of the Valley, Mistletoe, Morning Glory, Oleander, Poinsettia, Privet, Rhododendron, Rhubarb leaves, Sweet Pea, and Wisteria.

    This list is by no means exhaustive. Be sure to find out specifically about the ones in your home and garden, those around your apartment or condominium area.

    In her article entitled, "When Poisons are Pretty,"[6] Deborah R. Barchi gives some additional tips about flowers and plants...

    (1) Be sure to keep a list of those plants that you have in your yard, garden, and in the house. That list should include both the common name of each plant *and* its botanical name. In the event that a plant or flower is eaten, you will be able to quickly tell the Poison Control Center exactly what was ingested.

    (2) Label and store out of children's reach all bulbs and seeds.

Mom to Mom . . .

(3) Empty and wash all vases and pots that have held plants or flowers.

(4) Stress to your child from the earliest opportunity, *never* to put anything into his mouth without your approval or another trusted adult.

Even if you are diligent about protecting your child from the dangers of some plants, accidents can happen. In case your child does eat a possibly poisonous plant, Deborah Barchi suggests doing the following:

(1) Gently and quickly remove whatever pieces of the plant remain in your child's mouth. Be sure to check under the tongue and in the cheek pockets.

(2) Have your child show you the plant and try to determine how much was eaten.

(3) Then call the Poison Control Center and tell them the following:

    (a) The age and weight of your child.

    (b) The name of the plant and the amount and parts eaten.

    (c) Any observable signs of illness in your child.

BATHROOMS . . .

- *Begin to check under your bathroom and vanity sinks to see what might attract a little crawler's curiosity.*

    Again, you have an infant now, but infants begin to roll over and become mobile babies overnight. Begin your preparation *now* . . . that can't be stressed enough.

- *Keep all medicines and cosmetics <u>securely</u> out of reach.*

    Terri Ciosek adds this bit of advice about the medicine cabinet:

    > *Here's some advice I was given: Don't even let your child see what is in those forbidden cabinets and cupboards. It's amazing the*

Safety for Little Ones . . .

way a determined toddler whose curiosity has piqued can figure out those childproof locks!

- *Keep all personal care and cleaning equipment out of reach.*
- *Keep the toilet lid down and don't leave disinfectants in the bowl or tank.*

DINING ROOM . . .

- *If you use tablecloths, remember that they can be pulled by older babies.*
- *Keep all appliances being used at the table (e.g., food warmers, coffee pots) out of the reach of your baby.*
- *Candles should be kept out of your baby's reach.*
- *Take care not to pass hot food or platters over or near your baby.*

And, although this may be obvious, it ought to be mentioned anyway . . .

- *Be sure that anyone holding your baby isn't smoking or trying to sip hot coffee at the same time.*

KITCHEN . . .

- *Rearrange your kitchen drawers and cupboards to satisfy your little one's curiosity and still keep her safe.*

  For example, we pulled out the glass double boiler from our pots and pans cupboard and placed it in one of the upper cupboards. The remainder of the pots and pans were not a hazard but a joy for a little one to bang around with. Scissors in a utility drawer were placed in an upper cupboard, etc., so that the reachable drawers and cupboards didn't present any real hazard. However, we did let Maryanna know which cupboards and drawers were "her" drawers and cupboards and which were Mommy's and Daddy's. In that way, she learned not to get into those drawers that were not "hers," yet if she did when we weren't looking, there was nothing to fear.

Mom to Mom...

> We also created a drawer that really was hers—it had some little toys, a couple of books, a bell, and other little items that thrill a child's curiosity. She then learned that when she pulled all of those things out (as well as when she pulled out all of the pots and pans) that she was also to put them all back in.
>
> She was happy with this arrangement and so were we—we weren't worried about what she could get into, yet she was learning the difference between hers and ours, and about the responsibility of putting things back after she was finished.

- *Remember that some cabinets are reachable by climbing and some little ones climb before they can walk!*
- *If you're not already in the habit, be sure that pot handles aren't peeking over the front of the stove, inviting a curious crawler to pull himself up and reach for them.*

LAUNDRY...

- *Keep your washer and dryer closed at all times.*
- *Keep laundry products securely out of reach.*

LIVING ROOM...

It's far better for your baby if no one smokes in her presence, because studies have confirmed the ill effects of secondhand smoke on infants and young children. But, with that said, if smoking does take place around your baby...

- *Ashtrays should be unbreakable and be kept clean.*
- *Keep lit cigarettes, pipes, and cigars out of the reach of your baby.*
- *Table lighters, matches and cigarettes must be kept out of your baby's reach.*

Other...

- *If you live in an upper floor apartment, all of your windows should have guard rails or some other protective device.*

Safety for Little Ones . . .

- *Low furniture on which small children can pull themselves upon should not be placed near windows.*

FURNITURE AND EQUIPMENT . . .

Infant seats . . .

- *Infant seats should be used only for infants who are not active, turning, and kicking.*

    Once a child becomes more active, he can flip himself out of the seat or, if strapped in, can flip it over. This is especially dangerous if he has been placed on an elevated surface such as a chair or counter.

- *Never use an infant seat in the place of an infant car seat—they are two very different items.*

    The only exception to this is the model of infant car seat that has been especially made to fill both purposes. But, unless the infant seat that you buy specifically indicates that it fills both purposes, be sure that you have two separate seats, each which serves the purpose for which it is intended.

Jump or Bounce Seats . . .

- *Avoid using a jump or bounce seat.*

    These seats are very dangerous. As the baby becomes more active he can bounce and swing hard enough to slam into the door frame, causing head and/or shoulder injuries. Also, the supporting bar can loosen, dropping the infant/baby and possibly hitting him on the head.

Walkers . . .

- *Avoid using a walker.*

    Parents like the use of walkers because not only do they occupy the little one because they can usually bounce as well as "walk," but because they believe that the walker will actually help teach their child to walk.

Mom to Mom . . .

> According to Dr. Robert E. Hannemann . . .
>
>> *In reality, [walkers] do not do this and actually may delay the development of that skill. Numerous serious injuries have occurred when infants in walkers have kicked themselves to the top of a flight of stairs and then tumbled down.*
>>
>> *Other injuries occur when an infant propels himself at high speed across a slick, waxed floor and forcefully strikes a wall or a piece of furniture, flipping his head or shoulder against it.*
>>
>> *Walkers are so dangerous that the American Academy of Pediatrics has issued a special warning concerning the dangers of their use.*[7]

SLEEPY TIME . . .

- *Take care **not** to lay your infant on a waterbed or sheepskin rug.*

> The September 1989 issue of *Pediatric News* explains:
>
>> *Waterbeds and sheepskin rugs are not safe sleeping places for infants. There are nine known cases of infants who died from suffocation while sleeping on a waterbed. The babies were lying face down on the waterbed, forming a deep depression. They were unable to lift their heads to breathe and thus suffocated. The deaths usually occurred when the family was visiting a friend who didn't have a crib.*
>>
>> *Another unsafe place to put your baby is on a sheepskin rug. Four infants have died while sleeping on a sheepskin or thick rug. If the baby drools, causing matting of the sheepskin, and can't raise her head, she can suffocate.*

Safety for Little Ones . . .

> *Although the number of such deaths is not large, the risk nevertheless exists. Never leave an infant unattended on a waterbed or thick rug.*
>
> As quoted in *Pediatrics for Parents*
> January 1990, page 1
> Edited by Dr. Richard J. Sagall

- *Use fabrics and bedding treated with flame retardant.*

   Fabrics used in a nursery or child's room should be flame-retardant. This refers to curtains, ruffles, skirts on vanities, etc. Flame-retardant can be bought commercially or you can make your own mixture: Mix two quarts warm water, seven ounces of borax, and three ounces of boric acid. Soak the item, drip dry, and iron. Remember that whenever the item is washed, it must be treated again. Do not keep the mixture—it's toxic if swallowed.

- *Never put a pillow in the baby's crib because he may put his face in it and possibly smother.*

- *When your little one begins to pull up on the railing of the crib, be sure that the mattress is at its lowest level and the railing at its highest level.*

- *Mobiles and other toys hung above the crib should be removed as soon as your little one begins to push up with his hands and knees.*

- *It's best not to tie toys to the crib, but if you do, be sure that each toy isn't tied with a string any longer than 12 inches.*

MISCELLANEOUS SAFETY TIPS . . .

- *Newborns can turn over for the first time when you least expect it, so don't leave your newborn unattended on a bed or changing table, even for a moment.*

- *Don't use adult products to treat your baby.*

Mom to Mom . . .

> Such a suggestion may seem obvious, but there are good reasons for mentioning it. Adult skin is not absorbent, and so ingredients such as hormones, mercury, or insecticides don't seep into the skin and enter the bloodstream. On the other hand, the skin of infants and small children is quite thin and contains more blood and consequently readily absorbs products put on the skin. Ingredients in adult skin preparations and cosmetics can therefore be quite toxic for infants and little ones.

- *Never prop your baby's bottle to feed her.*

    By propping your baby's bottle to feed her while you attend to something else, choking can occur without your knowledge with tragic results.

- *Some important safety tips concerning pacifiers . . .*

    (1) Pacifiers are tossed and dropped frequently by a little one, which causes some mothers and caregivers to tie the pacifier onto a string and put it around the baby's neck. This is very dangerous, for the string can get wrapped around the baby's neck and strangle her, or it can get caught on something causing strangulation.

    (2) Pacifiers, if used frequently, can become worn. It's best to replace them frequently, before pieces of plastic begin to chip off and get caught in your baby's throat.

    (3) "Cutesy" pacifiers are especially dangerous because they have small plastic parts that can separate, causing the nipple to separate and possibly be aspirated by the baby which would be fatal.

    (4) Don't make your own pacifiers from bottle nipples. These homemade pacifiers can come apart easily, causing the baby to aspirate the nipple.

- *When throwing away dry cleaning bags in your various waste paper baskets, be sure to tie several knots in them—at each end and in the middle—so a little one can't drag it out and cover his face with it or crawl inside of it.*

Safety for Little Ones...

- *Write for an excellent safety checklist which is free:*

    The checklist is published by the Juvenile Products Manufacturers Association. You can receive one free by sending a self-addressed, stamped, business-size envelope to: "Tips for Your Baby's Safety," Juvenile Products Manufacturers Association, 66 E. Main Street, Moorestown, NJ 08057.

Linda Brosio, a mom from Grass Valley, California, makes this excellent suggestion:

> *Before your child goes to a new little friend's home to visit, you may want to ask the parents these very important questions:*
>
> *"Do you have a pool, pond, or creek at your house? Do you keep guns in your home?"*

---

[1] *Meditations for the Expectant Mother*, Herald Press, Scottsdale, PA, 1985, p. 19.
[2] *Buyer's Guide—The Safe Nursery,* U.S. Consumer Product Safety Commission, Washington, D.C., 4/85, p. i.
[3] "Research Briefs," *Growing Parent,* January 1989, p. 7.
[4] *Ibid.*
[5] Jean Caldwell, "How to Childproof Your Home," part of the Parenting Advisor Information Center, p.3.
[6] Deborah R. Barchi, "When Poisons are Pretty," Baby Talk, August 1986, p. 27.
[7] Robert E. Hannemann, M.D., "The Back Page," *Growing Parent,* November 1988, p. 7.

Mom to Mom . . .

Clips and Notes . . .

Safety for Little Ones . . .

Clips and Notes . . .

Mom to Mom . . .

Clips and Notes . . .

9

Traveling Away from Home Can Be Simple

> *As Deana approached her first birthday, she had traveled over 37,000 miles, and having her with us made our own experiences that much richer and more enjoyable. Our baby has opened doors for us from the Arctic's frozen seas to the Amazon's steaming rivers, from snow-blanketed Canadian northlands to dense and "unsanitary" jungles in Ecuador.... The joy of having her with us more than compensates for the rare moments of inconvenience.*
>
> Ivan Jirak
> "Babies on the Go ...
> Arctic to Equator with Deana"
> *Baby Talk,* May 1986

How true Ivan Jirak's words are! We have found the same to be true for us wherever we have taken Maryanna! We started taking her on trips when she was five months old, and by the time she was three, she had been to Hawaii twice, to England, to France, Italy, and Switzerland, and to several cities in the U.S. Babies are quite portable, as we very quickly discovered, and as she got older, Maryanna made our trips all the more pleasurable because of her company. Traveling out-of-town with a baby simply requires more advance planning—certainly more luggage—and a degree of flexibility in activity and scheduling. Go ahead—consider it! It's not nearly as scary as it might first appear to be in your imagination!

Mom to Mom . . .

But "traveling away from home" with a baby doesn't only mean out-of-town travel. It also means *short* trips away from home—to the store, to a friend's home, to an appointment, to the park, out for a walk—all of which may seem equally as scary as out-of-town travel to the new parent! Such short trips can be pleasurable too, if some advance planning and preparation become a part of your routine.

Simone Bloom beautifully expresses the beauty and pleasure of outings—short or long—with one's baby . . .

> *I am amazed (and secretly delighted) at how many people stop me to have a look at my baby. Motherhood seems to break all social barriers as conversations with strangers of all ages and backgrounds evolve.*[1]

How true!

Short Trips Around Town . . .

Suggested Contents for a Diaper Bag . . .

The contents of your diaper bag for an outing will vary according to the age of your baby.

For the newborn through four or five months:

(1) Several cloth diapers or disposables

(2) Clean diaper covers for the cloth diapers (2)

(3) Package of tissues or wet washcloth in a zip-type plastic bag

(4) Small container of water in the event none is available

(5) Large plastic zip-type bag for soiled and wet diapers

(6) Small plastic zip-type bag with one or two wet washcloths

(7) One change of clothes

(8) Small, travel-size container of powder (*If* you use it—most experts recommend that you *not* use it.)

(9) Desitin or A & D Ointment for rashes

(10) If you're using bottles, two or three bottles with a measured amount of powdered formula in each (You can then add the appropriate amount of water when it's needed.)

(11) A small receiving blanket

(12) A flannel-backed rubber lap pad

(13) A sweater or jacket

(14) A bonnet or hat

(15) A little music box

You will be amazed at how quickly a little music box can often quiet a fussy or crying baby!

Each time that you return to home base, be sure to replace the things that you used so that the next time you pick up the diaper bag, you won't be caught with some of the needed items missing.

From four or five months:

(1) The items from the above list

(2) Travel packs of baby wipes

(Baby wipes weren't recommended in the first list because they are best not used on newborn bottoms. The chemicals used in them tend to irritate a newborn's tender skin.)

(3) A couple of toys and teething rings

Plus, when you begin supplementing your baby's diet with solids:

(4) Plastic zip-type bag with clean teflon-coated baby spoons

(5) Plastic bib(s) (They can be easily wiped clean.)

(6) A plastic bag with damp/wet paper towels or package of baby wipes (for cleaning bibs, wiping off spoons, etc.)

(7) Jar(s) of various baby foods that your little one now enjoys.

Mom to Mom . . .

General Tips for Short Trips . . .

- *If the weather is cold, dress yourself first so your infant doesn't become too hot—and fussy!*
- *Prepare for "emergencies" by keeping a plastic grocery bag in the trunk of your car, filled with disposable diapers, paper towels, a small spray bottle (or baby wipes for an older baby), a small bottle of baby oil, a little box of tissues, and some plastic disposable bags.*

   Too often did I get caught because I was just going to "just be gone for a few minutes"—thus no diaper bag! Once I had my emergency supply readily available, my "quick trips" were not a problem.

Traveling by Car . . .

Some of the suggestions below may help make your short—and long—car trips a bit more comfortable and interesting for your baby and easier for you because he'll be at least temporarily satisfied.

- *Tape or pin pictures of faces and/or bright designs on the back seat of the car.*

   If placed in the most secure spot in the car correctly in his infant safety seat, your baby will be facing a very uninteresting back seat. Cut out some colorful pictures of faces and designs and "change the show" from time to time.

- *With a very short shoelace, tie a rattle or other noisemaker to the infant seat straps to catch your baby's interest and attention.*
- *Tie jingle bells on the ties of your baby's booties—again, for another interest-grabber.*
- *Keep one or two cassette tapes in the glove compartment to play when in the car.*

   Even infants love music! If you played any special music while you were pregnant, that music would be recognizable to your infant and give him a lot of pleasure. Such music may also be a calming influence if you're stuck in traffic and your little one begins to fuss.

And, don't underestimate your own singing! Your little one loves to hear your voice, so enjoy singing to your little one! Or, if you feel you need to concentrate more on your driving than the words to a song, how about making a tape of yourself singing? Our sitter has done that for Maryanna who is four years old now, and she still loves to hear "Rowie," as she calls her, singing to her on the tape!

- *If someone else is riding with the two of you, have the other person sit in back (if willing) with your baby.*

Your friend can still converse with you while at the same time giving your baby a much more interesting face to look at and listen to than those taped or pinned to the back seat! A real person's face moves! It smiles, it makes funny faces, it talks—what fascination!

Other moms had these suggestions . . .

> *Rather than buying an expensive "roll" for our infant car seat to keep our infant propped up during the first three months, we simply used a rolled receiving blanket. It was just perfect!*
>
> Janine Schooley
> San Diego, California

> *When a little one must be along on a shopping trip or during a church service, etc., include activities to involve him. An infant can hear the parent's voice as he or she talks to him, and can follow his parent's movements. (A front carrier or sling is perfect for this.) An older child can help bag items or select them. For a service or an office visit, Mom can hide*

Mom to Mom...

> *special toys in her purse that are available and handy only for such occasions.*
>
> Linda Bannister
> Cotati, California

Out-of-Town Travel with Infants...

- *If you will be traveling overseas, be sure to apply for your baby's passport well in advance.*

    Even a baby must have a passport—good for five years. This process may take two or more weeks, so apply as soon as you know that you'll be going overseas.

    And, while you're at it, be sure to check on yours, too! If you don't have one, apply for one. If you do have one, is it current? If it is, will it expire just before or during your trip? If so, you'll need to get a new one.

- *When making your plane reservations, tell the airline that you will have an infant with you.*

    The bulkhead area of most aircraft is equipped for attached bassinets that the airline would provide or gives enough space for an airline bassinet to fit on the floor in front of you. When making your reservations, inform them that you will have an infant with you and then ask if the aircraft to be used for your flight is equipped for an attached bassinet. Even if the aircraft is not so equipped, reserve that area anyway if it is available. The extra room will be much appreciated for the extra leg room and the occasional diaper changings.

- *Try to take a non-stop flight or a direct flight (one that does not require a change of planes) to your destination.*

- *If you are going to Europe from the West Coast, or the orient from the East Coast or any other similar "long haul," seriously consider breaking the trip mid-way.*

    It means getting to and from an airport hotel, but the break for some relaxation is worth it for both you (the parents) *and* your baby. Such a trip without a break is extremely difficult even for seasoned adult travelers. For an adult accompanying a baby and for a baby himself, traveling all the way in one fell swoop is *very difficult*.

If you choose to take a respite at an airport hotel, you may be able to store most of your luggage at the airport and simply take an overnight bag that you may have packed just for this purpose. That would make the overnight trip at the hotel much easier and certainly more hassle-free.

- *Take a late a.m. flight, if possible.*

    When Maryanna was still quite small, we found that it was much easier getting ourselves ready and to the airport if we followed a fairly normal routine in the morning. She was awakened (or she awakened herself) at her usual time, breakfast was at the usual time, etc. Getting her up and ready in the dark for a 7 a.m. flight did not go smoothly at all!

    Also, by still leaving in the morning, you will arrive at your destination at a fairly decent hour, still giving you a chance to leisurely settle in and relax in the evening.

- *When reserving a car in advance, reserve a car seat for your baby as well.*

    Most rental companies now have car seats available, but some don't. In order to ensure the safety of your baby, be sure to inquire first and then reserve a seat if it's available. If not, plan to take yours along as checked luggage. Not only will your baby be much safer, but you'll be abiding by the law.

- *And, if you reserve a car, reserve a BIG car.*

    The smaller, compact cars just don't have the necessary room for all of the paraphernalia that you'll be lugging with you.

    Tom and I used to pride ourselves on what light travelers we were! Once Maryanna joined the family, however, there were bigger suitcases needed because of all of her things that were

Mom to Mom...

needed, the diaper bag, the bag(s) of disposable diapers that had to be bought, the baby backpack and/or stroller, etc., etc., etc.!

- *When reserving a hotel room in a sunny vacation spot, you may want to request a ground floor room.*

   Janine Schooley from San Diego, California, has this suggestion:

   > When we went to Hawaii, we asked for a ground floor room. By being on the ground floor, we could still sit outside and enjoy the sun while our little one was asleep in her crib. We could be close enough to hear her when she awakened, and yet still enjoy the sunshine!

- *When reserving a hotel room, reserve a crib and other baby equipment if you need them.*

- *If you normally use a breast pump and would rather not take yours with you, call Medella at (800) 435-8316 and ask them for the names of "rental stations" at your destination that have breast pumps for rent.*

   You may then want to call one of the rental stations in advance and make a reservation. Some organizations will make arrangements to deliver the equipment and pick it up, saving you from the hassle.

- *If your baby has a stuffy nose,* **ask your doctor** *about the advisability of giving your baby a decongestant an hour before taking off and an hour before landing.*

   Your baby's ears are so sensitive and delicate, especially in the early months. If his nose is stuffy, this could lead to problems with his ears when the plane becomes pressurized. Be sure to ask your doctor for advice, both on the product to use and the amount of the medication to give.

- *Don't plan to do* **anything** *after your arrival the first day.*

   Relatives and/or friends may be very eager to see you—and you may be quite eager to see them, but if you're staying at a hotel,

Traveling Away from Home Can Be Simple...

settle in first and then begin your rounds the next day. A day full of traveling, entertaining your baby on the plane or in the train or car, securing a rental car, loading and unloading the car, and settling into the hotel—making up the portable crib, if you've requested one, unpacking, meeting the your baby's needs, etc.—is *plenty* of exhausting activity for one day.

- *Daddy... a word to the wise: Don't carry your pen and pencil in your shirt pocket!*

    Babies, once they have begun to grab at things, love those shiny objects in your pocket!

At the Airport...

- *Arrive at the airport early—don't skimp on your arrival time.*

    You'll have more luggage and more carry-on baggage to lug out to the gate—*plus* the baby to carry or wheel in a stroller. You will need plenty of time to check-in comfortably and to leisurely walk out to the gate. Also, your plans for the bulkhead or at least sitting together may evaporate if you're late. Some airlines will hold reserved seats only up to a half-hour before departure. If you're late checking in, you'll have to take pot-luck! So—a word to the wise—check in *early*!

- *If taking your stroller, do not check it with your luggage but check it at the gate instead.*

    By doing so, you not only will have its use allllllllll the way to your plane's gate, which always seems to be at least two miles from the check-in counter. Some airlines will then have it waiting for you as you get off the plane at your destination or connection point. You can thus avoid carrying all of your carry-ons and your baby from the gate to the baggage or customs area.

- *Include a small, thin quilt in your carry-on bags.*

    Sometimes flights are delayed or you have plenty of time before your flight departs. You can then spread out the quilt in a non-

241

Mom to Mom . . .

traffic area and give your little one a stretching and kicking opportunity. Try to use a quilt that has a different pattern or color on each side. Then you'll always know which side is the floor-side.

On the Plane . . .

- *Change your baby's diapers just before boarding your flight.*

   If your baby is dry, fine, but checking may eliminate *at least* one diaper changing in the cramped quarters of a plane.

- *Consider using your front carrier or sling to carry your baby on board the plane.*

   Not only will this keep your baby safe from possible bumps and jolts, but your hands will be free for carry-ons.

   Also, if you're accustomed to nursing your baby from the front carrier or sling, it's the safest restraint to use during take-offs and landings.

- *Do **not** strap the seat belt around you and your baby.*

   Ninety-five percent of all difficulties occur on the ground. Should the plane make a sudden stop, your body weight pushed against the seat belt restraint could seriously injure your baby if he were strapped in with you.

   Instead, it's best to securely cradle your baby with his head securely in the crook of your elbow and with your hands locked onto your arms.

   An older baby can be seated on your lap with your arms securely wrapped around his middle, your hands locked.

- *Nurse your baby during every take-off and every landing (or, if bottle feeding, have a bottle ready for every take-off and landing.)*

   By feeding your baby at these times, you ensure his continued swallowing which in turn will help keep his ears clear and free, or relatively free, of pain.

Traveling Away from Home Can Be Simple...

- *When meals are served, if you are traveling with someone, request that one of you be served first, the other served after the first has finished.*

   Flight attendants are very helpful in this regard. If you make this request, one of you can easily hold the baby while the other eats.

Packing...

- *Plan to use a whole suitcase for the baby.*

   "A *whole* suitcase?!?" I can hear you asking rather incredulously! When you consider the number of clothes you'll be taking because of changes needed during the day as well as day to day, the number of cloth diapers you will be taking for nighttime (I was convinced they were more comfortable than paper at night), and the bedding you'll be taking, etc., etc., you'll soon discover that the big suitcase you had planned to use for your baby's things *as well as yours* just won't be adequate.

   Also, you won't want to unpack everything. It's much easier to keep your baby's clothes and things all in one place—and it gives you a cherished feeling of organization!

- *Create your own standard "packing guide" so you will be sure to remember everything you'll need.*

   We travel frequently, so we have found that having a standard list that we use to guide our packing is quite handy to have. As Maryanna's needs change, the list is altered to reflect those changes. For example, when she was quite small, I wanted the crib in the hotel to be as much like home as possible, so I would include all of her own bedding, including her quilt. It would smell more like home and I thought that would help settle her. Whether having her own bedding made any difference, we'll never really know. But she seemed to have good nights most of the time, with the exception of her teething periods.

   The following is just a sample list that I used when I was packing for Maryanna at seven months. If you want to create your own

Mom to Mom . . .

standard packing list (using pencil so you can change it from time to time), you'll find a blank list at the end of this chapter.

PACKING LIST

Diaper Bag*	Plastic Bibs (2)
	Lap Pad
	1 Small Blanket
	____ Disposable Diapers
	(The number depended on the number of hours I was planning on from door to door plus two extra.)
	Small container of powder
	(This is included here just as a reminder, *if* you use it.)
	Extra outfit
	Bonnet or Hat
	Jars of food (if your baby has started solids)
	(Again, the number and variety depended on how long I thought it would take us to get to our destination. I was still nursing her several times a day, so this also influenced the number and kind that I carried.)
	Small plastic zip-type bag with teflon-coated spoons
	Small plastic zip-type bag with wet paper towels
	Large zip-type bags
	(These always come in handy, but they are especially handy for disposing of soiled diapers. It's not only more sanitary, but it's a consideration for others, considering the "aroma" that a soiled diaper can send out!
	2-3 favorite toys/teethers
Suitcase**	Linens: Fitted sheet(s), flannel-covered rubber pad, imitation lambskin pad, bumpers, quilt/blanket

Traveling Away from Home Can Be Simple . . .

Laundry Soap
(I always took a zip-type bag filled with Dreft.)
___ Cloth Diapers
(Again, the number depended on the number of nights we were to be gone and whether or not I would be doubling them. When Maryanna was about seven months old, I started doubling her diapers at night—it gave more absorption and kept her more comfortable.)
Plastic Bag for the cloth diapers
(This deodarized bag was from the diaper service that we used. I would rinse out the cloth diapers each morning, hang them over the shower curtain rod to dry, later fold them and put them into the bag that I kept in the bathroom. The day we left to return home, I would still rinse out the diaper(s), but would then put them in-between the dry ones in the plastic bag and put the plastic bag in the suitcase.)
Extra Diaper Covers
___ Outfits
___ Booty/Sock Pairs
___ T-Shirts
P.J.'s/Sleepers (2)
Blanket or quilt for the floor
(I sometimes carried this in a carry-on bag so I could use it in the airport and on the plane.)
Sweater/Jacket
Roll of Paper Towels
(We would use this to replenish the wet paper towels we carried each day in our diaper bag.)
Favorite Bath Toys (2 or 3)
Favorite Toys
("Lovie" plus two or three others. Inflatable toys are a good space saving idea.)

Mom to Mom . . .

Toiletries	Bath Towel(s) and Baby Washcloths
	(Baby towels and washcloths are so much softer and easier to manage with a baby.)
	Vitamins and/or Fluoride Drops
	(whatever medication your pediatrician has prescribed)
	Clippers (nail scissors)
	Baby Shampoo
	Bath Soap
	(I use Johnson and Johnson's Bath Mousse for face-washing because it's both gentle and won't hurt the eyes should some sneak in! I also use a very mild soap for her bath. Because hotels don't cater to these needs, I have always taken these items with us.)
	Thermometer
	Acetaminophen
	(Be sure to take this overseas with you. The warning against aspirin use with children under 15 is not world-wide. Consequently, pills bought or prescribed overseas may contain aspirin.)
	Triaminic (or other recommended child strength cold medication)
	Saline Solution
	(This is used to clear a stuffy nose.)
	Baby Nose Aspirator
	(This is used to suction out mucus from a stuffy nose.)
	Night Light
	(We have found that plugging in a night light in the hotel room's bathroom not only gives us some needed orientation in the middle of the night, but it also occasionally sheds enough light into the bedroom to provide the dim light needed for a night feeding and diaper changing.)

Traveling Away from Home Can Be Simple...

Equipment	Front Carrier or Sling—if infant is under five months (to be carried in diaper bag or suitcase)
	or Back Pack Carrier—if baby is five months or older
	and/or Stroller (to be checked at the gate)
	Infant or baby car seat (unless the car rental company has them available)
	Car Seat Cover
	(Most rental companies have the vinyl car seats. These can be very uncomfortable for a little one—either very hot during the summer or very cold during the winter. Consequently, it's a good idea to take your seat cover with you to use on the rented seat or to make the investment and buy one to be used on trips.)

Notes: *If you are bottlefeeding, be sure to include in your diaper bag all the bottles you'll need for the trip, each with a measured amount of powdered formula, ready to be mixed.

**The suitcase list above doesn't contain disposable diapers or extra jars of food. Except for a European trip, we always bought a bag of disposables and several jars of food at a grocery store when we arrived before checking in at our hotel or getting to a relative's home. Later, when Maryanna was a little older, we would also stock up on favorite snack items like oat rings, raisins, baby pretzels, and boxes of her favorite 100% juices.

And, as an additional note, you may want to consider including a day's *extra* essentials if you can squeeze them into your carry-on in the event your luggage is misrouted.

---

[1]*A Mother's Journal*, Running Press Book Publishers, Philadelphia, PA, 1985.

Mom to Mom...

YOUR PERSONAL PACKING GUIDE

Diaper Bag	
Suitcase	

Traveling Away from Home Can Be Simple . . .

Toiletries	

Equipment	

Misc.	

Mom to Mom . . .

Clips and Notes . . .

Traveling Away from Home Can Be Simple . . .

Clips and Notes . . .

Mom to Mom . . .

Clips and Notes . . .

10

Babysitters and Day Care ...

> *Before I got married I had six theories about bringing up children; now I have six children and no theories!*
>
> Lord Rochester[1]

One of the hardest things for a new mother to do is to give her little one to another to care for, whether it's for an hour or two, an evening, or a full day while she's away at work. Worry, guilt, and concern are just a few of the feelings experienced. And, while she's gone, her thoughts are often preoccupied with what's happening at home or at the sitter's.

Feelings such as these are very common to the mothering experience ... and I've been told that they never go away. Your child can be in college or off on his own—even married with a family, and the worry and concern continue! We may no longer feel the "guilties," but worry we will! It's just the nature of motherhood!

Because making that important move toward using an occasional sitter or in selecting and using full- or part-time day care is difficult for many, the focus of this chapter is to give you as much help as possible from other moms who have traveled that same path. You'll find many ideas on easing that transition and being comfortable with your decisions.

Some Initial Thoughts ...

Much has been written about the important bonding process that needs to take place between the child and its primary care-givers—the parents. Some of the literature written by experts in the field of child

Mom to Mom . . .

development suggests that if anyone other than the parent takes care of the child on a full-time basis there will be considerable interference with the bonding process.

There are also those experts in the field, however, who believe differently. They believe that no significant interference with the bonding process occurs when "loving parents leave their children with a carefully chosen care-giver. The key words, they emphasize, are 'carefully chosen.'"[2] And that's what this chapter will help you do . . . carefully choose your care-giver.

Both parents in so many of today's families must work full- or part-time to simply provide the minimum for their family. What then becomes necessary is for them to dedicate their after-work hours to their children. "(Parents) can't expect to raise well-adjusted children *if their after-work hours are dominated by civic or social activities outside the home.*"[3] (Emphasis added.)

Determining Your Requirements . . .

- *Determine what the ideal child care situation is for you:*

    (1) Do you want your baby cared for in your home or at the home of a sitter?

    It is believed that at-home care during an infant's first few months is best, since his exposure to other children could pose a health risk. Although this is often a more expensive option, an infant's immune system isn't fully developed for several months and thus needs the additional protection of being cared for at home, if at all possible.

    (2) Do you want your baby to be the only child cared for or are you willing to have your baby cared for along with one or two other babies?

    (3) What exactly are your needs?

    Are you wanting an occasional sitter who is on-call or do you need regular part- or full-time hours? Will you need someone once a week? twice a week? five days a week?

Babysitters and Day Care . . .

(4) Do you feel comfortable with a competent teenager for evening babysitting or during the weekends or would you feel more secure and comfortable with an adult?

(5) Do you feel comfortable with the idea of a babysitting cooperative?

(6) What do you expect of your sitter?

Do you want your sitter to simply care for your baby or do you want and/or expect some minor assistance with the housework?

(7) How much are you willing to pay?

Concerning this, San Diego mom, Jan Sundblad advises . . .

Pay the good sitters well—they'll come back and you'll be satisfied.

Sources of Sitters and Day Care-Givers . . .

Some of the best sources for information on good sitters and day care-givers are:

(1) Other parents

(2) Moms in the mothers' support group(s) that you attend

(3) Neighbors

(4) Relatives

(5) Church or synagogue organizations

(6) Health professionals (doctors, nurses, prenatal instructor, lactation consultant)

(7) A local nursing school

Sometimes students who are experienced in infant care are available for babysitting.

(8) Senior citizen centers or living complexes

Mom to Mom...

> You can post a "Grandma Wanted" notice on bulletin boards or in their newsletters.
>
> (9) A baby-sitting cooperative
>
> This option would not be considered for full- or regular part-time day care, but it is an excellent source of sitters you would know well. The mechanics of this option are explained in detail later in this chapter.

Just remember to thoroughly interview and check the recommendations that you receive from whatever source, even if your best friend raves about the sitter or day care-giver that she uses. As close as your friend may be and as much as you may seem to share similar parenting practices, you still may not be as comfortable with her recommendation as you might with another. So ... a word to the wise ... check *all* of the possibilities. It may sound like a lot of work ... and it is ... but it's worth every minute of your valuable time! It's hard enough to leave your little one behind; how comforting it is to be totally confident that you are leaving your precious little bundle in the arms of someone you totally trust and appreciate! It may be hard to find such a jewel, but the comfort and satisfaction and peace of mind are worth all the jewels in a queen's vault!

Interviewing Potential Sitters and Day Care-Givers ...

- *Prepare carefully for the interview.*

   > This piece of advice comes underlined from Linda Brosio, a mom from Grass Valley, California, who writes ...
   >
   > > *When interviewing, ask a previously well researched set of questions ... and pray!*
   >
   > Be well prepared for the interview by giving your interview format considerable thought beforehand. Write out your questions—even consider duplicating several copies of your "questionnaire" so that you can briefly jot some notes during or after the interview. Doing so will make it much easier to remember which person is which when you begin to make your selection(s).
   >
   > When preparing questions for the interview, create some "what-if" situations that might occur while you're away and ask each

Babysitters and Day Care...

person what she might do in those situations. Although no one knows for sure exactly what she would do in a situation until it really happens, you can still get a feel for her judgment which will either promote your comfort level with her or sound a warning signal.

During your interview, include a request for *several* references, not just one or two. Anyone can give their best recommendations when only one or two are required. But a better composite perspective can be gained from a minimum of three or more.

- *When interviewing a sitter or a day care-giver, include the following questions:*

    (1) Are you currently trained in infant CPR and first aid? Where were you trained and when?

    (2) Do you feed a baby on demand or on a schedule?

    (3) How do you handle a crying baby? Is he picked up immediately or left to cry?

- *During your interview, it's best to review your expectations and requirements so that the sitter isn't surprised and disgruntled the first time she sits for you.*

    For example, if you expect her to help with some of the housework while your baby sleeps, she had better know that during the interview. If she's not interested, then you both will avoid an unhappy first sitting experience.

- *For regular part- or full-time day care-givers, try to ensure whenever possible that the selection you make will be an on-going commitment on your part as well as the day care-giver.*

    Continuity is so important for your baby. Over time, a little one develops trust and a comfortable, loving relationship with his care-giver. Should that care-giver change frequently, there isn't that opportunity to develop those essentials of a baby-care-giver relationship. The result can be, and often is, an unhappy, confused little one.

Mom to Mom . . .

> We have been fortunate to have the "perfect situation." We have had the same care-giver for the last three and a half years. Although I work out of an office in our home, I use a wonderful sitter who lives just a few doors down from us. I returned to work when Maryanna was four months old—three hours a day at first, slowly working up to six hours a day. Since I was breastfeeding, our sitter would call when Maryanna was fussy and ready for a feeding, and I would walk down, cuddle and feed her, and return to work. As Maryanna grew, she and "Rowie" (Maryanna's pet name for her sitter, Rose) have become the best of pals. It has been and continues to be a wonderful situation for them both . . . and for me. I have never worried or felt terribly guilty because Maryanna not only has the time of her life with "Rowie," but she gets to interact with another adult on a regular basis who dearly loves her. I believe Maryanna has benefited tremendously! That definitely would not be the case had our "Rowie" changed frequently.

Suggested Process of Selecting Quality Sitters and Day Care . . .

First, write to Public Awareness About Child Care for important literature giving additional guidance in identifying and selecting excellent child care service.

> Address: Public Awareness About Child Care, Dept. P, P.O. Box 545, Station 12, 930 S. Monaco, Denver, CO 80224-1665.

Then, for sitters:

(1) Collect recommendations from the various sources you have available.

(2) Interview all prospects that appeal to you from the recommendations received.

(3) Check *each and every* reference provided.

> It is wise to have prepared questions for this process as well. Be sure to ask each reference specific questions about:
>
> (a) Why the reference liked or disliked the care-giver;

Babysitters and Day Care ...

    (b) Whether or not problems came up;

    (c) Whether or not the reference would recommend the caregiver.

(4) When making your final selection(s), use your intuition and select the person(s) you *trust*.

This means selecting someone whom you *believe* loves and enjoys babies, who provides a loving, sensitive environment, and who is stable and reliable.

Each of these characteristics must be present. The quality of the person is as important as reliability. Reliability is worthless to you if you don't believe that she *really* enjoys babies and/or *really* will provide a loving, sensitive environment.

I know of a mother who dearly loves her little ones, but as a single, working mother she has experienced her share of unreliable sitters. She finally found one whom she knows will be on the job each and every day—which is essential to her as a working mother. Yet, she confesses that the sitter isn't as thoughtful of her young son's feelings as she thinks she ought to be, and has often witnessed her assaulting his vulnerable self-esteem. She has called him a "cry baby" when he sometimes cries as his mom leaves him with her, etc. Her response is, "I'd rather she be more sensitive to such issues, but . . . she is very reliable and I absolutely need that."

As I said earlier, reliability is essential . . . but not at the expense of your little one losing his very delicate self-esteem! *All* characteristics must be present in the person you select: She provides a loving, sensitive environment, she loves and enjoys babies and little ones, and she is stable and reliable.

(5) Make sure that your sitter is clear on your expectations of her and her responsibilities.

What about venturing outside the home for an outing? Do you want her to only take your baby for a walk in her buggy or stroller or, if it's a longer day, may she take her by car to a park or . . . ?

Mom to Mom . . .

If you do allow your sitter to take your baby away from home in her car, be sure that she has access to your infant safety seat for the car.

(6) Try a "dry-run" before "the real thing."

Leaving your little one for the first time with someone you don't know, even if you were quite comfortable with the interview and *like* the person, can be a traumatic experience. You may find yourself quite uncomfortable. If that's the case, take a "dry run." Hire the sitter for a couple of hours to care for your baby while you are at home so that you can get some things done that you've been putting off or get some rest. You can then observe and listen to how things are going. Do understand that it's the first time for both of them to be together, so there will be some required "getting acquainted time" necessary. But, such a dry run should promote your comfort level a bit and give your baby the added benefit of having another face to laugh and giggle with for a couple of hours!

For Day Care-Givers . . . At Her Home or at a Center . . .

(1) Follow all of the steps above for finding and selecting a sitter.

(2) Visit the home or center early in the morning or late in the afternoon.

Are the children who are cared for happy and do they appear content? Are the care-givers still loving and patient, even after a long day? Etc.

(3) Check the following:

(a) The facilities

Are they clean? Are they well child-proofed and safe?

And, if it is a home:

Are televisions absent?

If so, wonderful! When there are no televisions in sight, it's a good sign that such an

Babysitters and Day Care...

electronic device won't be used either as a substitute sitter or a frequent diversion for the sitter when she should be devoting full attention to your baby or the few babies in her care. Some television programs are excellent for toddlers, but not if they are used as a substitute for human contact and interaction.

Is the environment loving and friendly?

Is there comfortable seating for feeding an infant and baby?

Is there a quiet room for napping?

(b) Adult to child ratio

If babies are under one year, the ratio should be no more than 3:1.

(c) Staff

Do they have yearly physicals, including a test for TB? Do they take care to wash their hands after changing a baby's diaper and before preparing bottles and snacks for other babies? Do they change diaper pads after each diaper change?

(d) Safety

Are toxic substances locked away? Is all furniture in good repair—not splintery or rickety or items that can easily topple? Are mobiles strung over only those cribs in which little ones younger than five months sleep?

(e) Activity

What do they do for activity for the little ones? Is any outdoor time given? Are they taken for walks in strollers or buggies? Etc.

Mom to Mom...

(4) Ask about their policies concerning:

   (a) Illness

   (b) Emergencies

   Are there enough staff members to cover in the event a little one must be taken to an emergency room?

   (c) Unscheduled visits by parents during the day

   (d) Parents late for pick-up

(5) Make sure that the two of you or the center and you agree with each other's requirements.

   These include:

   (a) Terms of payment

   (b) Number of days and hours needed

   (c) Specific policies regarding:

   *Sickness

   *Amount of notice required to terminate the agreement

   *Etc.

The process of finding a suitable day care situation for your baby can be a very trying, long and difficult experience. But doing it is absolutely essential if you want to feel at peace with your decision. Doreen Seldon, a working mom from San Diego, California, suggests a similar process in finding suitable day care...

> *Unless you are fortunate enough to have a loving relative to take care of your baby, this is one of the hardest decisions to make. If finding day care for your baby is necessary, I found it best to:*
>
> *(1) Begin searching for the best day care situation several weeks before returning to work. This allows plenty of time for investigation and decision-making.*

Babysitters and Day Care...

(2) When meeting each potential day care-giver:

(a) Look for cleanliness.

(b) Check the security—child-proofed? Back yard safe? Front and back doors always locked? etc.

(c) Observe the assistants, if there are any.

(d) Observe the day care-giver's attitude toward children—is she loving and attentive? How does she discipline? Does she communicate in a positive manner?

(e) Review the person's plan of the day.

(3) Ask for several references and <u>check every single one of them</u>.

(4) When you have made your decision:

(a) Explain your child's sleeping, eating, and playing habits so that the care-giver will know what to expect from your child.

(b) Give complete information on how to contact you or another designated person in the event of an emergency.

(c) Be specific about what you expect from the care-giver.

Remember, the environment in which your child will be placed is very important. If you begin this evaluation process early, you won't find yourself having to make a quick decision that may not be the best one for you and, most importantly, for your child.

- Write for an <u>excellent</u> checklist provided by the Child Care Action Campaign.

Mom to Mom ...

> Simply send a stamped, self-addressed, business-size envelope to:
>
> "Checklist"
> Child Care Action Campaign
> 99 Hudson Street, Room 1233
> New York, NY 10013
>
> Their phone number is (212) 239-0138.

A Great Babysitting Alternative—The Babysitting Cooperative ...

Several moms who contributed to this book were quite supportive of the idea of a babysitting cooperative. For example, Terri Ciosek from Poway, California, writes ...

> *I belong to a babysitting co-op which is a smart arrangement. The thing I like about it is that I trade sits with the mothers of kids that Katie sees often.*

Just what is a babysitting cooperative? It is a group of moms who agree to sit for each other for no fee in exchange for free time to do those things they need or want to do on their own. The size of the group or cooperative varies. Some moms prefer to keep them small—two or three other mothers whom they know and the children know each other well—and others run rather large cooperatives—15 or more mothers are involved.

One way to begin is to find two other moms who have little ones around the age of your own. If you're new to your area or just don't know other moms as yet, consider those who were in your Lamaze class or those who are affiliated with support groups such as La Leche League. Many smaller communities within large metropolitan areas have local community papers that are published once or twice a month. These will often list meetings of moms groups. The church or synagogue your family attends may be another source.

Once you have found two other moms who are interested in trying a cooperative, have each mom and their little ones spend some time at each

Babysitters and Day Care . . .

other's home—altogether or separately. In this way, you and your little one can become familiar with another's home environment, the mom, and her baby or children. Usually, this works out to be the start of a wonderful friendship as well!

There are many bonuses to a cooperative:

(1) It saves a lot of money!

(2) The sitters are experienced parents.

(3) The sitters are usually good friends whom your baby will know.

(4) It sometimes gives Daddy some much appreciated time with his baby or toddler alone if you're sitting for someone else's baby.

Whatever the size of the cooperative, some basic rules need to be established and agreed to. For example:

(1) Devise a method of keeping track of hours spent and owed so no one is left with the bulk of the sitting and few hours of "freedom" for herself.

(2) Agree upon an established set of safety rules.

(3) Keep a list of emergency numbers at each home's phone:

For example, include the numbers for the following:

(a) Where you and/or your husband can be reached

(b) Poison Control Center

(c) Police and Fire Departments

(d) The person you want to take charge in an emergency if you can't be reached (neighbor, perhaps, or a close friend or relative who lives nearby)

(e) Your pediatrician

(f) *And* your own address and telephone number should be included.

Often in an emergency situation, a person forgets his own phone number and address! If a friend or a sitter is calling in an emergency, she would certainly have difficulty re-

Mom to Mom...

calling the specific address and phone number. So, keep them posted at your phone as well.

(4) Have a well stocked first aid kit available at each home.

(5) Provide written directions for giving medications or vitamins, if necessary.

(6) Discuss home routines and child rearing practices so a sense of consistency is maintained.

Some Things Worth Reviewing with Your Sitter or Care-Giver...

It's a good idea to be sure that your sitter or care-giver knows when a baby or a child should be taken immediately to an emergency room or when an ambulance should be called.

Situations requiring a quick trip to the emergency room include:

(1) A cut, longer than half an inch, with significant bleeding, especially if it is on the hands or face.

(2) A puncture wound that does not stop bleeding after 10 minutes of applied direct pressure.

(3) A puncture wound that was caused by something rusty or dirty.

(4) The baby or child has a hard bump to the head, especially if accompanied by loss of consciousness, abnormal speech, abnormal walking, vomiting, or significantly altered behavior.

(5) The baby or child has a fever over 102.5 degrees Fahrenheit that is not reduced by acetaminophen or is accompanied by lethargy or vomiting.

(6) There is the possibility of broken bones.

(7) The child has burns, especially on the hands or face.

An ambulance should be called if a baby or child:

(1) Remains unconscious after a fall.

(2) Has seizures or convulsions.

If the child is epileptic and the sitter has been left with proper instructions, an ambulance is probably not necessary. The

Babysitters and Day Care . . .

sitter should be instructed on what circumstances *do* require an ambulance.

(3) Has severe shortness of breath.

(4) Has broken bones with deformity.

(5) Has chest, abdominal, or pelvic pain after a fall.

(6) If choking or the aspiration of food or small objects is probable.

Some Suggested Do's and Dont's Concerning Sitters . . .

Do's . . .

(1) Discuss and agree with your sitter or care-giver what you both expect her responsibilities to be.

(2) Give her a quick tour of the house, including where fire extinguishers, the first aid kit or materials are located, and where diapers and diaper changing needs can be found.

(3) Make your sitter feel at home . . . let her know what foods and beverages she may have in the refrigerator and, if you expect to be quite late, provide a blanket and a pillow on the couch, should she want to rest.

(4) Ensure that she knows first aid basics and CPR.

(5) Post the necessary numbers by your telephone.

See the list given above under the rules for a babysitting cooperative.

(6) Create a list of your baby's habits, favorite toys and/or blankets, best loved activities, and allowable snacks if solids have begun.

Although this list will frequently change, you may want to insert it in a plastic sheet so it can be used over and over again.

(7) Consider leaving a medical authorization and release form in the event your sitter must obtain emergency treatment for your baby.

Mom to Mom . . .

> See Chapter 7, pages 211-212 on the preparation of a medical release form.
>
> (8) Continue to collect names and interview potential sitters. You may have found a gem, but there may come a time when you desperately need a sitter and your "gem" has other commitments for that evening.

DONT'S . . .

> (1) Don't cancel your sitter at the last minute without an awfully good reason. If you must, offer to pay for a couple of hours or so. Remember, she may have turned down other sitting opportunities or an evening of fun with friends to honor her commitment to you.
>
> (2) Don't neglect to post those crucial numbers next to your telephone.

A Closing Thought on Beginning Day Care . . .

> *Whenever possible, ease into your day care situation. If you eventually will need a full-time situation, try to begin on a part-time basis, easing into a full-time basis. This is not only much easier for the little one, but much easier on you, the mother!*
>
> Lisa Wayne
> Portland, Oregon

---

[1] Lord Rochester as quoted in *A Mother's Journal,* Running Press Book Publishers, Philadelphia, PA, 1985.
[2] Peggy Epstein, "Bonding with Baby," *The Kansas City Star,* March 4, 1990, p.G-1.
[3] *Ibid.*

Babysitters and Day Care . . .

Clips and Notes . . .

Mom to Mom...

Clips and Notes...

SECTION TWO

A TREASURE OF GREAT IDEAS FOR BABY FROM SIX MONTHS THROUGH PRESCHOOL

A Treasure of Ideas for Baby from Six Months through Preschool...

> *We say "I love you" to our children, but it's not enough. Maybe that's why mothers hug and hold and rock and kiss and pat.*
> — Joan McIntosh[1]

ACTIVITIES WITH TODDLERS AND PRESCHOOLERS...

RECOMMENDED READING...

Playful Learning—An Alternate Approach to Preschool by Anne Engelhardt and Cheryl Sullivan

This is a marvelous book, chock full great ideas of things to do with preschool-age children (and a bit younger)! Although we chose to enroll Maryanna in a regular preschool and haven't regretted the decision, I appreciated gaining the perspective offered by these two mothers.

But, the book is not written only for those who want to create an alternative to preschool but also for parents who simply want and need hundreds of fun ideas to use to entertain and play with their children. *Playful Learning* has *marvelous* chapters packed with fun and exciting activities to do with children to build their imagination, to develop their muscles and coordination, to build their self esteem through creativity and productivity, to cook, to love music through singing and dancing, etc., etc., etc.!

Mom to Mom...

I highly recommend this book—I use it *frequently* and am able to consistently pull out some delightful ideas that Maryanna always thoroughly enjoys!

It is available from La Leche League International, P.O. Box 1209, Franklin Park, IL 60131-8209 or call (708) 451-1891.

Things to do . . .

Here are just a few ideas that may spark your imagination . . .

(1) Bird Feeding (at parks, beaches, harbors, zoos, etc.)

(2) Cooking

Even small children who are two or so can get involved in the kitchen. It takes some patience and a willingness on your part to enjoy whatever happens and whatever the results will be. If you're a perfectionist, toss your perfection out of the window for the morning or afternoon!

Little ones can help tear lettuce for the salad, they can use specially made knives for children that are serrated and quite dull to cut bananas and grapes and other soft items. They can help pour things into the mixer bowl and put muffin cups into the muffin tins. They can stir and even scramble eggs. There are lots of simple tasks they can help with if you use some creative thought!

There are even some "easy does it" type products out just made for little hands to help with. One such product is "Micro-Rave" by Betty Crocker. Everything is just mixed right there in the container that is to be used for baking in the microwave oven.

(3) Dance!

Put on some crazy music. . . or, even change that music every few minutes, and let the children dance!

A Treasure of Great Ideas . . .

Or . . . create a finger band with the various instruments that they hear and can pretend to play.

(4) Outdoor Concerts (in the summertime)

(5) Painting (finger-painting, water colors, water-based felt pens . . .)

(6) Picnics—for lunch or for snacks

(7) Playgrounds

Many children will swing endlessly . . . or as long as you're willing to push!

(8) Rides on Ferries, Buses, Trains, Trolleys, and Merry-Go-Rounds

Rides on public transportation, if they're not too long, absolutely delight little ones! There's so much going on outside of the windows—and inside as well!

(9) Special Events in Town

Fairs, parades, story hours at the library, open houses at the fire station and police station . . . the opportunities are endless!

(10) Sports

E.g., splashing in a wading pool or pool, learning to swim, riding a tricycle or bike, playing ball, etc.

(11) Walks

Just think of all the ants you can find, the cracks in the sidewalk you can follow, the different colored flowers and leaves you can collect, and the different colored houses you can see . . . not to mention the different colored cars that will pass by and the puffy clouds that will float by in the sky!

Mom to Mom . . .

PLACES TO GO . . .

(1) Airport

We have an international airport here in San Diego as well as several small aircraft airfields, one of which is close to our home. Both have always been big attractions for our daughter, as they are for most children!

(2) Botanical Gardens

(3) Harbors and Marinas

This is a wonderful place . . . not only for the boats and ships, but because of the sea gulls and pelicans you can often see—and feed, if you come prepared!

(5) Movies, Plays (for kids), and Puppet Shows

(6) Museums

More and more museums are creating delightful hands-on areas for children! And some cities like San Diego have a wonderful Children's Museum devoted entirely to children and children's interests.

(7) Nature Preserves

(8) Pet Shops

(9) Tourist Attractions

Local tourist attractions are usually those places the locals have never been! Give them a try . . . they're popular with the tourists for a good reason!

This can even include local farms, dairy farms, newspaper publishing companies, etc.

A Treasure of Great Ideas . . .

(10) Zoo

If your local zoo offers an annual family pass, it's usually a great investment! Our local San Diego Zoo also has the Wild Animal Park affiliated with it. The pass admits us to both at any time throughout the year. Without the pass, the fees would be prohibitive to just stop in for an hour or so . . . but with the pass, we're able to stop in whenever the mood strikes . . . which is often, and Maryanna *loves* it!

IDEAS TO KEEP IN MIND . . .

- *When going out on an outing specifically for your child, let him take the lead.*

Whenever you and your child are out, simply and purely for *his* enjoyment, let him be your guide. If you're at the zoo together, and he seems enthralled with the ants walking across the sidewalk, let him be enthralled . . . and revel in his pleasure with him! There may be delightful orangutans and exotic birds and roaring lions to see, but you'll be returning to the zoo time and time again. There's plenty of time for those wonderful sights and experiences.

When you begin such an outing—even if it's just a walk around the neighborhood, if you set your mind to letting your child do the guiding, you'll both enjoy the outing tremendously. The enjoyment fades, and perhaps never even flickers, if you begin with specific goals in mind. The outing then becomes really more for you than it is for him. Dallying for a young child is sheer delight; spending seemingly hours watching ants prance down the sidewalk is excitement for a child . . . and it's learning. So . . . enjoy! You'll find that you're discovering childhood for yourself all over again!

- *Go prepared.*

Plan ahead and determine what all of your needs might be while away. If it's simply a walk around the block, there's nothing too

Mom to Mom . . .

much to plan for. But if it's a morning's excursion into town or to the zoo or the park, you'll want to put some favorite snack items and boxed juices in your diaper bag or purse. And time your trip . . . begin heading for home *before* your child becomes too tired and exhausted.

- *Plan a regular outing.*

By planning to do something special every Tuesday or every Wednesday or whatever, it gives you and your child something to look forward to. It's especially fun to do it with another mother with a child who is of similar age.

Janelle Diller in her article "Tuesday Treats Brighten the Week," called these weekly outings "Tuesday Treats." She and a friend had only two rules: "We had to leave the house at least a portion of the time, and the activity had to appeal to preschoolers." She went on to share some other guidelines that she and her friend established:

(1) The day doesn't have to be expensive.

Tuesdays could be as cheap as the gas to get there or as expensive as our budget would allow.

(2) The activity doesn't have to be out of the ordinary—just out of your ordinary.

Just because it doesn't seem very imaginative doesn't mean your kids won't love it.

(3) If you make a bad choice, leave.

(4) Don't expect perfectly behaved children, but do lay some ground rules that must be followed.

A Treasure of Great Ideas...

We made it clear that the children could not shout, run freely, or touch displays in museums, for example. We also made it a point to not expect such behavior two weeks in a row, but we also tried to challenge them to their best behavior at least occasionally. If the children are interested in what we are doing, they aren't disruptive.

(5) Let the children decide what's fun at any given place.

from
"Tuesday Treats Brighten the Week"
by Janelle Diller
Growing Parent, September 1988, pages 1-2

BATHS AND HAIR WASHING...

- *To control the multitude of bath toys that accumulate, find a large wicker basket with a lid and place it near the bathtub.*

    This bright idea came from my mom after a recent visit. Prior to having this wonderful wicker basket, the toys dominated the bathroom counter. I had seen the mesh bags that can hang from the faucet in the tub, but the toys would never get completely dry, and I didn't want mold developing on any of them! So . . . Maryanna and her daddy or I would dry the toys after each bath and try to keep them collected in a colander on the bathroom counter. No luck . . . they easily overflowed after a few weeks or months! The wicker basket is perfect!

- *When washing your little girl's hair while she's sitting in the tub full of water, be sure you wash her hair last.*

    It has been found that shampoo rinsed out into the tub water that a little girl is sitting in can contribute to or cause urinary tract

279

Mom to Mom . . .

>infections and vaginal problems. If her hair is washed last, then her exposure to the rinse water is minimal and she can be easily and quickly rinsed off.

>Melody Leopard, a mom from Cardiff by the Sea, California, suggests . . .

>>*We don't have a sink or tub with one of those extended flexible spray nozzles. What I came up with was using our child's plastic child-sized flow watering can. It holds about three cups of water and is fun for her. I say, "Chin up!" and then pour water over her hair without any water getting into her eyes. She loves it! No more tears!*

BREASTFEEDING THE OLDER BABY AND TODDLER

- *If you choose to follow "child led weaning," you will want to read <u>Mothering Your Nursing Toddler</u> by Norma Jane Burmgamer.*

>When Maryanna was first born, I knew very little about breastfeeding other than it was the best food for an infant. I thought that an infant was naturally weaned by six months or so and the cup would be the next stage. But what I learned in the first six months about the added benefits of continued breastfeeding and of child-led weaning convinced me that I would continue to nurse her until she decided for herself that she didn't want it any longer.

>*Mothering Your Nursing Toddler* not only helped me see the wisdom in that decision, but it also gave me the needed encouragement whenever I had occasional doubts. I knew that many of the world's cultures practice child-led weaning, and all of those millions of mothers couldn't be wrong, but I still needed to receive occasional reassurance when I knew I was part of a culture that encourages early weaning.

A Treasure of Great Ideas . . .

If you are currently nursing your older baby or toddler, and you're feeling that you want to continue, I strongly urge you to do so. It was special for us and the weaning was so gradual and easy and gentle, for Maryanna and for me. Nursing was a gentle way to soothe the bumps and thumps that she experienced in her toddler days—her tears just didn't last very long. And, as she grew older, her nursing simply became a way of falling asleep. When she was three and a half, after several nights of very short nursing sessions, she suddenly said, "I don't want it anymore, Mommy," and that was it. She now just wants to be rocked for a few moments, have a lullaby or two, and then she crawls into bed for "just a short little story, Mommy." She then falls asleep—all on her own. As many moms had told me, it all really does happen in its own good time. She doesn't even come to bed with us in the middle of the night much any more! Her fourth birthday brought about some miraculous changes!

Again, if child-led weaning appeals to you, I highly recommend you read *Mothering Your Nursing Toddler*—it's excellent!

CLOTHING AND DRESSING . . .

SHOES . . .

- *Don't be in a rush to put shoes on your little one.*

Many pediatricians believe that no shoes are best for children until they start walking, and even then, they should be allowed to walk barefoot in the home.

The November 1989 issue of *The Edell Health Letter* explains:

> *A study from the Department of Physical Therapy at the University of Southern California compared the walking patterns of toddlers shod with different types of footwear.*
>
> *Leather shoes actually made walking and balancing more difficult. Sneakers, being*

Mom to Mom . . .

> *more flexible, make balancing slightly easier. No shoes were best. Without shoes babies could balance and walk better than with either types of footwear.*
>
> As quoted in *Pediatrics for Parents*
> December 1989, page 5
> Edited by Dr. Richard J. Sagall

- *Buy your child's first pair of shoes when . . .*

    (1) Your child is taking many steps at one time for a week or longer;

    (2) *And* your child begins walking on hard surfaces such as concrete or linoleum rather than just on soft surfaces like rugs.

- *Buy shoes that eliminate ankle support and stiff soles.*

    Very young children who are just beginning to walk don't have the weight necessary to bend stiff soles. Such shoes, especially those with ankle support, remove much of what a child uses to balance properly. According to Dr. William A. Rossi, a former podiatrist and currently a consultant to the shoe industry:

    > *"When you constrict the movement, you restrict the muscle and tendon development of the foot. The shoe becomes like an old-fashioned corset, weakening muscles so they can't do their natural work."*
    >
    > from
    > "Buying the Correct Shoes for Your Child"
    > by Sandra Engeland
    > *San Diego Parent Magazine's Health Supplement 1989*

- *Don't buy tennis shoes for your new little walker.*

A Treasure of Great Ideas . . .

Tennis shoes aren't the perfect choice for little ones either. Tennis shoes don't come in various widths, only lengths. Plus, they don't breathe, they cause the feet to sweat excessively, and the soles are usually thick and inflexible.

Shoes that breath and have soles that bend easily are the best selection.

CLOTHES SHOPPING SUGGESTIONS . . .

- *Buy clothes a size larger so that there is room to grow.*

- *Look for those clothes that are easy to care for and don't require special handling.*

- *Consider buying the less expensive clothes—they will last as long as your child needs them (usually) and they often get spotted with indelible marks and wouldn't be "neat and pretty" for a hand-me-down.*

- *Allow your child to help shop for his clothes—not only can you start early showing him what to look for in clothing when shopping, but he'll be more eager to get dressed in the morning when he's had a say in what he has hanging in his closet.*

- *Train your school-age children to understand the magic of "classic separates" and how to change outfits by mixing and matching and accessorizing.*

HASSLE-FREE DRESSING . . .

- *Snowsuits are much easier to put on over your little one's shoes if you put a plastic bag over the shoe first.*

- *Expect your preschool-age child to dress slowly.*

    Young children just can't dress quickly . . . negotiating buttons and zippers and determining where the labels are and whether

Mom to Mom . . .

they go in front or back, getting the heels of socks on the heels instead of on the tops of their feet . . . these tasks all take considerable thought and time. They haven't had nearly the number of years' practice that we've had, and they need time to figure each of these things out, one . . . at . . . a . . . time!

- *Select clothing choices that are easy for your child to put on.*

- *At first, give your child just a few choices to choose from when getting ready in the morning.*

It won't be long before your child notices that there is a whole closet full of other things to choose from, not just the items you selected. But at first, she'll limit her selection from those that you pulled out for her.

- *When she does turn to the whole closet for her selection, have her pick out the clothes she wants to wear the night before.*

This has worked wonders in our house! Since there isn't any rush in deciding what to wear, Maryanna generally makes her decision in a matter of minutes. When we started this idea, we also agreed that there wouldn't be any changes the next morning. So far . . . no changes have been requested, and this has been going on for months!

Lori Buschmann of San Diego also suggests . . .

> *When your child insists on picking out her own clothes, avoid power struggles ahead of time by pinning coordinating tops and bottoms together. She will be satisfied that it was her choice and you can be satisfied that her clothes match!*

- *Understand how important some special pieces of clothing may be to your child.*

A Treasure of Great Ideas . . .

Some children, especially those going to school for the first time, will want to wear the same thing or same two things time and time and time again. This might even be a certain pair of shorts that he wants to wear in the dead of winter! It's important for us to realize that children often establish close attachments to some of their clothing as they do to a special "lovie" (teddy bear, blanket, etc.). It can mean a piece of home that is with them, it can mean a bit of security, it can mean a variety of *special* things to your child. Honor these feelings as best you can by working to incorporate his wishes into what would really be best—have him wear warm corduroy pants over his shorts!

- *Make getting dressed a game!*

    Sing, rhyme, play peek-a-boo—try to make getting dressed a time to look forward to in the morning!

A Couple of Great Ideas . . .

- *Make your own skid-proof socks and slippers!*

    Non-skid socks are a wonderful invention, especially for the active toddler who loves to run everywhere! But, those skid-proof socks can be expensive. You can make your own artistic creations by using paint designed for painting on T-shirts. The designs dry raised, and presto! Non-skid, *inexpensive,* beautifully designed socks!

    Another alternative is to stick on self-adhesive bathtub strips and designs to the bottoms of socks and slippery fabric slippers. They work wonders!

- *Store outgrown clothing in sturdy cardboard boxes with covers from print shops.*

    Print shops usually are only too happy to give away the wonderful cardboard boxes that they trash every day. These boxes are sturdy and have secure lids on them as well.

Mom to Mom . . .

>As your little one outgrows his clothes, put them in one of these print boxes and label the box with the approximate sizes and types of clothes that it contains. If you do this as your little one grows out of his clothes, it will never be a formidable task a year from now.
>
>The advantage of storing and labeling the clothes is obvious if you have another child in the future . . . or if you eventually decide to either give the clothes away or sell them to re-sale shops. Whatever you decide to do with them, they will already be sorted and ready for use!

CREATING MEMORIES . . .

>I created this topic just so I could include the recommendation of a *wonderful* book: Let's Make a Memory by Gloria Gaither and Shirley Dobson. It's full of terrific ideas for building family traditions and togetherness. Ideas include those for making memorable holidays and special days (e.g., birthdays, Christmas, Passover, New Year's, ordinary days), making memories through the seasons and in special places (e.g., the woods, a new home, the desert, etc.), and making memories with special people (e.g., grandparents, people in the community, couples, people who are ill, etc.). This is another book that you'll turn to time and again if it's on your bookshelf.

COMMUNICATING WITH YOUR LITTLE ONES . . .

RECOMMENDED READING . . .

>The books I recommend below have given me some excellent guidance, and everyone I have recommended them to have found them as helpful and as informative as I have. As Maryanna gets older and at times more challenging (in every sense of the word!), I find that I'm awfully glad I read them *before* I needed them!
>
>*How to Talk So Kids Will Listen and Listen So Kids Will Talk* by Adele Faber and Elaine Mazlish

A Treasure of Great Ideas . . .

Siblings Without Rivalry by Adele Faber and Elaine Mazlish

Loving Your Child Is Not Enough—Positive Discipline That Works by Nancy Samalin

- *Be as aware as possible what your words actually convey to your child.*

Some parents simply don't recognize what meanings their thoughtless and unkind remarks can actually communicate to their children. For example, consider the following statements we've all heard, either from our own parents or from other parents we've overheard at the grocery store or elsewhere:

> "Are you *blind*?"
> "What's the matter with you anyway?"
> "I wish you'd never been born!"
> "What are you, *deaf* or something? Can't you hear?"
> "Don't be so *stupid*!"
> "If I've told you once, I've told you a *thousand* times . . . !"
> "Can't you do *anything* right?"
> "How could you do something *so stupid*!"
> "You're so *clumsy*!"
> "I've had it with you! You'll never learn to do anything!"
> "You might as well quit now because I'm through trying to teach you how to . . . ."

Need I continue? Questions or statements such as these erode a child's feeling of self-worth and undermine his potential. *Please* listen to what you say . . . and *how* you say it. It could mean a big difference in how your child sees himself, his world, and his relationship with you.

And, if we expect others to communicate respectfully with us as adults, then we should in turn communicate respectfully with

Mom to Mom . . .

others, *including our children*. Children who feel of equal value to other people will speak to others with courtesy and respect.[2] Consider the following two statements. Which statement would *you* rather hear . . . and in what tone of voice?

"David . . . pick up your toys!" (a command)

"David . . . pick up your toys, please." (a request)

Children really do learn to mirror our behavior. Just listen to a little girl playing by herself with her dolls to get a good idea of the mirroring process!

If we listen attentively to our children, they will learn to do the same. If we are respectful of them, their feelings, and their worth, they will learn to be the same toward us and others.

- *Give your child some advance notice prior to changing his activity or removing him from any activity.*

    We all appreciate advance notice—and so do our children. Doing so is both thoughtful and considerate.

    For some examples . . .

    If your child is chasing bubbles and you want to move on to another part of a park or on to another activity . . . "Let's pop seven more bubbles and then we'll go . . . ."

    Or . . . "We have five more minutes before we have to put our things away and get ready for bed."

    Or . . . "Let's watch three more waves and then we'll . . . ."

    Or . . . "Take three more runs down the slide and then we'll . . . ."

Here are two more thoughts worth considering from some special moms . . .

> *Here's an example of how we train our children without realizing it or intending to do so:*

A Treasure of Great Ideas . . .

When I call one of the kids to do something, I want them to come right away, but they'll often respond with, "Just a minute," and take <u>forever</u>!

Sure enough, when I listened to myself, that's where they picked up on that habit. Andy: "Mom!" Me: "Just a minute, Andy."

Peggy Takaaze
Hilo, Hawaii

As a learning specialist at a private school for children ages three through ten, I am seeing children who have been so overpraised by their parents that they have little sense of the worth of doing anything unless the teacher turns cartwheels in praise of the effort. Children seem to internalize their own self-worth better if their efforts are met sometimes with encouragement rather than praise, that is, "You must feel happy after working so well on that painting," instead of, "That's a wonderful painting!"

Pricilla Cowell
Portland, Oregon

DAY CARE AND SITTERS . . .

- *Create a list of the words that your child is beginning to use and their "translations."*

Creating such a list and keeping it updated helps your child's regular caregiver understand just what your little one is trying to communicate. When the caregiver understands her nearly as well as you do, your little one will feel quite successful in communicating and will feel all the more encouraged to continue communicating!

Mom to Mom . . .

- *Be sure that your sitter or caregiver knows when a trip to the emergency room or a call for an ambulance is appropriate.*

  A review of these situations is provided in Chapter 10, pages 266-267.

- *Try to determine if there is a lot verbal interaction with the child or children by the caregiver.*

  Growing Child Research Review, Volume 5, No. 12, reports:

  > *New research indicates that children in day care profit most from a verbally stimulating environment in which adults and children are frequently engaged in conversation with each other.*
  >
  > *Some other findings:*
  >
  > - *Verbal interaction with peers, perhaps because it replaces the more important caregiver talk, appears to have negative effects on social development.*
  >
  > - *Both parents and caregivers in centers with higher amounts of adult-child talk rated the children as more considerate. Caregivers also rated them more sociable, intelligent, and task-oriented.*
  >
  > - *Caregivers in centers with higher levels of child-to-child talk rated the children as more aggressive and anxious.*

- *Review the suggestions on how to find and interview appropriate day care for your little one.*

A Treasure of Great Ideas . . .

This information is located in Chapter 10, pages 256-264.

In addition, if you are interviewing for full day care, include the following suggestions in addition to those provided in Chapter 10:

(1) Drop in for a visit early in the morning when children are being dropped off, or late in the afternoon.

(2) Observe the children—are they generally happy and comfortable? Is the care-giver loving and affectionate with each of the children? Does she seem to be patient and enthusiastic . . . even after a full day?

(3) Can the children crawl and explore safely? Is the home well child-proofed? How about outside? Is there ample room to play? Is there play equipment available and if so, is it in good repair? Are the fences and gates well secured?

(4) Are there plenty of stimulating objects available for the older baby, toddler, or preschooler?

(5) How many children are cared for each day?

This is important—the fewer children the better. But, four or five children to one adult should be the maximum.

(6) If a license is required, is it up-to-date?

- *Write to Public Awareness About Child Care for literature giving important additional guidance in identifying and selecting excellent child care service.*

Public Awareness About Child Care, Dept. P
P.O. Box 545, Station 12
930 S. Monaco
Denver, CO 80224-1665.

Mom to Mom . . .

> Lisa Wayne of Portland, Oregon, suggests . . .
>
> *Our family is big on pictures and our little one loves to look at pictures of family members who live far away as well as pictures of himself when he was a baby! Consequently, we have taken Polaroid pictures of each of the sitters we use so that when we are planning to be away and a sitter will be with him, we are able to show him the picture of the sitter who is coming for the evening, talk about how special she is, and that she is coming to visit him to play and have some fun. It works wonders! I've shared this idea with others and some moms even put these pictures in a plastic cube and call it the child's "special sitter box."*

Dining Out . . .

Dining out with your children can be a great experience, providing that the restaurant chosen is appropriate to the child's age and behavior. We all need to get out and do something different at mealtime occasionally, but do some advance planning so that it is more likely to be a delightful experience rather than one you'd not want to repeat.

Choosing a restaurant . . .

- *Save the candle lit, romantic restaurants for the evenings that you and your husband have alone.*

    Older babies, toddlers, and preschoolers just aren't ready for that kind of atmosphere. Their behavior will be as expected—age appropriate, which will most likely not be appropriate for the candle lit, soft music environment!

A Treasure of Great Ideas . . .

- *Select a restaurant that is known for being a "family restaurant."*

    This doesn't mean having to go to your neighborhood fast food restaurant. Those restaurants are often noisy and distracting—not necessarily the peaceful experience you may have been looking for!

    Many family-run restaurants welcome children of all ages, as do some very well known chains. Most Chinese and Mexican restaurants also welcome children. If you have any doubt whatsoever, simply call ahead and make sure that they welcome little ones. If, when you ask the question, there is a horrified silence, you'll intuitively know the answer!

    Such restaurants also generally have food that will appeal to small children. Soup and salad bar restaurants are another good choice, since there's an abundance of nutritious things that little ones enjoy.

- *Avoid going to any restaurant at peak hours.*

    Not only will you be seated quickly and served quickly, but you'll most likely not feel that you're disturbing other diners in the event of a little squabble or disturbance.

- *If your child is hungry before you leave for the restaurant, give him a little snack to tide him over.*

- *If you have chosen a restaurant that really doesn't serve appropriate food for your little one (10 months or 16 months of age, for example), take along a little picnic you've prepared just for him.*

    When Maryanna was still a toddler and we first started going to what has become our favorite Mexican restaurant near our home, I would always take little two-ounce plastic jars with food that Maryanna enjoyed, e.g., peas, carrots, cheese cubes, cut up pieces of fruit, etc., so she wouldn't have to have the Mexican fare. Now that she's four, she loves Mexican food . . . but as a

Mom to Mom...

toddler, although she was loved by the restaurant staff, the food just wasn't for her quite yet.

- *Be prepared with some nibbles and other little snacks to keep their fingers, mouths, and tummies happy in the event the food takes a while to arrive.*

- *Be prepared to deal with boredom.*

   Older children will enjoy having crayons or colored markers and paper or a coloring book and little ones will enjoy wind-up toys, little toys that are silent (rather than rattles, etc.) and other little diversion-type items.

- *Enjoy the children . . . don't expect this to be an evening or an outing for adult conversation.*

- *When leaving the restaurant, praise your child (when it's appropriate) for his behavior and let him know that you truly enjoy his company!*

An additional tip from Stevie Wooten, a mom from Seattle, Washington . . .

> *When we took Sean to a restaurant the first time and he got bored in his high chair and started to squirm, we got him back on track by giving him small pieces of ice cubes to push around. This kept him distracted so we could eat in peace. It was a technique that worked for several months!*

DIAPER BAG CONTENTS FOR THE TODDLER . . .

- *Keep a supply of elbow straws in a zip-type plastic bag in your diaper bag.*

   Many restaurants have straws but few have the elbow straws which are much easier for a toddler and preschooler to use and thus cause fewer accidents.

A Treasure of Great Ideas...

And, once your toddler no longer needs a diaper bag, continue carrying some elbow straws in your purse. Even a preschooler often has difficulty getting up to the top of a straw when the glass is tall!

- *Keep two or three boxed fruit juices in your bag along with Carton Cagers™ to keep them in.*

Boxed juices were just made for moms, toddlers, and preschoolers! And what made them even more perfect was the invention of Carton Cagers™! The juices don't have to be refrigerated and are ready for use whenever your little one is thirsty, and the Carton Cagers™ prevent the boxes from being squeezed and thus prevent the inevitable squirts that come from those wonderful boxes! They also provide a means of resealing the box so that if the box isn't emptied, it can be stored for later use without spills.

The only place I know of where Carton Cagers™ are available is through the *Right Start Catalog.* See page 394 in Appendix B, "Indispensable Resources for Mommies and Daddies."

DISCIPLINE . . .

This is a difficult topic. We've all witnessed the results of permissiveness and the lack of any training or discipline, and it isn't pleasant for anyone.

For myself, I *strongly* believed that spanking was totally inappropriate. If I were trying to teach my child that hitting and spanking were not appropriate behaviors, I felt that I too should not resort to spanking to get my point across. I felt that I as a parent was supposed to be the model of self-control and that giving a spanking, even if it was comprised of only a swat or two on the bum, was definitely exhibiting out-of-control behavior.

I deeply believed this—so much so that when my husband once or twice gave Maryanna a little swat on the bottom, it *really* made me

Mom to Mom . . .

angry. My method had always been to talk with her, to have her take a time out for a certain length of time, and then "talk about it."

Such a method worked until she was about three. She is nearly always a very cooperative, loving child. But occasionally, she can become very uncooperative, defiant, and disobedient. She soon figured out that there was nothing to hold her in that chair in the corner . . . she didn't "have" to stay there if she didn't want to! So . . . I resorted to putting her in the bathroom until she cooled down and was ready to talk. That worked for just a time or two until she figured out that she didn't have to stay in that bathroom . . . she could walk out any time she wanted! Nothing prevented her from doing so except me holding the door handle! In the meantime, I found that I, who am usually very, very slow to anger and am extremely patient by nature, was getting hotter and hotter under the collar from her defiant, uncooperative, and disobedient behavior! Nothing really was being resolved, and these conflicts were going on interminably! I was really desperate for another means of handling this situation.

About this time, I fortunately bumped into Dr. James Dobson's *Hide or Seek—How to Build Self-Esteem in Your Child.* He thoroughly discusses his philosophy on positive discipline which includes spanking for three situations: defiance, disrespect, and disobedience. He also discusses this measure's abuse, making it clear what he is suggesting. After reading and rereading his book, especially the sections on discipline, and after much debate within myself because this meant a dramatic shift in my thoughts, I decided to adopt his reasoning and give it a try. Dr. Dobson's books, such as *Dare to Discipline,* had been highly recommended to me by several moms who contributed their ideas for this book, and they were all moms I knew to have loving, respectful children with good self-concepts as far as I could tell. So, with the next episode of defiance, the method was tried. The results were quite successful, in more ways than I had anticipated. We had a much more open talk afterwards, which is exactly what Dr. Dobson had predicted, and, equally important, I wasn't feeling the anger that took many minutes to subside after the confrontation.

A Treasure of Great Ideas...

I haven't had to use "the method" very often. But when I do, the event is quickly over, Maryanna and I are soon in good spirits and are able to enjoy one another.

If you are having any difficulty with those three "D's"—defiance, disobedience, and disrespect, I highly recommend you read Dr. Dobson's books, *Dare to Discipline* and *Hide or Seek*.

EQUIPMENT...

FURNITURE...

- *High Chair*

    "What's there to selecting a high chair?" I can hear you ask! Actually, there's plenty, which I learned the hard way! I selected a comfy looking high chair that was all vinyl, that had a back that tilted backwards, and a stand that could be adjusted to any height. It even had a tight vinyl strap that held the table down and at the same time would keep the little one from slipping down and off of the high chair. It even had a sturdy ribbon safety belt! Vinyl—should be easy to clean; the straps made it safe, what could be better?! I won't go into the details of what turned out to be wrong about this design, but I will give you a list of things to look for in the one you purchase so you can avoid all of the mistakes ours contained! (I won't even give ours to a charity re-sale shop! I wouldn't wish all the problems on anyone else!)

    Be sure that the high chair you select:

    (1) Is made of wood and has no "seams" or difficult-to-reach or impossible-to-reach areas to clean.

    There are many attractive fiber-filled tie-on covers for the wooden high chairs that make them much more comfortable for little ones than the hard wood seat. These covers obviously need cleaning frequently, but they are much easier and it is certainly more sanitary to throw it into the washer than to try and get into the seams of a vinyl seat where food and grime collect and collect and collect!

(2) Has a table with just a raised area around the edge rather than a vinyl ribbing.

The vinyl ribbing can come off and is nearly impossible to replace, and it also catches food underneath its ridge.

(3) Has a safety belt that is both easy to adjust and is easily cleaned.

Some belt adjustments practically require an instruction manual to make any adjustments and if the belt is made of fabric, it will become grimier and grimier, regardless of what you use to clean it and how often you clean it! Even if the belt is detachable, it still will require a lengthy cleaning and drying process.

(4) Has a table that is easily attached and removed.

Some high chairs have a table that swings over from the back, over the child's head, and rests in front of him. This is great... until the child is still needing a high chair but is too tall for the table to easily swing over his head!

(5) Can be folded and stored.

These are hard to find and the convenience is not a necessity, but it is one of the "nice to have" options. As Terri Ciosek, a mom from Poway, California, says...

I wish we had a wooden high chair that folds. Our high chair sits unused in the kitchen—in the way. If we could fold it, it would be easier to store until we decide if we'll ever need it again.

A Treasure of Great Ideas . . .

- *Old Plastic Shower Curtain or Flat Plastic Sheet*

    These are wonderful to place under the high chair to keep the inevitable mess from soiling your carpet or creeping into the cracks of your kitchen tile!

- *Small Table and Chairs*

    Children *love* to be where their mommies are, and mommies often spend a lot of time in the kitchen preparing meals or other goodies. What children love second-most next to mommy is water painting, coloring, cutting, drawing and/or pasting while you are busy at your tasks.

    For ourselves, we found that a little table and chairs and plastic stackable baskets (or a nearby drawer) for art supplies, play dough, etc. have been the perfect additions to our kitchen. Not only do they provide Maryanna with a perfect area all of her own, but, when I'm in the kitchen preparing a meal and she's not wanting to get involved as she sometimes does, it gives her a space to do her own thing and have me within sight to just talk with or to show her masterpieces to! These few pieces of children's furniture truly are a mommy's sanity saver in the kitchen!

OTHER ITEMS . . .

- *Carton Cagers*™

    As mentioned above for diaper bag contents, Carton Cagers™ are used with boxed juices and prevent the boxes from being squeezed, thus preventing the inevitable squirts that come from those wonderful boxes! They also provide a means of resealing the juice so that if the box isn't emptied, it can be stored for later use without spills.

    The only place I know of that Carton Cagers™ are available is through the *Right Start Catalog*. See page 394 in Appendix B, "Indispensable Resources for Mommies and Daddies."

Mom to Mom . . .

- *Sleeping Bag and Bed Tent*

    One thing that we found to be a wonderful purchase for Ben as a young child was a sleeping bag. Marimekko had some especially pretty ones which could also be unzipped and used as warm bedspreads. When we went to friends' homes to play bridge in the evenings, we simply took his pillow and sleeping bag along and he went peacefully to sleep. He also used to enjoy being where we were when we had company over and would sometimes put his sleeping bag down on the carpet and go to sleep there. He has had his about five years now and still likes it on his bed.

    Another great purchase that Ben really enjoyed was a tent attached to a fitted sheet that made his bed into a tent!

    Joyce Mattson
Great Falls, Virginia

Fears . . .

- *When dealing with the fears of a child of three or four, keep these do's and dont's in mind:*

    Do:

    (1) Respect his fears.

    (2) Assist the child to gradually become accustomed to the fearful situation. This means getting acquainted with what is feared while still "protected" by you.

    (3) Examine the fear or fears; then try to avoid exposure to them for a while.

A Treasure of Great Ideas . . .

>(4) Realize that the child will outgrow them. Meanwhile, allow a reasonable period of withdrawal from the situation before you re-expose him.
>
>**Don't:**
>
>(1) Don't criticize or make fun of him.
>
>(2) Don't shame, force or pressure him to confront the thing which is feared until you know he is ready.
>
>(3) Don't feel it is bad or unnatural for children to have some fears.
>
> Growing Child
September, 1988
Page 1

FEEDING TODDLERS AND PRESCHOOLERS . . .

- *When preparing a plate for your little one, keep in mind a good measure for portions that many doctors recommend: One tablespoon of each food served for each year of your child's life is a proper amount.*

    Example: If your child is three, then three tablespoons of each food being served would be an appropriate amount.

- *CAUTION . . . Be sure that the foods you prepare for meals and snacks are not those that could promote choking.*

    Children can't grind their food in their mouths until their back molars come in, which is around four years of age. Consequently, you should keep that in mind when preparing food for their meals and giving them various snack foods.

    Until their back molars come in, it's best to avoid giving your child anything that is small, hard, round, or has a slippery

301

Mom to Mom . . .

surface. Examples of these are: hot dogs, hard candy, nuts, unpeeled grapes, meat sticks, celery and carrot sticks, and chewable tablets. These can slip down a child's throat and get caught in her windpipe before being properly chewed. These food culprits mentioned have caused over 40% of choking deaths in children. Bites of hot dog have been the biggest offender; they have caused more choking deaths in infants and young children (17% of that 40%) than any other food.[3]

Peanuts and popcorn are two other real hazards—peanuts because of their size and popcorn because, although it can be chewed fairly easily, small pieces of it can be easily aspirated.

- *Teach little ones table manners which can prevent their choking.*

    Asking your child to take small bites rather than large ones, to sit while she eats, and to not talk or laugh with her mouth full are manners that can be real life savers. Most children like to lie on the floor, and some even do this while snacking. So keep a watchful eye and be sure that they understand the reasons for your "rules" and concern.

- *Chocolate milk does have merit.*

    For those of you like me who feel that chocolate milk should be avoided because of the added sweetener of chocolate with its caffeine, may feel better about it when you consider this:

    > *According to <u>Environmental Nutrition</u>, an eight-ounce glass of chocolate milk contains only five milligrams of caffeine. The average 12-ounce soft drink has 32 to 65 milligrams of caffeine. The added calories in the glass of chocolate milk are less than half of those in the 12-ounce serving of cola. And chocolate milk is a good source of calcium, something lacking in soft drinks.*
    >
    > Dr. Richard J. Sagall
    > *Pediatrics for Parents*
    > January 1990, page 4

A Treasure of Great Ideas . . .

Some additional ideas from other moms . . .

When children get older, instead of a bib, use an apron around their necks. It covers their legs also. I still use one of mine for Greg since he eats breakfast after he's all dressed for school. It saves me a lot of morning hassle.

Sue Brandes
Des Plaines, Illinois

One thing that I feel I've done right (and was told so by a psychologist) was my "Take it or leave it" food policy. I cooked dinner for everyone—no special items for any one person—no "short orders." If they're hungry, I figured they'll eat it. If not, they won't, and they can wait and see what's on the menu for the next meal. I was right. We have no picky eaters, and as a matter of fact, they are quite willing to try new foods when we travel, or when we visit.

Ann Gaines
Nevada City, California

I freeze juice in popsicle form and always save an "emergency popsicle" for a cut lip, a fever in the middle of the night (the frozen juice helps restore liquids while bringing the fever down faster than the Tylenol; it also helps so the child does not receive medication on an empty stomach.)

The popsicle helps soothe a fussy child during the 15 to 20 minutes before dinner can be served. Since I use only all-juice in my popsicles, appetites are not spoiled.

Mom to Mom . . .

A favorite snack, guaranteed to cure the blahs . . . my children have called it "Ants on a Log" and "Ants on Land." "Ants on a Log" is simply a banana cut in half, then sliced longways. Spread peanut butter over the slice, then sprinkle with raisins (or nuts or raw sunflower seeds, depending upon their age). "Ants on Land" is peanut butter on a graham (or other favorite) cracker with raisins lined in rows across the cracker.

Joanne Soukup
Holland, Michigan

Now that Katie is a toddler, I love making my own popsicles for her treats.

Sometimes food is more appealing to Katie if it has "sprinkles" on it or if she can "dip" it. "Sprinkles" might be ground pepper, Parmesan cheese, wheat germ, etc. "Dips" are ketchup, salad dressing, and even mashed potatoes (for turkey or roast beef).

Terri Ciosek
San Diego, California

My older son was a terrible eater at six months of age—he just wouldn't eat well when I fed him. Thanks to some advice from my mom who suggested that I allow him to eat some things on his own, his eating hasn't stopped since! Consequently, at an early age, around six months, I allowed my children to eat certain foods by themselves. I sliced bananas and gave things that would dissolve in their mouths. It encouraged them to eat more.

Now, at ages three and five, I serve them very small portions of food (about a tablespoon). They both feel real good about eating because after eating a small portion of peas, corn, carrots, broccoli, or spinach, they will say, "Mom, I ate all my _____." And, they will sometimes ask for more!

Doreen Seldon
San Diego, California

Cook and puree separately in a processor a variety of vegetables. Then put the various vegetable purees in ice cube trays. Defrost a variety of flavors for a more exciting meal. Works with meats or fruits also. A microwave helps to thaw and reheat.

Sue Brandes
Des Plaines, Illinois

Caution: Be sure to stir microwaved food so the heat is well distributed... some thawed items may be too hot in some places, just right in others, and still cool in others. Thus, your little one could easily get his mouth burned when you thought his food felt just right.

HEALTH...

ADMINISTERING MEDICATIONS...

- *When using insect repellent sprays on children over two (repellent use is not recommended on children under two):*

    (1) Use a spray repellent that contains no more than 20% DET;

Mom to Mom . . .

    (2) "Apply the spray only once every four hours;"

    (3) Wash the repellent off when the child goes indoors.[4]

While on insect repellents, mom Terri Ciosek has this suggestion . . .

> *Did you know that Avon's "Skin So Soft" oil works as an insect repellent? It even comes in a spritzer. Last summer in Michigan the Avon reps were bombarded with requests for it because of all the "skeeters"!*

- *Remember that "teaspoons" are not all alike.*

> *Teaspoons are like snowflakes—they're not all the same. In fact, they can vary in size from 3 ml to 9 ml, which might be fine for putting sugar in a teacup but not for giving medicine to your child.*
>
> *To be sure you're giving the correct dosage, buy a standard (5 cc or 5 ml) teaspoon from your pharmacy. And ask for the kind designed especially for kids—it will help you get the medicine in, not on, them.*

                                Dr. Richard J. Sagall
                                Pediatrics for Parents

- *To help your child swallow medicine that doesn't taste very good . . .*

> *If you have trouble getting your child to swallow unpleasant-tasting medicine, try the old ice-cube trick:*
>
> *Have your child suck on an ice cube for a few minutes before taking the medicine. This*

A Treasure of Great Ideas...

numbs the taste buds and makes it a little easier and less traumatic to get the medicine down.

Dr. Richard J. Sagall
Pediatrics for Parents

- *To give eye drops with ease . . .*

Children don't like having eye drops put in. The combination of having to lie down and feeling the cold eye drops is unpleasant, but there is another way.

With the child sitting up, pull down his lower eyelid and put the drops in the pocket. If you hold the lid down and wait a few seconds, the drops will warm up to body temperature. When you release the lid and the child blinks, the drops will be just where they should be.

If your child is especially squiggly, try having him lean his head back with his eyes closed, and put the drops where the upper and lower lids meet near the nose. When he opens his eyes, the drops will go in easily.

Dr. Richard J. Sagall
Pediatrics for Parents

- *If your child is fussy about taking liquid medications . . .*

Many antibiotics come in two strengths—125 milligrams per 5 milliliters, about a teaspoon, and 250 milligrams per 5 milliliters. The next time your physician prescribes an antibiotic, ask him for the more concentrated medicine. Then, if the dose is 125 milligrams, you'll only have to get your child to swallow a

Mom to Mom...

> *half teaspoon of the more concentrated medicine instead of a whole teaspoon of the less concentrated type.*
>
> Dr. Richard J. Sagall
> *Pediatrics for Parents*

CARING FOR A SICK CHILD . . .

- *Call the doctor if:*
    (1) If your child has a temperature of 104 degrees or more.
    (2) If the temperature is over 101 degrees for more than 24 hours.
    (3) If the temperature is over 100.5 degrees for three days or more.
    (4) If the fever is accompanied by rash, constant crying, unusual listlessness, cough, persistent vomiting, rubbing and/or pulling at his ears, or convulsion.[5]

- *Review the story told by D. J. Strauss on pages 192-194 in Chapter 7: Health.*

    D. J. illustrates through her experiences with her son how vitally important it is to question, question, question your child's doctors so that you understand what your child's illness is and what the medications are and specifically when they must be taken.

- *You can send your child back to school when there has been no fever for 24 hours, he feels and looks better, and the symptoms are under control.*

- *When your little one has diarrhea or an upset stomach . . .*

  > *. . . doctors often recommend clear liquids. But what temperature should they be?*
  >
  > *Cool liquids may stimulate the intestines, causing an increase in contractions and*

A Treasure of Great Ideas . . .

a feeling of the need to defecate. Cold liquids have also been associated with an increase in the rate food travels through the intestines as well as with diarrhea.

So, if you're giving your child liquids, remember to avoid cold drinks and give, instead, drinks that are room temperature or slightly warm.

Dr. Richard J. Sagall
Pediatrics for Parents

- *To rehydrate your child who has diarrhea or is vomiting . . .*

   Feed your child small, frequent feedings of fluids that contain simple sugars. These feedings can be two to four ounces every one to two hours.

   Older children can be given frequent sips of fluid and chips of ice or popsicles.

   Remember—your goal is to replace the fluids that he is losing.

- *A good diet guide for a child with diarrhea is the following:*

   After 24 to 48 hours, if your child is not losing weight and the diarrhea has lessened somewhat, add semi-solid foods such as rice cereal (without milk) and mashed bananas. Continue the regimen of small, frequent fluid feedings. As the stools continue to improve gradually, add applesauce, saltine crackers, gelatin, and yogurt. As a general rule, as your child's stools become more solid, so can his diet.

Dr. William Sears, M.D.
"Summer Ailments"
Baby Talk, August 1988
Page 36

Mom to Mom . . .

Recommended foods are as easy to remember as "A B C"—applesauce, bananas, and cereal (rice).

- *Some fruit juices may cause diarrhea in some children.*

    Many fruit juices are high in natural sugars. Some children have trouble breaking down carbohydrates, including natural sugars, and will therefore develop diarrhea after drinking juice. The worst juice in this situation is pear juice, although grape and apple juices can cause similar difficulties.

    If you're unable to determine a cause for your little one's diarrhea, try eliminating fruit juices for a while to see if that helps.

- *Do not give tea to a child who is sick.*

    Tea is a common folk remedy for illness, but especially shouldn't be given to children. Caffeine, which is in tea, stimulates the body's digestive juices and may in turn cause or aggravate diarrhea. It can also cause wakefulness in a child (and adults), just when the child especially needs sleep and rest. Consequently, tea is really counterproductive.

- *Some important information on strep throat . . .*

    The following information has been quoted from *Growing Parent,* June, 1988:

    > *"Strep throats are virtually unheard of in the first year of life," according to the <u>Harvard Medical School Health Letter</u>.*
    >
    > *Parents intent on stopping the spread of strep infections should also know that:*
    >
    > > ** Strep is not likely to be present in the youngster who has common cold symptoms along with a sore throat.*

A Treasure of Great Ideas...

> * The small child with a strep infection frequently has a stomach ache in addition to the sore throat.
>
> Throat cultures pinpoint strep but the traditional technique necessitates a wait of 24 to 48 hours.
>
> Ask the doctor about a new quick way to confirm a strep throat. Results of the office test are available in an hour or less.
>
> Growing Child Research Review
Vol. 7, No. 2

- To care for a little one with chicken pox...

    (1) Be sure to clip your child's fingernails to prevent scratching and avoid scarring.

    (2) Apply calamine lotion or (believe it or not) milk of magnesia on the spots to relieve the itching.

    (3) Give cool baths with added baking soda to relieve the itching.

    (4) Give acetaminophen to help relieve the discomfort and fever from the disease.

HOSPITALIZATION . . .

Recommended Reading . . .

A Hospital Story: An Open Family Book for Parents and Children Together by Sarah B. Stein, Walker & Co., 1974

Elizabeth Gets Well by Alfons Weber, Thomas W. Crowell Co., 1977

Eric Needs Stitches by Barbara Pavis Marino, Addison Wesley, Reading, Massachusetts, 1979

I Have Feelings by Terry Berger, Human Sciences Press, Inc., 1977

Mom to Mom . . .

The Hospital Experience by Janovic Nerenberg, Berkley Publishing Co., 1985

- *Prepare your child in advance for possible hospitalization.*

  Of course we all hope that our children will never have to be hospitalized, but since we can't guarantee that they won't, it's a good idea to acquaint your child with the hospital environment in a positive way before she ever needs to stay in one. Consider attending hospital fairs where tours are often given of a hospital facility, and local children's hospitals often have "show and tell" days. If you have a children's hospital in your community, call and ask about such a program and plan to attend one if they do have one.

- *To prepare for your child's stay at the hospital . . .*

  (1) If you can choose a hospital, try to use one that has an experienced pediatric staff and that either permits rooming-in or 24-hour visiting for the child's parents.

  (2) Take some of your child's special belongings along for the stay, such as his favorite stuffed toys, a favorite blanket, his bed-time "partner" (favorite teddy or . . .), etc.

  (3) If your child is still quite young—a toddler or preschooler—remember, he won't understand what's happening to him and will not be able to understand why you are leaving him in such a strange place. It will be perfectly normal for him to protest your leaving and to be angry when you come to visit.

  (4) Your child will need all the cheer he can get, so stay positive, and be as loving *and cheerful* as you can be. If you're terribly worried—and show it—your little one will pick up on it and reflect it!

  (5) If you have to leave him, do reassure him that you're coming back.

(6) This can be a very frightening experience, regardless of all the love and attention and presence you give him. Recuperation from his illness and hospital stay won't be just physical recuperation but emotional as well, so be prepared to give all the extra love and attention your child will need.

Your big job while your child is in the hospital is that of moral support. Sara Flowers in her article, "Helping Your Child in the Hospital" made the following suggestions:

> *Play games with your child, read together, and just talk....*
>
> *Make sure your child knows what's going on with his or her body....*
>
> *You may need to explain the illness, the treatment, and the prognosis—and you may need to do it several times. We found that a children's illustrated book about the body was very helpful, not only to the hospitalized child, but to his brothers at home as well....*
>
> *Explain as much as possible, even to very young children. They are not able to express well their fears and imaginings, and factual explanations help to bring those out into the open and allay them....*
>
> *We did "get well" exercises. We concentrated on the part of the body that was sick and told it to get well. It may sound silly, but it helps to give the child a feeling of control and it helps to develop a positive attitude, which can actually speed recovery.*
>
> *Touching also helps. Even though your child may be nearly inaccessible in a high crib*

Mom to Mom . . .

> *or attached to tubes and wires, you need to find some portion of his body to touch...Do it often. Touch is vital; don't let the hospital intimidate you from your natural responses....*
>
> *You may want to take over some aspect of his personal care, such as bathing. There may be some forms of treatment you can learn about and help with. Ask the nurse, the respiratory therapist, the physical therapist, or the occupational therapist if there is some part of the job you can take over....*

from "Helping Your Child in the Hospital"
by Sara Flowers
Growing Parent, August, 1987, pages 2-3

- *If your child is scheduled for surgery, do everything you can to stay with your child while she is being readied for the operation—right up to the administration of the anesthesia.*

The August 1987 issue of *Growing Parent* reported that doctors at the Yale New Haven Hospital in Connecticut found that "youngsters are calmer before surgery and recover more smoothly when they are not separated from their folks." At that hospital, parents are permitted to be with their child as he "goes under" and are present in the recovery room when he "comes to."

SOME IMPORTANT MISCELLANEOUS ITEMS ON HEALTH . . .

- *Remember the threat of secondhand smoke to your child's health.*

Infants and young children who are consistently exposed to secondhand smoke experience upper and lower respiratory infections more often than those who are not. Many studies have shown that children of parents who smoke develop bronchitis, pneumonia, tracheitis, and other respiratory illnesses more

A Treasure of Great Ideas . . .

often than those children whose parents are nonsmokers. They also experience more ear infections. And, both their ear infections and respiratory infections require hospitalization more often than those infections in children who are not often exposed to secondhand smoke.

- *Insist that your young ones wear sunglasses and a hat whenever there is enough sun to cause sunburn.*

Growing Child Research Review (7:6) explains:

> *Still another study reminds that protection against the harmful ultraviolet rays of the sun should begin in childhood, but this one attaches the familiar warning to a new danger.*
>
> *Research at John Hopkins links cumulative, prolonged exposure to ultraviolet B to later development of cortical cataracts, the type that accounts for one-third of the cataract operations performed on elderly Americans every year.*
>
> *. . . . The expert's advice: Insist that children wear a hat with a brim and sunglasses whenever there is enough sun to cause sunburn. The hat reduces the eyes' exposure to ultraviolet B radiation by 50 percent, "and even cheap plastic sunglasses absorb 85 to 90 percent of ultraviolet B radiation."*
>
> As quoted in *Growing Parent*
> November 1989, page 7

- *Insist that your little ones learn the clean hands habit.*

> *. . . On each inch of unwashed skin, 40,000 microscopic bacterial organisms swarm and multiply. Beyond spreading colds,*

Mom to Mom...

these organisms can cause food poisoning, diarrhea and Type A hepatitis. But a brisk washing with warm water and soap will remove 95% of those unseen beasties.

Hands should be washed after:

*Using the toilet

*Handling money

*Blowing your nose

*Touching your hair or any private part of the body

*Handling an animal

*Helping care for someone who is ill

*Coming home from any public place

A little made-up song sung along with the routine will help set a good habit.

"This is the way we wash our hands, wash our hands, wash our hands, This is the way we wash our hands after we go potty"

Use the same song for other handwashing occasions, changing the last phrase:

"... before we eat our dinner."

"... after we play with doggie."

"... when we come home from school."

Encourage vigorous lathering with soap (friction is the prime cleansing factor), rinsing with plenty of warm water, drying on a clean towel.

from "Clean Hands Feel Good"
by Connie Soth and Marietta Sorenson, RN
Growing Parent, March 1988, pages 1-2

A Treasure of Great Ideas . . .

- *Consider making and using your own brand of insect repellent.*

  I think you'll like this recipe—it's not too oily and the ingredients needed can be bought at a health food store.

  > *Purchase one fluid ounce of unscented body lotion, one ounce pennyroyal oil, and one ounce oil of citronella. Mix the two herbs into the lotion and keep it in the refrigerator so that it will be soothing in hot weather. Take it with you, of course, on trips to the buzzing world outside.*

  from "Your Baby's Skin in Summer"
  by Mary Hilton
  Baby Talk, June 1988

- *Christmas tree needles can cause serious injury to little ones' eyes.*

  Christmas trees are beautiful and delightful to have in the house during the holidays, but for little ones—crawling infants and unsteady toddlers—an eye's bump into the trees needles can cause serious problems. These include scratches on the cornea and other difficulties such as blurred vision, pain, redness, sensitivity to bright light, all of which can last as long as up to a year. And if that weren't enough, the needle's scratch on the eye can also introduce difficult bacterial or fungal infections.[6]

- *If your child enjoys swimming, you can take some precautions to help prevent swimmer's ear (an infection of the outer ear canal).*

  > *. . . It's important to keep water from getting trapped in the ear canal. Sometimes bacteria or fungus enter the ear with the water and remains there. Infection can then follow.*
  >
  > *Rubbing alcohol to the rescue: Putting a few drops into the child's ear after a swim*

Mom to Mom . . .

> *helps the water evaporate and dries the ear. To take this remedy to the beach, put a few cotton balls in a small medicine bottle and pour some alcohol over them. When an ear gets wet, simply take out a cotton ball and squeeze a couple of drops into the ear. If your child finds the rubbing alcohol too harsh, mix equal amounts of white vinegar with the alcohol, and use the mixture the same way; the vinegar will be soothing. If an infection does develop, a visit to the doctor is in order.*
>
> Dr. Richard J. Sagall
> *Pediatrics for Parents*

We have found that using the inexpensive wax ear plugs are also quite helpful in keeping our little one's ears dry. The wax is somewhat sticky and is easily molded and consequently stays put in the outer ear, keeping water from entering the ear's canal.

- *Send for a copy of the child-health bibliography prepared by the Pediatric Clinic at the Henry Ford Medical Center in Sterling Heights, Michigan.*

This two-page bibliography recommends some excellent health care reading for parents. To receive a copy, send a self-addressed, stamped envelope to:

Head Nurse
Pediatric Clinic at the Henry Ford Medical Center
145000 Hall Road
Sterling Heights, MI 48078

- *Prepare a medical release form to have on hand for any caregiver to use in an emergency should emergency personnel not be able to reach you for consent to treat your child.*

You may have done this when your little one was an infant, as it was highly recommended in Chapter 7. But if not, it's important enough to repeat it here.

A Treasure of Great Ideas...

Doctors are able to administer treatment without consent of a parent or guardian *only* if the situation is life-threatening or delay in treatment would result in the loss of a limb. Consequently, it is a good idea to have a medical release form prepared and ready for use in the unlikely event that such a situation would occur.

Such a form should be dated and include your baby's name. You should then state that as the parent you are authorizing any licensed physician, dentist, or hospital to give emergency medical treatment upon request of the person presenting the release form. You should then sign it, as should your husband, and have a witness sign it as well.

An excellent "consent-to-treat" form that you can reproduce that has space to include your child's detailed medical history, can be obtained free by sending a postcard request to:

Communications Department
McNeil Consumer Products Company
Camp Hill Road
Fort Washington, PA 19034

The American College of Emergency Physicians was involved in developing this form. It's a good one, and I recommend that you get a copy, complete it, and keep it with the information you regularly provide your baby's caregiver.

- *When visiting the doctor, include your child in the discussion of his health and the prescribed treatment when appropriate.*

Many children understand what is said about their condition, whether they are visiting a doctor for a well-child check-up or for an illness. It is their health that is being discussed, and including them in the discussion of care and treatment involves them in their health and promotes their awareness of what they can do for themselves to keep themselves healthy or help get themselves well.

Mom to Mom . . .

HOLIDAYS . . .

- *Costumes for holiday parties and for stage productions (even paper costumes) can be made flame retardant by treating them with commercial flame retardant sprays or with a home preparation. (See Chapter 8, page 227.)*

A great idea for handling that mound of Halloween candy received every October 31st . . .

> *On Holloween, a mother of one of my daughter's preschool friends lets her four-year old go trick-or-treating. But, instead of letting her eat all of the candy she has collected, the mom tells her that she can pick a piece of candy for each year of age she is. These she is allowed to keep and eat. The rest, she was told, should be put under her pillow that night, for the tooth fairy to take so the tooth fairy can help protect her teeth! When she wakes up the next morning, the tooth fairy has left a super duper present (special toy) in exchange for the candy!*
>
> Sue Wexler
> La Jolla, California

Learning the true meaning of giving and receiving . . .

> *This is the most popular tip among all of our family and friends. Since I am married to a wonderful man who for 22 years has found letter writing, gift shopping, or any other similar project so terrible that he never does it, I decided to train my boys differently. We had several Christmases which I was appalled at the greed of opening and discarding of gifts that I decided to change that. They displayed*

A Treasure of Great Ideas...

no interest in anything except opening their next gift.

Three years ago I began making the boys either make or personally buy gifts for everyone who gave them one. The money which they earn doing various chores comes from their piggy banks. We make a list, we plan all year long and pick up special items as we see them—just as I have always shopped. They have to make the selections, they must provide the money or the energy to make the items, and they have to wrap the presents themselves.

This has created a "miracle" at Christmas. While their excitement over receiving gifts is still there in abundance, it is equalled and in some cases surpassed by their excitement over <u>giving</u>. They no longer shred the wrap off their gifts, but we all take turns and open things one at a time. And now, since they also get thank you's for their gifts, they are much happier about writing thank you's of their own. I get more compliments on my boys at gift-giving occasions than at any other time.

Stevie Wooten
Seattle, Washington

Having little ones make their own cards for all occasions is not only great fun for them but it helps promote thoughtfulness!

Terri Ciosek
Poway, California

Here's some needed encouragement to use form letters to help with the mound of cards and correspondence required at Christmas . . .

Mom to Mom . . .

> *I sure recommend that if other moms are like me, a "form" Christmas letter becomes a necessity if there is to be any letter at all!!! So which is it, friends? Nothing, or this little "generic" ditty?? I personally prefer generic news to no news, but I didn't realize that until after our children came along!*
>
> Karen Johnson
Satellite Beach, Florida

That's ditto from me as well! I always felt that cards with a long personal message from me were the absolute requirement for Christmas cards each year . . . until Maryanna arrived! Each year thereafter, the cards went out later and later—even by Easter one year! It was then that the form letters took over with just a quick personal note on the bottom of each one! Friends are *friends,* and they understand!

PARENTING SUGGESTIONS . . .

Over the years, I've collected a wealth of excellent pointers and guidance that I've picked up from an abundance of sources. My files are bursting, but the selections below seem to package all the information fairly concisely. I think they will give you some outstanding food for thought:

(1) Earl A. Grollman and Gerri L. Sweder wrote *The Working Parent Dilemma* (1986) in which they discussed what kids want their parents to know. Consider these eight crucial tips *that come from kids themselves:*

      (a) *Discuss your work.*

      (b) *Don't overwork.*

      (c) *Don't come home grumpy.*

      (d) *Don't go out too often.*

A Treasure of Great Ideas ...

(e) Listen to your child.

(f) Start the day right.

*(g) Make your home safe.*⁷

(2) *When children are praised for their efforts, rather than their accomplishments, they learn that the process of learning is important and that mistakes are all right....*

Children most often live up (or down) to the expectations their parents have for them. Once you set an expectation you will consciously and unconsciously convey that to your child.

"How to Raise a Positive Child"
by Laurajean Downs
Growing Parent, July 1987
page 5

(3) Ray Maloney wrote *Vibrant Life* (1985) in which he gave some advice that *Reader's Digest* said was "advice no parent can afford to be without." His main points were:

(1) Love them.

(2) Build their self-esteem.

(3) Challenge them.

(4) Listen to them.

(5) (Give and) *Expect respect.* (Addition my own)

"*Morals are caught, not taught.*"

(6) Limit them.

(7) Make God a part of their lives.

(8) Develop a love of learning.

(9) Help them be community-minded.

Mom to Mom . . .

        (10) Let them go.[8]

(4) In the article, "You're the Greatest!" by Julius Segal, he suggests "seven ways for parents to help children build up that 'world beater' attitude that is so critical to both their emotional and intellectual development."

    (1) Accentuate—and reinforce—the positive.
    (2) Help your child set realistic goals.
    (3) Offer rewards for brave attempts even if they end in failure.
    (4) Avoid stigmatizing your child with labels.
    (5) Accept—and appreciate—the uniqueness of your child.
    (6) Offer this simple message: "You're the greatest!"
    (7) Don't treat your child like a fragile doll.[9]

(5) James T. Webb, author of *Guiding the Gifted Child*, gives the following suggestions on how to be more positive in dealing with your kids:

    (1) Focus on the child, not the achievement. For instance, "I really feel proud of you for that good report card," rather than, "That's a good report card."

    (2) Watch your words. Don't say, "Son, that was a pretty good game, but I bet if you tried harder, you could do better."

A Treasure of Great Ideas . . .

> *(3) Encourage effort. Make it clear you expect progress though, not perfection.*
>
> *(4) Expect your children to act intelligently and responsibly. Your attitude is more important than words.*
>
> *(5) Share activities so you children can see your enthusiasm and learn your values.*[10]

Two moms who contributed to this book offer their advice . . .

> *If I were to give any advice to new moms it would be, "Don't think you are alone when you are at the end of your rope!" I never wanted to admit that there were times that I simply wanted to disappear from the stress of parenthood, but the first time I verbalized to someone other than my spouse, I discovered that I was definitely not alone, and consequently a great deal of the guilt I was carrying around disappeared. It is best not to talk this out with a spouse, because inevitably your worst day is his/her best day and consequently that brings out criticism rather than understanding. Instead, find some other equally exhausted parent who is questioning their own sanity at having kids, and talk out your frustration. Doing so helps me to get back in and try again.*
>
> Stevie Wooten
Seattle, Washington

> *Children <u>love</u> to be with their mothers; they're not content to play where you aren't. Enjoy the adoration while it lasts! Don't push*

Mom to Mom...

> *them away . . .the separation comes all too early these days!*
>
> Sandy Price
San Diego, California

PETS . . .

RECOMMENDED READING . . .

> *Raising Better Children—How A Pet Can Help* by the Pets Are Wonderful Council
>
> This 16-page booklet produced in consultation with Dr. Lee Salk is excellent! It covers a multitude of topics such as pet selection, how pets can strengthen your child's self-image, when to bring a pet into the family, tips for training a puppy or kitten, how pets help children learn to interact with their peers, and much, much more. It's amazing just how much information the Council was able to pack into 16 pages!
>
> To order, write to Pets Are Wonderful Council, 500 North Michigan Avenue, Suite 200, Chicago, IL 60611

- *Consider the selection of a pet very carefully—think of all the possibilities with each type.*

> For example, we were told by many that a bunny would be the "perfect" first pet for our three-year-old. We were delighted! What fun a little bunny would be hopping about the house! But alas, it was quite a mistake! First, although our daughter was very gentle with the neighborhood cats and dogs, we just didn't realize that a bunny wouldn't be as receptive to petting and attention. Consequently, whenever she tries to gently pet it, it tries to run away, causing her to grab it, squeezing much too hard to keep it with her.
>
> Secondly, it's not the playful companion we had hoped it would be. A kitten/cat and especially a puppy/dog normally love

attention and play. Not so with a bunny. It much prefers to wander about, sniffing and *chewing* and doing its own thing.

And thirdly, as I intimated above, bunnies chew! They can be litter-box trained or trained to do their thing back in their cage, but they absolutely cannot be trained not to chew the carpets and the many wires (for lamps, television, stereo, etc.!). Our living room, consequently, has become rather unique in its decorating scheme—we have unusual barriers placed in several places to keep our bunny from going behind the couch, behind the television set, and behind other areas where wires might be or where we can't see her chomping on the carpet!

Cats may claw furniture and drapes, but they can be taught and trained not to behave so destructively. But . . . bunnies cannot. Bunnies are delightful little animals and may be an appropriate pet for an older child. But a bunny definitely will not be the companion that a dog or a cat might be.

- *Consider how much time, space, and money you as a parent have to spend on an animal.*

    Remember . . . veterinary bills can run into hundreds, even thousands of dollars, during a pet's lifetime.

- *Be sure to determine that no one in the family is allergic to the pet <u>before</u> it is brought home and your child falls in love with it and becomes very attached.*

- *Help your child cope with the loss of a pet when it dies.*

    A parent can do a great deal to help a child deal with his grief over the loss of his pet. If he learns to handle it well, this will help him handle future deaths of other animals and loved ones more successfully. Susan Isaacs and Cecilia Soares offered excellent guidance in their article, "Animal Magnetism," on how to help your child cope with the loss of a pet:[11]

Mom to Mom...

> *(1) Be truthful with your child.*
>
> *(2) Help your child express her feelings.*
>
> Children go through the same stages of grief that adults do—denial and then feelings of anger or guilt. Help your child talk about his feelings and, as the authors suggest, "see those feelings as stages that will pass in the process of grieving."
>
> *(3) Acknowledge the power of grief.*
>
> Grief is as real for a child over a lost pet as it is for an adult over the loss of a loved one. Show understanding and acceptance of your child's feelings and perhaps even use the opportunity to explain how grief subsides over time and share your thoughts on life and death.
>
> *(4) Don't automatically replace the pet.*
>
> *(5) Reassure your child that she's not at fault.*
>
> *(6) Celebrate her pet's life.*
>
> This can be a little "memorial service" that celebrates how special the pet was to your child.
>
> An excellent children's book that illustrates this beautifully is:
>
> *The Tenth Good Thing About Barney* by Judith Viorst, published by Atheneum in 1972.

Other moms offer these thoughts . . .

> *My suggested best time for a pet would be six to seven years of age. As for the animal . . . a dog or a cat. At six or seven, a child will*

be old enough and physically better able to handle his pet without strangling the poor thing and also big enough not be be continually knocked down by a boisterous puppy. He would also better be able to take care of his own animal.

Sandy Price
San Diego, California

Dogs are great for under high-chair clean-up! And our one-and-a-half-year-old and three-and-a-half-year-old <u>love</u> our new aquarium!

Linda Brosio
Grass Valley, California

Pets . . . we have everything! All pets are fine as long as the pet is the <u>parent</u>'s pet, not the child's. I think a small child is incapable of the many daily rituals involved in handling a pet and parents who say, "This is your doggy so you'll have to feed and bathe it," are letting themselves in for anger when the child forgets. Both Sean and Ryan feed all of our animals on a regular basis, happily, but it is not their "chore." Animals are too insistent on their own attention to have much patience for a forgetful child. My kids walk the dog, help with the baths, help a lot during visits to the vet and give lots of hugs and kisses, but they still do not have the burden of total responsibility.

As for selection, I do think that pets that die easily, e.g., hamsters, some birds, possibly bunnies, can either cause undo distress or

Mom to Mom . . .

> *possibly generate an "easy come, easy go" attitude.*
>
> Stevie Wooten
> Seattle, Washington

PLAYTIME . . .

RECOMMENDED READING . . .

First Fun by Shelia Gregory and Diane Melvin (one of the Mothercare Nursery Guides)

> This little book is packed with wonderful ideas! If you have ever had any doubts about what to do with an infant, baby, and toddler in terms of play, this book will guide the way! The authors include developmental charts which help you look for the exciting progress that he is making in becoming a child. Each chapter, devoted to a certain developmental stage, lists toys to buy and toys to make that are appropriate for that stage. Each chapter also includes highlights on safety for each developmental stage. This book is little . . . but it's mighty, and well worth having on your bookshelf!

The Read Aloud Handbook by Jim Trelease

> I'm amazed at how many parents are unaware of this incredible resource! Jim Trelease gives excellent advice on introducing books to children—how and when, and includes ideas on how to coax children away from television. As the Washington Post said in its review, "This book is about more than reading aloud. It's about time that parents, teachers, and children spend together in a loving, sharing way." He suggests the how's and when's and then provides an extensive annotated list of books that children love.

BOOKS . . .

- *Make books easily seen and accessible.*

A Treasure of Great Ideas . . .

Little ones select their books according to the pictures they can see on the cover . . . and sometimes because of the pictures in the books. To make it easier for your little one to select a book to "read," place his books flat on a shelf or put them in a low box or little tub so that they stand up and can be easily flipped through.

- *Special books for 6 monthers and older . . .*

   As I mentioned above, Jim Trelease gives an excellent annotated list of books to read, but there are several that are favorites of ours that I want you to be sure to know about.

   Hawaii is a Rainbow by Stephanie Feeney and Jeff Reese

   This is a beautiful book produced by the University of Hawaii Press. I am convinced that this book was the most responsible for Maryanna and the little ones we bought it for as gifts knowing their colors at an incredibly young age. Although Maryanna is now four, she still loves to look through this beautiful picture book. She now uses the pictures to tell stories!

   As an added endorsement for this book, Terri Ciosek writes, "We loved this book to tatters!"

   Good Night, Moon by Margaret Wise Brown

   This is a true classic. Your little one will want it read over and over again in a single sitting. And, when you read it, be sure to see if you can spot the mouse in each of the colored pictures! True to his nature, he doesn't sit still!

   Peter, Good Night by Alison Weir

   This was published in 1989 so there hasn't been time for Jim Trelease to include it in his list. It's beautiful, not only in its written imagery but in the artwork as well. It gives such a dreamy send-off to a lovely night!

Mom to Mom . . .

> *Love You Forever* by Robert Munsch
>
> > This is another that will eventually be included in Jim Trelease's list! It's for the preschooler and older, showing how little ones grow and they grow through various stages of life. Although life can be trying for a mother sometimes, she will always love her "little one" forever, even when he is an adult and she is an old woman. It's beautiful! It includes a little song that the mom sings over and over, and although it doesn't show the music, I made up a tune for it, and it now is one of Maryanna's favorite good-night songs!
>
> Pop-up books are wonderful! I remember being captivated by them when I was a child. Many tell delightful stories, and some encourage little ones to look for hidden delights and treasures. There are eight that are exceptional that you may not be aware of simply because they are not available in the bookstores. They are the *National Geographic Action Books,* available only through the National Geographic Society. Their detail and intricacy are a marvel and I highly recommend that you invest in one set or all four. They are sold in sets of two, each set selling for $19.95 plus shipping. It sounds expensive, but *they are well worth it!*
>
> > Set 1: *Hide and Seek* and *Amazing Monkeys*
> >
> > Set 2: *Creatures of the Desert World* and *Strange Animals of the Sea*
> >
> > Set 3: *Dinosaurs* and *Animals Showing Off*
> >
> > Set 4: *Animal Homes* and *Explore a Tropical Forest*
>
> For a catalogue and ordering information, write to: National Geographic Society, Washington, D.C. 20036.

- *Use Baby Talk Magazine, not only for yourself but with your older baby and toddler as well!*

  > Maryanna *loved* this magazine and would look at the pictures of

A Treasure of Great Ideas...

babies by the hour, pointing to each one she saw.

- *Make your own storybook tapes.*

  Tape any child's book and ask relatives and friends to tape books also. Use a bell or any noise to help child turn pages. Both narrator and reader will love it!

  Sue Brandes
  Des Plaines, Illinois

Toy Selection

- *Be aware of the possible hazards of rattles, teethers, and squeeze toys.*

  Rattles, teethers, and squeeze toys must be large enough so that *no part* of them can fit into your baby's mouth. Babies, even as old as 11 months, have choked on such toys, either by partially swallowing rattles or their handles while sucking on them, or falling on them with handles or other parts in their mouths, causing that part of the toy to be jammed into their throats. The largest size rattle, as of 1985, involved in a tragic choking accident, involved a rattle, the ends of which were *1 5/8 inches in diameter!*

- *Follow these general guidelines for appropriate toy selection.*

  When selecting toys for your children, choose their toys according to their age, skills, interest, and needs.

  Other guidelines are:

  Six to nine months: Because your little one is sitting up and can use his hands more capably, good choices would be balls, shape sorters, busy boxes, and nesting toys. You may want to introduce some simple picture books during this time period. Push and pull toys are great, especially those that make delightful

Mom to Mom . . .

Nine to twelve months: sounds, even if your little one won't be walking for a bit yet.

Because of your little one's growing abilities, he will be able to create all sorts of uses for all of the toys he now has. Continue introducing picture books. He'll love them!

Also closely follow the recommended age guidelines *on the packages* of all toys you buy for your child.

For detailed guidelines, write to the Toy Manufacturers of America. They publish two pamphlets: "Learning About Labels," detailing age-grading on toys and "The ABC's of Toys and Play," which includes additional information on toy selection. To get your free copies of these two pamphlets, send a postcard request with your name and address, including zip code, to:

Toy Booklets
P.O. Box 866,
Madison Square Station
New York, NY 10159

- *Test all toys that are brought into your home for your little one to be sure that there are no small removable parts like wheels or eyes or noses, etc.*

Even though the toys from major toy manufacturers are carefully tested, still recheck the toys frequently. Teddy bear eyes, for example, if chewed on long enough by a little one or pulled on long enough, *will* come off. Maryanna's favorite Teddy is now on his third set of eyes, and he was made by one of the best of the stuffed toy manufacturers.

- *When you bring new toys into your home, label it for appropriate age.*

It may be appropriate for your child's current age, but will you remember in a year or two when a younger sibling comes along or a friend's little one comes to visit? Toys are made according to age, and those made for three-year-olds are definitely not appropriate for a one-year-old.

- *Check the safety of all of the toys brought into your home by older siblings and their friends.*

  For example, a seven-year-old's ball is harmless for his little eight-month-old sister, but his friend's bag of jacks could be lethal if left within reach of the baby sister.

Stevie Wooten, a mom from Seattle, Washington, had this to suggest...

> *We discovered our oldest son's favorite toy when he was given a wooden spool my Grandmother handed him as a distraction! He preferred it to all the fancy toys that lined the shelves in his room!*

Note: Be sure that the spool is a sturdy one and cannot easily chip if gnawed on. The chips could get stuck in your baby's throat.

PRESCHOOL...

Once a little one or two are on the scene, the days, weeks, and months fly by like they never have before. And before you are even ready for it, decisions about school will begin to pop into your mind. Should we send her to preschool? Should we wait until she's old enough for kindergarten? If we wait until then, will she be behind the others in intellectual development? And, if we keep her home until kindergarten, won't she suffer or be behind in socialization skills?

Do these questions sound familiar? I'm certain they do because they were questions that haunted us long before our daughter was ready for preschool. Fortunately, there are some excellent books to help you make these difficult decisions. They can't make the decisions for you, certainly, but they can give you plenty of information to help you make an informed decision.

Mom to Mom . . .

RECOMMENDED READING . . .

Your Growing Child by Penelope Leach

I have recommended this book a number of times throughout *Mom to Mom* because of its outstanding guidance.

The section entitled "School" provides an excellent discussion on the pros and cons of early schooling and of parent-led play groups or preschool groups versus public or private preschools.

Playful Learning—An Alternate Approach to Pre School by Anne Engelhardt and Cheryl Sullivan

This is a wonderful book! After all of the reading we did and all of the discussions we had with other parents and with those in education, we went ahead and decided to put Maryanna in preschool at three and a half years of age. But, this book gave me a some excellent guidance and helped me weigh our decision.

Perhaps the best thing about this book is its *marvelous* chapters on hundreds upon hundreds of wonderful activities to do with children—fun and exciting activities to build their imaginations, to develop their muscles and coordination, to build their self esteem through creativity and productivity, to cook, to love music through singing and dancing, etc., etc., etc.!

If you're looking for a way to provide preschool education at home, this is the book to give you the sound guidance you need. If you're looking for interesting activities to do with your child and his friends that are not only delightful but educational, too, this is the book you won't be able to part with!

Eileen Carroll, a mom from La Jolla, California, also suggests:

For making those important decisions about school, read anything by John Holt, e.g., How Children Learn, How Children Fail, and Teach Your Own.

A Treasure of Great Ideas . . .

PRESCHOOL ENTRY . . .

- *Prepare your child for his first experience in preschool as much as possible before the first day of school.*

    Consider doing some or all of the following to make your child's transition into school much happier and smoother:

    (1) During the summer before school starts, ask the school's office for a list of the parents and children who are assigned to your child's class.

    (2) Call the parents on the list and try to create a play group that can meet once or (better yet) twice a week.

    If your child's class will have 12 children and only five families want to participate, that's great! At least your child will have four good friends in his class before the beginning of school! The more children who can participate, the better. But if your child knows even just one other child, the whole experience of being in a new environment will seem just a bit more familiar, making the adjustment a bit easier to handle.

    (3) Take your child to the school several times to walk around and "get a feel for the place."

    You might also make arrangements with the school to allow you to visit a classroom a couple of times while it is in session. If you know before June what teacher your child will have in September, all the better. Make arrangements to visit that particular classroom so your child can get a better idea of where he will be and what he will be doing and with whom.

    (4) Take pictures of your child's school from her point of view and level.

    Include everything that she will experience—the playground and its equipment, the classroom (from every angle you can imagine!) and its various activity centers. If your

Mom to Mom...

school has a library that the children go to for stories and even to borrow books, include it in your picture series too. Whatever your little one will be doing, include pictures of it. You can then talk about the school and what it looks like in detail and what the various parts of the room are for. You can talk about the playground and what she can do on all of the equipment. By the time school is ready to begin, she'll be very familiar with the "new" surroundings and won't feel as though she's in a completely strange and new place. You can then use the pictures to talk about the day when she comes home!

- *On the first day of school, be very clear about what will happen, when, and with whom.*

  Spend some time with your child describing what his time at school will be like and then be *absolutely specific* about what will happen at the end of school.

- *When leaving your child at school, spend some time with him pointing out friends and other things familiar.*

  We have discovered that if we take Maryanna to school just before it begins, she is much more comfortable. Rather than just leaving her with a very short, brief "good bye" which is what the teacher had originally recommended, we have found that by staying a few minutes with her and asking, "Who's here from your class?" she feels much happier and less "abandoned."

  When we first started taking her to school (her school runs up to the 5th grade), we didn't realize that school starting at 8:15 didn't really apply to the preschool department. We didn't want her to be late, so we were dropping her off at 8:00. The preschoolers, however, are actually taken to their classroom from their playground at *8:45!* Consequently, many of her little classmates didn't even arrive until around 8:30! So until we realized what was actually happening, our little one's happiness level was close to zero when we'd leave.

  Now that we are getting her there when all her little friends are arriving, she is much happier and runs off very quickly to play.

A Treasure of Great Ideas...

What a difference a few minutes in arrival time and a few friends present have made!

- *For the first day... the first week or two... be sure to be there to pick him up the minute school is over.*

    We learned this suggestion the hard way! We were told by our daughter's preschool that the children could be picked up anytime between 11:45 and noon. It didn't even occur to us that we should be there right at 11:45. Yet, when we arrived at 11:53, our daughter and one other child were *the only ones left!* As secure as our child has always been, she had just had a very new experience in a very new place with total strangers, and she was actually quite afraid that she was going to be left there and that no one would be there to pick her up. Although we had reassured her when we left her at school that we would be there to pick her up, she began to doubt it as she watched all the other parents come and go. Her reaction then was anger and our relationship with her was on rocky ground for a short while after that!

PRODUCTS WORTH KNOWING ABOUT...

- *Carton Cagers™*

    I've mentioned these wonderful holders for boxed juices a couple of times before, but because this is an alphabetical section, you may have missed their description.

    Carton Cagers™ prevent the boxes of juice from being squeezed and thus prevent the inevitable squirts that come from them! They also provide a means of resealing the box so that if the box isn't emptied, it can be stored for later use without spills.

In addition, Terri Ciosek, a mom from Poway, California, recommends these great finds:

- *Elastic sweat bands*

    These are used around the ankles of footed pj's that are too big. That way the feet don't get out of place and flop around and possibly trip the little one. (Right Start Catalogue)

Mom to Mom...

- *Plastic bibs with velcro closures*
- *Onesies T-shirts or "piluchos" from Penny's*
- *Links from Discovery Toys and other manufactures that keep toys attached to the stroller, backpack, and car seat.*
- *Magnetized frames to insert the little one's art work and hang on the refrigerator.*

  These frames really make the art work look special and the refrigerator looks neater, too! (Lillion Vernon Catalogue)

Sue Wexler, a mom from La Jolla, California, suggests the following periodicals for preschoolers:

> *I love both* Highlights *and* Turtle *magazines.* Turtle *is more for preschoolers, and* Highlights *is good for preschool through about age 8. Dana loves getting her own mail, and it's a treat to sit down with her every month and read through the latest issue. They have games and puzzles, so it's a little more interactive than the usual storytime session.*

To subscribe to either or both of these:

Turtle Magazine
P.O. Box 1003
Des Moines, IA 50340

Highlights for Children
P.O. Box 269
Columbus, OH 43272-0002

Children do love to get their own mail. Other *excellent* magazines that you may want to consider are:

Sesame Street Magazine (for ages two through six) 10 issues for $14.97

Kid City Magazine (for ages six through ten) 10 issues for $13.97

A Treasure of Great Ideas . . .

3-2-1 Contact Magazine (for ages eight through 14) 10 issues for $15.97

Each of the three above can be ordered by writing to:

> Sesame Street Magazines
> P.O. Box 55518
> Boulder, CO 80322-5518

Lady Bug (for ages three through seven) and *Cricket* (for ages eight through 14)

$2.95 for single copy; 12 issues for $29.97; 24 issues for $49.97

To order a sample copy or to subscribe, call (800) BUG-PALS or write to:

> *Lady Bug* or *Cricket*
> Box 52961
> Boulder, CO 80322-2961

SAFETY . . .

IMPORTANT PHONE NUMBERS TO BE POSTED AT YOUR TELEPHONE . . .

For example, include the numbers for the following:

(a) Where you and/or your husband can be reached

(b) Poison Control Center

(c) Police and Fire Departments

(d) The person you want to take charge in an emergency if you can't be reached (neighbor, perhaps, or a close friend or relative who lives near by)

(e) Your pediatrician

(f) *And your own address and telephone number*

Often in an emergency situation, a person forgets his own phone number and address! If a friend or a sitter is calling

Mom to Mom...

an emergency number, she would certainly have difficulty recalling your specific address and phone number. So, keep them posted at your phone, and be sure that she knows that they are there for quick reference.

PREVENTING POISONING ...

- *Always store potentially hazardous liquids in their original containers or CLEARLY label a new container.*

    An example of this is storing vodka in the refrigerator in an unmarked bottle. I know of an older child who was preparing a powdered drink for his little sister and wanted to use ice-cold water to mix it with. Thinking that he was using a bottle of ice-cold water, he mixed the drink with vodka. Alcohol ingestion can be lethal, depending on the amount ingested.

    Some other examples of liquids to be mindful of are:

Mouthwashes	They often contain 20-40% alcohol, are beautiful colors, usually taste good, and don't have safety caps.
Colognes	Children's and adults' colognes can contain as much as 90% alcohol.

- *Be aware of the prime times for accidental poisonings.*

    Poisonings most often occur in the early morning—between 7 a.m. and 9 a.m.—and late afternoons, because these are normally hectic times in the household and care may not always be taken.

    According to Suzanne Colby in her article, "The Enemy within the Home," "5 p.m. is the 'arsenic hour.'" At 5 p.m., children are usually hungry and want something to satisfy their hunger. Consequently, Colby suggests that parents serve their children mid-morning and late afternoon snacks to tide them over these usually hungry times.

A Treasure of Great Ideas...

- *Be aware of "look-alike" products.*

   For small children, these products can be rather confusing. Consider the cleaning product, Pinesol. It has the color of apple juice. Cough and cold medications often look like fruit punch. Medicine tablets are often pretty colors and look like candy.

- *To avoid accidental poisonings, use these guidelines:*[1]

   (1) Don't ever leave your child alone with a poisonous substance, even for "just a second."

   (2) Develop the habit of putting away cleaning materials and substances immediately after use.

   (3) Be sure that all containers of poisonous or hazardous liquids and powders are *clearly labeled.*

   (4) When giving your child a medicine, never tell her that it "tastes just like candy."

   (5) Always read the label carefully before administering any medication.

   Even if you know "exactly which bottle the decongestant is," even in the dark, turn on the light and *be sure.*

   (6) Don't discard old medicines in the trash—flush them down the toilet instead.

   (7) Store all of the following out of reach and out of sight of children:
   (a) Medicines
   (b) Sprays
   (c) Powders
   (d) Cosmetics
   (e) Mouthwashes
   (f) Personal hygiene products
   (g) All household cleaning products
   (h) All garden and garage chemicals

Mom to Mom . . .

(8) Keep all cleaners, household products, and medicines in their original containers.

(9) Don't use familiar containers that suggest safety to a child, like milk gallon containers and juice containers, for poisonous or hazardous liquids.

Occasionally a person may choose to mix a whole batch of garden poison spray and use a milk gallon container to store it in. For a young child, the milk container represents something "OK" and "safe" because he has seen you pour milk from a similar container and drink its contents.

(10) Train your children to always ask permission before they eat or drink anything that you or a sitter haven't given them.

CONCERNING MEDICINES . . .

- *Use a locking device on your medicine cabinet.*

  If it is at all possible to install a key lock of some kind, that is by far the most preferable. However, if that is impossible, try using a lock box of some kind, even an old cosmetic case from a set of suitcases. Store all of your medicines and even disinfectants in it.

  Remember—child-proof caps aren't necessarily child-proof. Even if all of your medications are stored with child-proof caps, it is still important to lock them up. I have occasionally noticed that the caps don't always go back on straight, and the medications are consequently left virtually open. If that isn't noticed, and they aren't locked up, a real tragedy can occur.

- *Be sure that medicines that visitors use aren't left on kitchen or bathroom counters.*

  These can either be locked away in your cabinet or, for your visitor's easy access, in their locked suitcase.

A Treasure of Great Ideas . . .

- *Be sure that your purse and those of your visitors are placed out of reach of your little ones.*

    Purses often contain various medications such as aspirin and other over-the-counter drugs that can represent a real danger for little ones.

CAR SAFETY . . .

- *The best insurance that your child will grow up accepting the confines of a car seat and later a seat belt is by the example you set.*

    If you faithfully put on your seat belt every time you get into your car, you set an important example for your child that could some day save his life. And if you are relentless in putting your child in his car seat every time he is in the car from the very beginning *with no exceptions made*, he will become accepting of its necessity. Begin explaining the importance of safety seats and safety belts, even when he may not understand any or all of what you are saying. You may find that he will become the "seat belt police" in your car, reminding others such as visiting grandparents that they don't have their seat belts on!

- *If your child wants to sleep in the back seat when traveling long distances, use large pillows to prop him up and buckle his seat belt properly.*

    Many parents believe that their children are still safe if they are lying down in the back seat with the safety belt loosely strapped around their bodies. Unfortunately, this practice may *increase* their chances of serious injury. When children are strapped in while they are in a reclining position, the belt reaches diagonally across their waists rather than being snug across their pelvis, the boney area that would protect their internal organs if they were in an accident that thrust them against their seat belt. If they are lying down in such an accident, their bodies would jackknife around the belt, causing possibly serious internal injuries.

Mom to Mom . . .

- *Remember that the driveway of your home is the riskiest place for a toddler.*

    The typical fatality of children under five occurs in the driveway of their own home. Unfortunately, I didn't record the source of the following information when I jotted down the following notes, but I think it's worth sharing with you here:

    (1) In 76% of the driveway deaths, the vehicle was a light truck or van.

    (2) In 71% of the deaths, the driver was a member of the child's family or a visiting friend.

    Those conducting the study determined that there were a combination of factors involved:

    (1) The child was too young to recognize the danger of a backing vehicle.

    (2) The child was too small to be seen by the driver of the van or truck.

FURNITURE AND EQUIPMENT . . .

- *High Chairs . . .*

    Some tips to keep in mind . . .

    (1) Check the high chair to be sure it is stable and not easily toppled over by a wiggly tot.

    (2) Ensure that the safety straps (waist and crotch) are in good repair.

    (3) *Always* use the safety straps . . . the tray by itself will not keep a child from slipping down under it and falling off of the chair.

    (4) Never leave your child unsupervised.

- *Playpens . . .*

    The most serious injuries tend to involve strangulation and suffocation. Consequently, keep these thoughts in mind . . .

A Treasure of Great Ideas...

(1) The weave of the mesh should be less than a quarter of an inch by a quarter of an inch. Anything larger can catch buttons on clothing and cause strangulation.

(2) Never use a mesh playpen with one of the sides down. Doing so creates a pocket and even infants have rolled over into the pocket and have suffocated.

(3) Be sure that mesh pens have to tears or holes which can trap children and cause strangulation.

- *Hook-on Chairs . . .*

    These chairs are so convenient to use because the little one can be right at the table with you, either at the restaurant or at home. However, injuries can occur if the child dislodges the chair. To prevent this, remember to . . .

    (1) Never attach the chair where the child can reach table supports, a wall, or a chair to push off from with his feet.

    (2) *Always* use the restraining straps.

- *Toy Chests . . .*

    Toy chests can be very special. Often times they are made for our little ones by favorite family members or very close family friends. Sometimes they are prized hand-me-downs. As special and delightful as toy chests are, there are some important safety precautions to keep in mind.

    Be sure that:

    (1) If the toy chest has a hinged lid, the support hinge will firmly hold the lid open in any position it is placed.

    If the lid is hinged with an adjustable friction lid support, it is not safe and should be changed or the lid removed.

    Severe accidents have occurred when children, usually under the age of two, tried to pull themselves up on the toy chest when the lid was in the full open position or when they

Mom to Mom . . .

tried to open the lid themselves. As the children were reaching in the chests, the lids fell either on their heads or on their necks, causing severe injuries.

(2) If a child were trapped inside the chest, that there would be some ventilation, either by holes that will not be covered if the chest is against a wall or by a space between the underside of the lid and the sides or front of the chest.

There have been some reports of suffocation when children have crawled in toy chests to hide or sleep.

(3) The chest lid does not have a latch.

If your toy chest doesn't meet these safety suggestions, consider temporarily removing the lid of the chest or installing a spring-loaded lid support that will not require adjustment periodically. Such a support will hold the lid open in any position.

PREVENTING SUFFOCATION AND CHOKING . . .

- *Teach your child as early as possible to never run with food in his mouth.*

- *Watch the size of the food pieces that you give your child to eat.*

    Until your child has a good set of teeth and chews well, be sure that the pieces of food that he is given aren't big enough to block his small airway.

    Examples of food that can easily become chokers are: grapes, nuts, bites of hot dog, popcorn, small hard candies, anything else that is small and either round or cylindrical, making them high-risk foods for choking.

- *Don't give your child foods that she can bite off but not chew well.*

    Examples of these are some raw fruits and vegetables, such as apples and carrots.

- *Be sure that seeds, pits, bones, and shells have been removed from food before you give it to your child.*
- *As soon as your child is old enough to understand the danger of choking, warn him and explain to him about the dangers following:*

    *Stuffing a lot of food into his mouth at one time.

    *Talking and laughing with food in his mouth.

    *Not chewing food well.

    *Eating in a reclining position.

    *Walking or running with food in his mouth.

- *If your child starts to cry at the table, remove whatever food is in front of her until she has stopped crying.*
- *Know the signs of choking.*

    A baby or small child has no knowledge of choking nor of how to tell anyone that she is choking. The following are the signs of choking:[13]

    (1) Violent or ineffective coughing

    (2) High-pitched noises (crowing)

    (3) Bluish tinge of lips, nails and skin

    (4) Inability to breathe, speak or cry

    (5) Unconsciousness

- *Know what to do if you child is choking.*

    (1) At first, if your child is making noises (crying, speaking, crowing), do nothing—see if he can cough up the obstruction himself.

    (2) Never give him water to drink—it's the windpipe, not the esophagus that is blocked.

    (3) If he stops making noises and can't breathe, then begin life-saving maneuvers appropriate for his size, e.g., the Heimlich maneuver or CPR.

Mom to Mom . . .

    (4) While doing what you can to free the obstruction, send someone to call for emergency help—otherwise dial 911 yourself while assisting your child.

    (5) Be persistent when trying to resuscitate your unconscious child.

    (6) If you are successful in dislodging the obstruction, still take your child to the doctor because damage to the respiratory tract can result from a severe choking incident.

- *Take a CPR course from the American Heart Association or the American Red Cross and renew that training every two or three years.*

    The course will not only teach you the life saving CPR procedures for infants, children, and adults, but it will also include the Heimlich maneuver for infants, children, and adults. Taking this course could save the life of your child or another loved one. If you haven't had this training, or you're rusty in the techniques, sign up for the course now!

- *Keep large and small plastic trash bags out of the reach of small children.*

    Trash bags are often kept under the kitchen sink which provides easy access for a little crawler who enjoys exploring and pulling things out of the cupboards. Plastic trash bags, if opened and pulled over the head, can mean suffocation since the little one won't know how to remove it quickly enough. So store plastic trash bags up and away from little crawlers and climbers.

- *When throwing away dry cleaning bags, tie several knots in them before putting them in the trash.*

    Dry cleaning bags are very filmy and can cause suffocation if a little one gets one of them put over his head in any way. By tying several knots into it, a bag no longer can be opened at any point and if pulled out of the trash can't be "worn." However, they can be chewed on, and pieces of the thin plastic can be aspirated. So use caution when throwing away dry cleaning bags.

A Treasure of Great Ideas . . .

BACKYARD AND PLAYGROUND SAFETY . . .

- *Allow your child to explore the out-of-doors freely, only when you are watching him every minute.*

    So many wonderful things attract a little one's attention—flowers, grass, dirt, bugs, snails. . . but they all are to look at or touch, but *not* to put in the mouth which he'll often want to do. Dirt is delightful to play in—it can be squished if it's wet, it can become mud if water is added, it can crumble—it's wonderful! But, again, it's not for the mouth. It can have pesticides in it, bugs and worms, etc.!

    Water, too, is delightful, and the wading pool is a favorite outdoor activity for the backyard. For little ones, the pool shouldn't have more than six inches of water in it. That's enough to thrill him and to play with. He can still fill buckets with it and pour it and splash it. But even six inches is enough to produce tragic results if he isn't watched very carefully. Drowning is the third most common cause of accidental death among young children.[14]

    Plants and flowers are so inviting to touch and pick. But be aware of those in your own backyard and in the area in which you live which are toxic. Some common garden plants, for example, that are toxic are lily of the valley, iris, sweet pea, daffodil, and autumn crocus. Check out a book at your local library that illustrates the common (and not so common) toxic plants that your backyard may contain.

- *Keep in mind these recommendations from SAFE KIDS, The National Coalition to Prevent Childhood Injury:*

    (1) Check the playground's surface.

    The surface under play equipment should *not* be asphalt or concrete. Instead, the surface should be cushioned in some way. The best is eight to ten inches of shredded mulch or sand. Others are rubber mats, synthetic turf, or other artificial materials that are softer than asphalt or concrete.

Mom to Mom . . .

> *(2) Maintain equipment properly.*
>
> > (a) Equipment should be mounted in concrete footings, should be placed away from walls, fences, and other equipment.
> >
> > (b) Climbing and gripping parts should have slip-resistant surfaces.
> >
> > (c) Metal equipment should be either galvanized or painted to prevent rusting and wooden equipment should be treated with a nontoxic preservative.
>
> *(3) Watch for moving swings.*
>
> Wooden or metal swing seats are heavy and dangerous when swinging. Lightweight plastic or rubber seats are much safer.
>
> *(4) Supervise young children at play.*

HOLIDAY SAFETY REMINDERS . . .

- *Remember the dangers that alcohol represents.*

  Alcohol in all of its forms can have some serious, even fatal, consequences for little ones. Be sure not to leave bottles of perfume and cologne under the Christmas tree where young children can easily open, smell *and drink* the contents.

  And, although you may be tempted to clean up after a party "in the morning," be sure to empty the contents of all glasses before turning in for the night. Early rising young ones may find it fun to sample what remains of the alcoholic drinks.

- *Some popular decorations can cause poisoning or suffocation.*

  Tinsel and icicles are usual made of plastic, tin, or lead. Not only can the lead cause internal problems but a child's airway could be blocked if he tried to swallow the filmy material.

- *Pine needles can cause serious eye infections if they brush or scratch a young child's eye.*

A Treasure of Great Ideas . . .

- *Snow sprays are propellants and solvents and can be dangerous if inhaled or sprayed in or near the eyes.*

MISCELLANEOUS . . .

- *Check your garage door opener to be sure that it reverses if it touches an obstruction of any kind.*

  Older models of door openers do not, and there have been several tragic accidents involving children getting caught under closing garage doors.

  According to the *San Diego Tribune,* March 21, 1990, quoting UPI:

  > *The government warned parents to disconnect and replace garage door openers that do not reverse when blocked, saying the devices have accounted for the deaths of more than 40 children since 1982. The Consumer Product Safety Commission says when children are present, garage door openers should be disconnected or replaced if they are not certified as meeting the requirements of the "ANSI-UL 325-1982" or later voluntary standards.*

- *Beware of the dangers that batteries represent.*

  Children should not be allowed to play with batteries or insert them for a number of reasons.

  (1) All consumer batteries contain dry chemical fuels that can leak out and cause serious burns if not washed off immediately.

  (2) Batteries can explode if they aren't used properly. Examples of improper use are:

   (a) Batteries left in toys after the batteries are "dead."

Mom to Mom . . .

       (b) Two different types of batteries are used together, e.g., an alkaline with a carbon-zinc.

       (c) Newer batteries are used with older batteries.

       (d) Attempting to recharge disposable batteries.

       (e) Batteries aren't aligned properly with the positive and negative terminals.

  (3) The small button cell batteries are particularly dangerous, because they can be easily swallowed.

If your child swallows a button cell battery, take her to the emergency room immediately. Most often the batteries pass through the intestinal tract without causing harm, but should it get caught somewhere along its route through the body, it can cause serious, even fatal, internal chemical burns.

To prevent accidents, you need to supervise the installation and change of batteries if your child is allowed to do it, and any dead batteries must be disposed of immediately.

- *Some important items to keep in mind about those wonderful balloons . . .*

  (1) Keep balloons at a safe distance from toddlers.

It has been found that balloons can cause serious eye injuries if they explode near the eyes of young children.

  (2) Remember the dangers of uninflated balloons and pieces of popped balloons.

Small children love to try to blow up balloons, but can very easily suck in a balloon when taking a deep breath to blow into the balloon.

Also, small children love to chew on pieces of popped balloons and to stretch the pieces of balloon across their mouths to try to make bubbles by blowing out or sucking in. Pieces of rubber balloon sucked in accidentally can be

A Treasure of Great Ideas . . .

deadly because they mold to the air passages and prevent air from passing in either direction.

(3) Always blow balloons up for small children.

(4) Carefully watch children under six who are playing with balloons.

(5) Caution older children of the dangers of chewing or blowing on pieces of popped balloons.

(6) Pick up and throw away all pieces of popped balloons.

(7) Remember that mylar balloons can be a real hazard if they escape and get tangled in the power lines! The power supply to an entire area can be messed up temporarily due to their mischief!

- *Be ever mindful of deadly hiding places.*

    (1) Check your home and storage areas for appliances and *ice chests* that are hazardous.

    Extend this search to include relatives' and friends' homes when you're staying for an extended period of time and the children will be playing somewhat unsupervised.

    (2) Ensure that old locking-style appliances that are no longer in use are child-proofed.

    Either completely remove the door or disable the lock if it cannot be removed. As a last resort, chain and padlock the door shut with no give in the chain so a child could not squeeze in and then see to it that it is removed *as soon as possible*.

    (3) Warn children of the dangers of playing inside an appliance.

    Be absolutely certain that they know that they should *never* play inside an appliance or a cooler.

    (4) If you can't find a child, check appliances and coolers *first*.

Mom to Mom . . .

- *Recliner chairs can be dangerous for children to play on.*

  The August 1988 issue of *Growing Parent* gave this warning:

  > *Children who play on the raised leg rest of a recliner chair are in a dangerous position.*
  >
  > *The Consumer Product Safety Commission reports a number of deaths and serious injuries to children from 12 to 36 months old who were climbing or playing on reclined chairs. The children were hurt when their heads got stuck in the opening between the chair seat and the leg rest and their own body weight forced the leg rest down.*
  >
  > *The agency recommends that recliner chairs always be left in a closed and upright position and that children not be allowed to play on them.*[15]

- *Always check the toys your little one plays with to ensure that each toy is in good repair.*

  If a toy is broken, fix it or discard it. Little pieces can break off, causing a choking hazard, or sharp and/or jagged edges can cause some nasty cuts.

- *Begin to prepare your children to handle emergencies and dangerous situations by playing the "What If. . ." Game.*

  This is a great way to build your child's self-confidence and a good way for you to follow his development and awareness.

  This little game can be played just about anytime, anywhere. You can play it while the two of you are baking a cake, riding in the car, working in the garden, or taking a walk. You simply begin by suggesting that the two of you play the "What If . . ." Game, and begin by asking, "What if . . ." or "What would you do if . . ."

A Treasure of Great Ideas . . .

For example, "What would you do if you and I were at the shopping mall and we became separated?" The object of the game is for your child to come up with some answers and you then reinforce his thinking by praising and approving the good ideas he suggests. The "What If . . ." Game may take a little practice at first and may need some little nudges from you, but encourage your child each time you play the game to come up with as many ideas as he can on his own.

The "What if's . . ." can include topics about dealing with strangers, friends who play with matches, friends who begin offering drugs, a fire in the house, a stranger who comes to the door, etc.

- *Safeguard the front door by installing a deadbolt lock near the top of the front door.*

    Several months ago I was visiting Stan and Melody Leopard in Cardiff by the Sea, California, and I noticed a marvelous idea that they had come up with! To ensure that their little Ari didn't wander out the front door unaccompanied, they had installed a deadbolt lock at the top of their front door! It also occurred to me that it was an excellent security measure for the home, regardless of whether or not there were wandering little ones who lived there!

HELPFUL LITERATURE AND PRODUCTS . . .

- *Write for the Buyer's Guide: The Safe Nursery, published by the U.S. Consumer Product Safety Commission.*

    This excellent booklet can be obtained by sending a request to the U.S. Consumer Product Safety Commission, Washington, D.C. 20207.

- *Create a identification record of your child using "Kinderprint Fingerprinting Kit."*

    We don't ever want to think of our little ones ever being kidnapped or lost, but you may want to consider be well prepared just in case.

357

Mom to Mom . . .

"Kinderprint Fingerprinting Kit" helps you prepare an excellent identification record of your child by giving you the means to prepare a complete fingerprint record, physical description, and photo file. The kit also includes some excellent reminders for keeping your child safe.

You can obtain one of these kits by sending $1.00 for shipping to: The Clearinghouse, P.O. Box 770, Amsterdam, NY 12010

SECURITY ITEMS—LOVIES . . .

"Lovies" or security items like blankets or favorite stuffed animals are very important to little ones. Some children don't develop a strong attachment to a special toy or blanket, but many children do.

Many moms wonder how they can possibly *clean* those blankets and stuffed animals that get dragged everywhere by their loyal masters! The secret to cleaning those prized possessions was shared with me by the "Teddy Doctor" who specializes in the the care and repair of all special teddy bears! I met her at what Maryanna calls "the Teddy Bear Convention," a bi-annual convention of antique dealers in dolls and Teddy Bears. To safely wash the stuffed animals of today:

(1) Double a pillow case by putting one pillow case into another.

(2) Put the Teddy bear or other stuffed animal inside the pillow cases.

(3) Close the pillow case securely by using a rubber band.

(4) Put the pillow case in the washing machine along with the rest of the laundry.

(5) When finished in the washer, put the pillow case (complete with rubber band!) in the dryer, set on medium.

(6) If, after the cycle, the animal isn't completely dry, just hang him up with clothes pins and a hanger in the fresh air for a short while.

I followed her advice hesitantly because Maryanna's Teddy was a precious treasure . . . to her! But it worked beautifully, not only on Teddy

A Treasure of Great Ideas ...

but on several other stuffed animals in her menagerie! The pillow cases keep the eyes protected so that they won't crack or chip. And the rubber band, believe it or not, does not melt or make any marks on the outer pillow case. We were delighted!

SELF-RELIANCE ...

Kids love to do things on their own, especially when given the chance when they're quite young.

Allow your children to do small tasks by themselves that you know they can do. For example:

(a) Put your cup in the sink, please.

(b) Put the paper in the trash, please.

(c) Put your toys away, please.

(d) Put your dirty clothes in the hamper, please.

(e) Etc.

Remember to always thank them and give praise for a job well done.

Doreen Seldon
San Diego, California

SIBLINGS AND THEIR RIVALRY ...

RECOMMENDED READING ...

Siblings Without Rivalry by Adele Faber and Elaine Mazlish

Too many families are experiencing the stress of constant bickering, teasing, and tattling that drives most parents to distraction. The two authors of this book are specialists in teaching communication skills to parents. They have developed simple

Mom to Mom . . .

yet very effective ways to reduce antagonism between siblings. It's an excellent resource in guiding you to help children accept one another and to get along with one another—a skill that will last them a lifetime.

SUGGESTIONS FROM OTHER MOMS . . .

Once our younger son was born, we had some very difficult problems with our older son, Sean. We thought we had handled it all in advance, but that second child still means competition—in capital letters! The one thing we have done which seems to keep our lives at a more even keel, is we "divide and conquer"—one parent takes one child and the other parent, the other child, and off we go here and there on free time. We still do a lot as a family, but individual time is highly prized and has most DEFINITELY helped Sean. His self-worth has improved remarkably since we began doing this.

Stevie Wooten
Seattle, Washington

We think it's very important for each child to have some time alone with each parent. They really open up one on one. For example, our Pastor used to alternate taking one of his three daughters to breakfast Saturday mornings.

Our kids look forward to a little Christmas "tradition" we started a few years ago. They each get a turn going to dinner and to do

A Treasure of Great Ideas . . .

their shopping with me one night at Christmastime.

Peggy Takaaze
Hilo, Hawaii

SLEEPY TIME . . .

- *To ensure that your child's room remains a special, happy place, use some other place for time outs when they are necessary—never the bedroom.*

We've used a corner in our living room and one of the bathrooms for time outs, but never Maryanna's bedroom. Her bedroom is her palace and should always represent a happy place for her.

SUGGESTIONS FROM OTHER MOMS . . .

We found "Solving Your Child's Sleep Problems" by Richard Ferber to be very helpful. It may not suit everyone, but it helped us to get Katie to sleep through the night and several other mothers I know were so thankful for the method described in that book.

We have a rather unique bedtime ritual! For months, Rick has been "flying" Katie into her crib. Her tummy is laid out on Rick's arms and her arms are spread out like a bird! Whenever I say that it's bedtime or nap-time, Katie asks right away, "Who's going to fly me?" Grandad even got in on this!

Another thing that helps Katie accept bedtime is my "setting the buzzer." When I say that bedtime (or anything else she may not want to do) is coming soon, she asks me to "set the buzzer" (the kitchen timer). For some reason, when that timer goes off she goes to bed (or takes her bath, or puts her toys away . . .) unquestioningly! It works even if I've only "set the buzzer" for two minutes.

Terri Ciosek
Poway, California

Mom to Mom . . .

> *When your child is afraid to sleep in the dark and insists on having the light left on, install a dimmer switch. Gradually work on getting him or her used to the dark by dimming the light more and more over a period of time.*
>
> Lori Buschmann
> San Diego, California

> *I bathe my children at night and wash them off in the morning. My children sleep better after a nice warm bath and a treat of warm milk. This has always worked and still does at ages 5 and 3. The bath and warm milk really seem to relax them and put them right to sleep.*
>
> Doreen Seldon
> San Diego, California

STORYTELLING . . .

Children love to hear stories, especially when they come from Mom and Dad! Reading favorite books—and new ones, too—is a special activity, but for some reason, storytelling straight from Mommy and Daddy's heart seems to appeal like no other story can.

What sources can you use for such storytelling? Some little ones (and not so little!) will delight in stories of your days as a child. And, you can spin some yarns, so to speak, of your very own. That's really not as hard as you might think. I know I thought it would be difficult, but I found, once I got started, that it wasn't very difficult at all.

One night Maryanna asked me to tell her "a little story" as she climbed into bed. At first, I gulped, thinking what story could I tell her?! I loved to read stories to her, but tell her one of my very own without any planning or jotting notes ahead of time? It seemed impossible, but . . . anything to please! I suddenly had an inspiration—I would tell her a story

A Treasure of Great Ideas . . .

about Tom Thumb. And, since she loves rainbows and flowers, I would somehow weave those into "a little story." By the time I was finished, I was amazed at myself. I had had Tom sliding down rainbows to a magic pond where he loved to hop on the dragon flies and fly over all the beautiful flowers, etc., etc., etc.! It now has become a ritual. Maryanna asks to hear another story about Tom Thumb every evening, sometimes even specifying the "plot," such as, "tell me about Tom Thumb when he was sick, Mommy." Or, after she celebrated St. Patrick's Day at preschool, "Tell me about Tom Thumb and the leprechauns, Mommy!" We've had some real fun—she's been quite happy and I've had a lot of fun!

TEETH AND TEETHING . . .

- *If you are still breastfeeding your older baby or toddler, you may want to read Pamphlet #31 by the La Leche League: "Breastfeeding and Dental Caries."*

    This pamphlet is described in detail in Chapter 7 on page 202-203. There are many doctors and dentists who discourage night-time nursing after a little one's teeth have begun to come in because they believe it causes "bottle mouth." This pamphlet presents research to prove otherwise.

- *Take your child to see a dentist for the first time before he is 24 months old.*

    If you plan to use your own dentist for your child *(and only if he or she is known to be wonderful with children)* an excellent "strategy" for introducing your child to a dentist's office and the examination and cleaning is to take your little one in with you for your own appointment. Take some toys for him to play with while you are having your teeth examined and cleaned by the dentist or the dental hygienist. Then, make your next six-month appointment for exam and cleaning with a first appointment for your little one. You can then have your exam and your little one can follow. By taking him along "just for the ride" the first time, he can see that it is a non-threatening situation. Then, when he

Mom to Mom...

has his first appointment, he has already watched you again having your teeth examined and cleaned.

- *To find a dentist for your child . . .*

Follow the same procedure that you did for finding a pediatrician:

(1) Create a list of referrals from recommendations of friends with children, your pediatrician, friends of friends who have children, doctors and nurses you may know.

(2) Prioritize the list, first according to recommendation and then by location.

(3) Select the top three and call for an interview.

Some new parents feel very uncomfortable interviewing a potential pediatrician. For some reason, they feel even more uncomfortable about calling a dentist for an interview. But, if you are wanting a friendly, welcoming atmosphere and environment in a dentist's office for your child, then a visit is well worth the time and trouble.

(4) Interview each of the candidates carefully.

(5) Make your selection.

Other moms offer these suggestions . . .

> *When teaching your toddler and preschooler to brush their own teeth, have them hold the toothbrush with their index finger placed above the bristle area of the brush so that they "point" while brushing their teeth. Doing this rather than holding the toothbrush at the end of the handle gives them more control over where the toothbrush goes and adds some strength in the brushing.*
>
> Lynn Carlson
> (a mom *and* a dental hygienist!)
> San Diego, California

A Treasure of Great Ideas . . .

> *As soon as little teeth start coming through, put a toothbrush in their hands. By the time they are two years old, start taking them to the dentist with you so they are familiar with the process and aren't afraid.*
>
> Jan Sundblad
> San Diego, California

> *Keep a second set of toothbrushes and toothpaste in a cup in the kitchen. It saves precious minutes in the morning if your bathroom is on another floor and your child's teeth will be clean!*
>
> Sue Brandes
> Des Plaines, Illinois

TELEVISION . . .

As parents, we are all concerned about the incredible amount of time that we're told that the average American child spends in front of the television on a weekly basis. As of 1989, the average is 16 hours *per week*—and that's for an average preschooler!

When Maryanna was just a few months old, I shuddered when a neighbor said to me, "My 16-month-old grandson is so easy to care for! I just sit him in front of the television and he'll stay there for hours!"

It's probably because of that experience and because of the stories that I so frequently hear via the news media about children and television, that we have chosen to use very little television with Maryanna. And, when we do, we're certain to watch it with her and interact with her so that it isn't simply an "intake process" but an exchange as well. A good example is the local program, "Animal Express" with Joan Embry and the San Diego Zoo. We'll turn it on for Maryanna occasionally, but we all watch it together and talk about what we're seeing and what we like about the various animals.

Mom to Mom . . .

Peggy Takaaze from Hilo, Hawaii, who has three children ages 9 through 16, explains why they have no television at all.

Since we've watched <u>them</u> instead of TV, they have kind of a sense of pride knowing that they're more important to us so they haven't minded, plus it's a treat to watch Tuesday nights (after mid-week church service when we go to Dad Takaaze's for dinner). They then have an idea of what's going on and aren't out of touch completely. Also, re-runs are new for us!

I could write a lot about the advantages of not having had a TV. Of course, it's much easier never having had one than if we would have had to "unplug" our kids. It avoids all that bickering over who wants to watch what, when. Mostly, we've found that there isn't enough time in the day without television as it is! So we can imagine what a big bite out of the day <u>any</u> amount of television watching would take.

We think our children are more creative and active and well-rounded than perhaps they would have been otherwise. Our little nine-year-old girl especially LOVES to read. All three do well in school. They are very good at card games from their little days—they started with Crazy Eights and built up. Since there is so much chance involved, winning doesn't depend upon age. They play lots of board games, too, including Trivial Pursuit, Pictionary, and now Balderdash. Adults find our children fun to play games with. They laugh and talk a lot.

A Treasure of Great Ideas...

Homework crowds out some family time, but TV doesn't. Holidays we usually have time to watch video movies together.

How do we watch video movies without a television? Our VCR is hooked up to a special monitor!

When Jay and I go out on Friday nights, the kids usually have a movie that they watch on the VCR—a movie that we have previewed in advance.

TOILET TRAINING . . .

- *Just as all of the books say, DON'T push your child into training.*

  It really does happen when they're ready and not before, and the timing has nothing to do with how bright the child is! Be sure not to fall into the trap of comparing your child's progress (or the lack of it) with other children, both boys and girls. In general, boys supposedly train later than girls, but that doesn't mean your daughter will decide to train before her little friend who is a boy. The key word there is *decide*. They truly *decide* for themselves when they are ready! When they are ready, then they are truly ready and not before. You may *encourage,* perhaps, but *do not push with nagging, hollering, or punishment*. It will make no difference other than to *delay* it all the longer.

  However, once they have the very strong idea of what's expected and are performing fairly well, you may want to play Sherlock Holmes to figure out the last few wrinkles in the training.

  For example, our daughter, soon after her third birthday, decided that she would use the potty and stay dry (most of the time) during the day. But after a while, she started to soil her panties—frequently—rather than use the potty. At first, I didn't make a big deal out of it and simply cleaned her up and sent her on her

Mom to Mom . . .

way. But after it continued, I decided that there may be more to it than I could perceive.

I then told her that she would have to clean herself up—I would help her, but she was a big enough girl that she could start cleaning herself up instead of me doing the entire job. I'd stand her in the bathtub and she would have to remove her pants—carefully—and then wipe herself. There were a lot of tears at first, but the new procedure soon caught on. Once she was washed up, she would then have to wash out her panties, again something she didn't like—at first.

But . . . we didn't go anywhere with this new procedure. The soiling still continued! However, one day a little friend who was older was over to play when an accident occurred. We excused ourselves, got her cleaned up, and then I left her to wash her panties by herself. She howled! I explained that it wasn't polite to leave her guest alone and that since she was occupied, I would entertain her guest until she was finished! She pleaded, "Stay with me, stay with me, stay with me, Mommy!" It then dawned on me that one of the reasons she may be doing this was to keep me with her for additional one-on-one attention.

That evening, when another soiling accident occurred, I did the same thing—I left her alone to do her washing. She howled and howled, but I told her I needed to spend time doing other things, that when she was finished, we could read together or do a puzzle, or whatever she wanted. But until she was finished, I would be busy doing my own things. Presto! That was it. There hasn't been a soiling accident since!

TRAVELING AWAY FROM HOME . . .

- *Use a little suitcase (toy size) or a little backpack (toddler or preschool size) or both to carry all the favorite activities and toys on a trip.*

Until Maryanna began packing her little pink suitcase and her little backpack herself, I would pack the following:

A Treasure of Great Ideas . . .

* A zip-type bag full of crayons and watercolor-type felt tip pens
* A large pad of blank paper
* A thin coloring book
* Several new paperback-type books (not hardcover because they're too heavy)
* A puppet
* An inflatable ball
* A favorite small doll or two
* Cloth activity book (the type that has shoe laces to tie, buttons to button, zippers to zip, etc.)
* Some new activity, i.e., sewing cards, story boards with restickable "stickers," etc.

Her backpack would contain a sweater and her favorite furless stuffed animal, Teddy, and some other odds and ends that were treasures at the time.

Now that she does her own packing of these items, they still contain many of the same items, but a few changes have occurred. She enjoys taking her scissors for some creative artwork, and we've even taken along some Glue Stic™ which is much better than any liquid glue that could spill.

- *Create a "visiting bag" that your little one never sees except for such a special outing.*

  To create this bag, find several age-appropriate, very intriguing toys and books and stuff them into the bag. The bag itself can be made from some colorful quilted fabric that just calls your toddler to come and investigate its contents! You will find that such a bag really keeps the little one occupied . . . although she may be so thrilled with its contents that she will want to show and share each one with you. However, it does help to keep her hands on her own things rather than on the many things that she would find of interest in your friends' homes!

Mom to Mom . . .

Terri Ciosek of Poway, California, has some excellent ideas when it comes to traveling a great distance by car with a little one. She has a lot of experience—her little family frequently drives from California to Michigan and back! She suggests the following:

- *Travel during naptimes whenever possible.*
- *When on a long trip (more than one day of travel), start early, stop early in the day, and try not to have your baby travel in the car after you get to the hotel.*

  To avoid taking her in the car any more for that day, we either walk to a restaurant or one of us goes out for take-out food.

- *Have a surprise for each day of travel.*

  This can be an inexpensive toy or book that the child can play with in the car. You can even wrap them like presents.

- *Collect some toys that are perfect for the car.*

  For example, colorforms, sticker books, paint with water books, bubbles, small dolls or tiny figures.

- *Take along cassette tapes—they're a necessity!*

  Cassette tapes are great! The tapes of songs are wonderful for everyone to sing along! The tapes that have accompanying books are even better—the little one(s) get all the more involved in the songs or stories.

- *Take along a lot of nutritious snacks, too.*

  Even semi-messy snacks are okay—just have a big bib handy that covers the little one and the car seat's straps and just place a large towel on the seat underneath the car seat.

Other moms have these suggestions . . .

> *A must for traveling away from home with a toddler or a preschooler is a cassette player with headphones. Bring children's*

stories, songs, or record your own containing your child's favorite songs and stories.

Lori Buschmann
San Diego, California

I think it's important to give a child a good "brief"—how long the trip will be, whether they'll be expected to sleep on the plane or in the car, when meals will be, etc. If it's an overnight flight (to Europe, for instance), take pajamas for a young child—up to five or so—and go through the whole bedtime routine: brush teeth, read a story, etc. Make their seat into as comfortable a bed as possible (and loosely buckle their seat belt).

Tell them all about it ahead of time. Don't get nervous; act like it's the perfectly normal way to do it.

After the age of about three, buy the small traveler a backpack. Let him or her select what to take along, and limit what he takes to what fits in the backpack. Put them in charge of their own belongings early. Later, they can help pack by bringing their clothes to you to be put into their suitcase. As soon as they can they should carry their own suitcase; by age ten or sooner they'll be able to pack on their own.

Ann Gaines
Nevada City, California

Make your trips away from home during the day as short as possible—this takes some

Mom to Mom . . .

real practice! Don't give your little one too much time to become restless. Always take a favorite toy, stuffed animal, or book, whatever your child seems to enjoy. The shortest trips can be exhausting and challenging! Be sure to always take a few surprises in your purse—a few of his small toys—and a small snack or two (e.g., crackers, graham crackers, oat rings, raisins—if he's old enough for them—etc.) Snacks can sometimes take a little one's mind off being confined.

Doreen Seldon
San Diego, California

A Treasure of Great Ideas...

[1] Joan McIntosh as quoted in A Mother's Journal, *Running Press Book Publishers,* Philadelphia, PA, 1985.
[2] Anita Remignanti, "Tips for Teaching Children Positive Communication," *Growing Parent,* July 1989, p. 4.
[3] Sharon Lynne Anthoney, "Children's Health," *Baby Talk,* November 1986, p. 28.
[4] Gary Holt, Ph.D., R.Ph., "Medicine Chest," *Family Circle,* July 25, 1989, p. 50.
[5] Adapted from a Patient Information Flyer on Fever by Frederick A. Frye, M.D., San Diego, CA.
[6] "December Almanac," *Parents Magazine,* December 1986, p. 13.
[7] Earl A. Grollman and Gerri L. Sweder, "Tips for Working Parents," condensed from *The Parenting Dilemma* in *Reader's Digest,* February 1986, pp. 107-110.
[8] Ray Malony, "Ten Ways to Turn Out Terrific Kids," condensed from Vibrant Life in *Reader's Digest,* pp. 148-150.
[9] Julius Segal, Ph. D., "You're the Greatest," *Parents Magazine,* May 1986, pp 84-88.
[10] Included in the article, "Push Your Kids Without Shoving," by Norma Peterson, *U.S.A. Today,* Tuesday, October 25, 1983, p. 6D.
[11] Susan Isaacs and Cedilia Soares, "Animal Magnetism," *Parents Magazine,* March 1987, p. 98.
[12] Adapted from guidelines provided by Suzanne Colby in her article, "The Enemy within the Home," *Baby Talk,* October 1985, p. 38.
[13] Anthony, p. 30.
[14] Janice T. Gibson, "Safety in Your Own Backyard," *Parents Magazine,* June 1988, p. 187.
[15] *Growing Parent,* August 1988, page 7.

Mom to Mom . . .

Clips and Notes . . .

A Treasure of Great Ideas . . .

Clips and Notes . . .

Mom to Mom...

Clips and Notes...

A Treasure of Great Ideas . . .

Clips and Notes . . .

Mom to Mom . . .

Clips and Notes . . .

SECTION THREE

APPENDIX

A

A Scrapbook of Thoughts to Ponder . . .

A Mother's Prayer

*Give me patience when little hands
Tug at me with ceaseless small demands.
Give me gentle words and smiling eyes,
And keep my lips from hasty, sharp replies.
So that when in the years to come my house is still,
Beautiful memories its rooms may fill.*

Author unknown
Submitted by Peggy Takaaze
Hilo, Hawaii

"How do you divide your love among four children?"
"I don't divide it. I multiply it."

Reproduced from "The Family Circus is Us"
Fawcett-Columbine Books, November 1990
with permission of Bil Keane

Mom to Mom...

> *This is an age when men value organizations more than their members. When we force children to conform to our convenience, our schedules, our boundaries, and our locked doors, we show them that we value the system more than we value them.*
>
> Dr. James Clark Moloney[1]

> *Bitter are the tears of a child:*
> *Sweeten them.*
> *Deep are the thoughts of a child:*
> *Quiet them.*
> *Sharp is the grief of a child:*
> *Take it from him.*
> *Soft is the heart of a child:*
> *Do nothing to harden it.*
>
> Lady Pamela Wyndham Glenconner[2]

> *When kids feel right, they'll behave right.*
>
> Dr. Haim Ginott
> quoted in
> *How to Talk So Kids Will Listen and Listen So Kids Will Talk*
> by Adele Faber and Elaine Mazlish
> Page 2

Scrapbook of Thoughts to Ponder . . .

A contributing mom wrote:

> *I remember reading Judith Viorst, the author of wonderful children's books, on things she wished she had done differently in raising her children. She regretted that she had not been more <u>charming</u> with her children. There is a lot to be said for charm, which implies to me tact, respect, friendliness, and admiration.*
>
> Priscilla Cowell
Portland, Oregon

One of the mothers who contributed to this book is one of three children. Her parents wrote the following to her and her husband after the birth of their second child:

> *Dearest Peggy,*
>
> *As your family grows, each child becomes THE MOST PRECIOUS and THE BEST LOVED. We know . . . ours are!*
>
> *Mom and Daddy*

And, finally, here is the Foreword for Tine Thevenin's book, *The Family Bed*, written by Herbert Ratner, M.D., Editor of *Child & Family Quarterly*. It's shared here with you thanks to the kind permission of Tine Thevenin. I include it here not only because of its endorsement of the concept of the family bed, but also because of its important support of *intuitive* mothering and parenting and its relationship to healthy development. The piece offers an abundance of food for thought for any parent.

> *Were modern society thriving with high level wellness at all ages and stages of life, physicians and others*

Mom to Mom . . .

interested in childrearing would have a right to dismiss a book promoting the old-fashioned notion that the parental bed be converted into a family bed. With modern society, however, suffering from a marked dysfunctioning and harboring doubts that there will be a viable society to turn over to the next generation, we can afford to be open minded about a practice which purports to contribute to the emotional security of a human being.

The indices of a sick society—alienation and psychiatric illness, suicide attempts and suicide, alcoholism and drug misuse, infidelity and divorce, pornography and perversion, sexual restlessness and impotency, juvenile delinquency, child abuse and violent crime—have been steadily rising since World War I. Psychiatry, for the most part, has responded remedially and ineffectively: at the technologic level with an unawareness or insensitivity to nurturent needs and with a permissiveness which, severed from controlling social norms, reflects an excessive counter-reaction to a preceding Victorian age.

Unfortunately, today's mental health movement is a movement primarily concerned with the management of mental illness, not with the promotion of mental health, the latter being hardly more than a platitudinous window-dressing. Physicians in general, and psychiatrists in particular (neither of whom are especially competent in their own family life or even partially immune from personal psychiatric problems), preoccupied with patient problems and lulled by the blandishments of drug companies and the ready promises of the prescription pad, fail to reflect on and explore the true nature of a mental health movement—one directed to the preservation, promotion and perfection of the initial mental health with which man is endowed at birth.

Scrapbook of Thoughts to Ponder . . .

For though nature turns over to us more than three million babies a year, virtually all of whom are psychologically healthy, the fact is that the majority of these, despite continuing medical attendance (or because of it), grow up emotionally insecure, and one out of ten newborns enters a mental institution sometime in the course of his or her lifetime. Now, especially that it is becoming virtually impossible to supply enough psychiatrists, psychiatric social workers, nurses, and psychiatric facilities to handle the mounting number of patients needing help, it would seem that society should turn its attention to the earlier years to see when and how things went wrong. It is perhaps our only hope for stemming the tide of psychiatrically crippled human beings.

What we must be mindful of it we have any respect for nature is that she has accumulated a built-in wisdom born of a vast clinical experience over millions of years, out of which a reciprocal fitness between the living thing and its environment has evolved. In mammalia this is found particularly in the intimate relationship of mother and and young. The mother is nature's "prepared environment" for the newborn! We cannot afford to ignore this wisdom. Literally this is what the natural sciences are about: to discover the wisdom of nature; that is, the laws, nuances and subtleties of nature which enabled our species to survive and prosper. In the meantime, to bridge the gap between what we already know (or think we know) and what we have yet to learn—what is yet to be discovered by the activities of countless researchers in thousands of laboratories—the prudent and sagacious man must seek his cues and clues and norms from the operations of nature. Here we must remember that medicine, in its broadest sense, is a normative art.

The fatal mistake we have made in medicine, not only in psychiatry but even more so in pediatrics and

Mom to Mom . . .

obstetrics, was to introduce practices which deviated from normal physiologic and psychologic processes without first firmly researching the full implications and wisdom of man-imposed changes. This is best exemplified by the ignorance inherent in the ready substitution of bottle feeding for breastfeeding as if, to recall Oliver Wendell Homes, the two hemispheres of the contemporary pediatrician's brain is superior to a pair of mammary glands in the art of compounding a nutritive fluid for infants. We forget that the root of the word <u>physician is phusis</u> which means nature, and that medicine is a cooperative art because it cooperates with the active mechanisms of nature and the goal of nature which it shares. (The same mistake is also seen by our having made the drugged and operative hospital delivery the prevalent as opposed to the natural delivery.)

The fitness of the environment for the living, whose fitness is reciprocal to the environment, is not only a matter of the physical, such as water, oxygen, nitrogen, carbon and trace minerals, but also of the psychologic, as seen by the maternal and parental environment without which the young of mammalia cannot survive or emotionally mature. Here it must be stressed that it is the family, not the individual, which is the proper unit of care, because the family, especially as it concerns the psyche, is the maker or breaker of health.

The fact that modern medicine and technology, despite its many brilliant accomplishments, has not given society high, or even low, level wellness (nor has the huge amount of money we have expended, as if health were a commodity that could be bought in the market place) nor even slowed up the prevailing malaise that is enveloping our country should make us reconsider our problem and its solution.

Scrapbook of Thoughts to Ponder...

Accordingly, it is incumbent upon the reader, particularly those who are professionals in the medical and behavioral sciences, to approach <u>The Family Bed</u> with an open mind. It cogently brings to life the manner in which a family functions or may function in attaining its purpose—the giving of mature adults to society at large. Enough studies now exist to document with finality that the first years of life are vital if not crucial to adult maturity; that the indices of a sick society are symptomatic manifestations in later life of insecurities generated in earlier years. Even academia—the Harvard studies under Dr. Burton White—reaffirm the importance of full-time attention of a mother (or a mother substitute) to the dependent child in his or her first two or three years of life for the child's optimal emotional development. The time is long overdue for parents, physicians, social agencies and government experts to realize that they have been working at the wrong end of the age scale in seeking basic solutions. We must recognize that the dysfunctioning family should be corrected and helped to function properly in its work as the prime health maker for society.

<u>*The Family Bed*</u> *is a case in point. The author's thesis is that there is something natural, right and salutary in the desire of young children to convert the parental bed into a family bed. The exposition of her thesis is substantial. In fact, it is as if Maria Montessori whispered in her ear, "If you want to understand the needs of children, observe and study the child." That very young children, always and everywhere—in contrast to older children—prefer the family bed to their own bed or their own room communicates a convincing message. Since man is not only a social animal but a gregarious animal as well, the ramifications of interfering with such a universal, inborn natural inclination may be extensive.*

One of the great strengths of <u>The Family Bed</u> stems

Mom to Mom...

from the author's recognition of the experience and convictions of mothers who accept rather than reject motherhood as a vocation and who make a point of trying to enrich their vocation by participating in mothering organizations such as La Leche League International. Many of these mothers have large families, mothers whom Sir James Spence characterized as really good at motherhood. Such mothers, practitioners as opposed to theorists, are the real experts. They contrast to the Spocks and Salks, who, when they are right, are simply echoes of what the good mother has learned by being attentive and responsive to the voice of nature. Profundity characterizes the simple conclusion of a mother that "Babies' wants and needs are one and the same thing"; or of another, "Society has taken away the right of a baby to be dependent upon his mother."

The Family Bed is most readable. It will bring joy and support to parents who refuse to reject the silent (and sometimes not so silent) importunings of their children and who refuse to banish them to isolated, solitary outposts. It will help other parents take a second look at what parenthood is all about. Parents tell me that the best advice I gave them as young couples entering marriage and parenthood was first, to invest in a king-size bed, and second, to never forget that the fastest road to furthering independence in their children is total attention to the needs of their children in their dependent years.

---

[1] Tine Thevenin, *The Family Bed*, Avery Publishing Group: Wayne, N.J., p.xvii.
[2] *Ibid.*, p. 71.

Scrapbook of Thoughts to Ponder . . .

Clips and Notes . . .

Mom to Mom . . .

Clips and Notes . . .

Scrapbook of Thoughts to Ponder . . .

Clips and Notes . . .

Mom to Mom...

Clips and Notes...

B

INDISPENSABLE RESOURCES for MOMS and DADS

Parenting really must be a hobby of mine! I've spent several years reading parenting materials of all kinds, clipping and filing, talking with other moms—experienced and inexperienced— and taking notes, all of which has given me a marvelous supply of information! I even carefully review each baby- and child-oriented catalogue that finds its way into our mailbox, and have often found some ingenious products that way.

I'm often asked where I found a certain wonder product, or where I found a certain book that I recommend or where I found various delightful ideas. It has taken a long time to bump into the various resources that have been responsible for my finding those products or books or wonderful ideas. None, of which, I might add, had been recommended to me. I just found these resources "by accident"!

Below is a list of the resources I've found to be the *most* helpful, most of which I continue to use on a consistent basis. I am quite confident that you will be pleased with any of the resources listed below.

Catalogues:

La Leche League International Catalogue

This catalogue is distributed several times a year. It has excellent books on not only breastfeeding, but nutrition, childbirth, and parenting as well. Some excellent children's books are also available.

Mom to Mom . . .

To be included on their mailing list, call (708) 455-7730 or (708) 451-1891, or write: La Leche League International, P.O. Box 1209, Franklin Park, IL 60131-8209.

One Step Ahead Catalog

You'll find this to be a wonderful collection of products for baby and toddler. They offer many innovative products that are especially helpful in making travel, feeding, bathing and diapering easier. All products are thoroughly tested by their Mother's Panel for quality, safety, durability and play value, and are 100% guaranteed.

To be included on the *One Step Ahead* mailing list, call (800) 274-8440 or write to *One Step Ahead,* Box 46, Deerfield, IL 60015.

The Natural Diapering Handbook

This little catalogue is not only filled with excellent "tried and true" products, it also is loaded with some great suggestions and tips.

To be included on the mailing list for this catalogue, call (609) 737-2895 or write to The Natural Baby Company, Rd. 1 Box 160S, Titusville, NJ 08560.

Newsletters:

Growing Child/Growing Parent

These two monthly newsletters are excellent. A subscription to one is a subscription to both. I read them both cover to cover the day they arrive and have yet to be disappointed. They're wonderful resources and I find the information to be quite useful. Each newsletter comes three-hole-punched, so they can easily be kept for future reference.

Indispensable Resources...

For subscription information, call or write: Growing Parent/ Growing Child, Dunn and Hargitt, Inc., 22 N. Second Street, Lafayette, IN 47902. (317) 423-2624.

New Beginnings

This is the bimonthly journal of La Leche League International. If you are breastfeeding your child, you will find this journal to be a wonderful source of support. Sometimes, a breastfeeding mother can feel discouraged, especially during a growth spurt or, if she chooses to follow "child-led weaning," she may feel as though she may have made the wrong decision. This is another resource that I read cover to cover the day it arrives in our mailbox.

A subscription comes with your membership in LLLI for an annual fee of $25 or you may just subscribe to the journal for an annual rate of $15.

To subscribe, call (708) 455-7730 or (708) 451-1891, or write: La Leche League International, P.O. Box 1209, Franklin Park, IL 60131-8209.

Pediatrics for Parents

Pediatrics for Parents is a monthly newsletter edited and published by Dr. Richard J. Sagall, a practicing pediatrician and the "Pediatricks" columnist for *Parents Magazine.* In his monthly newsletter, Dr. Sagall provides up-to-date pediatrics information, clearly explains medical terms and concepts that we as parents may hear about but may not understand, provides important information concerning your child's health, and includes articles that are written by health care professionals and medical writers.

To subscribe, write to: *Pediatrics for Parents,* P.O. Box 1069, Bangor, ME 04401. (By sending $2.00 to the same address, you can receive a sample copy if you would rather read a copy before committing yourself to a full year's subscription at $15.00.)

Mom to Mom...

Magazines

Parents Magazine

This monthly magazine is an excellent collection of articles and columns that never fails to help, encourage, and inspire. As with others I've mentioned above, this too is read from cover to cover as soon as it arrives. Pick up a copy at a news stand or book store and see if you don't agree!

To subscribe, complete a subscription card found in a copy of the magazine or call (800) 727-3682. If you call, be sure to inquire about the subscription rate. Some magazines run specials on the subscriptions from time to time, and the rate on the post card *or* the rate over the telephone may be cheaper, depending on the promotion.

Focus on the Family

Focus on the Family is an outstanding monthly magazine, Christian-based, and obviously centered on the family as its title suggests. It is edited and published by the Focus on the Family organization headquartered in Pomona, California, which was founded by Dr. James Dobson, the organization's current president. Dr. Dobson is the author of a number of excellent books on family concerns that have been recommended by the mothers who contributed to this book. Each edition of the magazine contains articles that not only give you support and guidance in parenting, but provide a tremendous amount of food for thought.

Perhaps the greatest news about this wonderful magazine is that a subscription is *free*. Simply call 1-800-A-FAMILY.

Mothering

This magazine may be hard to find at the newsstand because it is published only four times a year. Several moms who contributed

Indispensable Resources...

to this book recommended it and, after finally finding a copy, I can certainly agree with their recommendation! It provides a rich diversity of articles to match the great diversity among its readers. I ordered several back issues that are still available and read each one from cover to cover. I'm now eagerly looking forward to my regular subscription!

The best times to find issues at the newsstand would be January, April, July, and October, since it's published on a quarterly basis. Back issues are $4.00 each and an annual subscription is $18.00. For more information, California residents can call 1-800-354-8400; outside California, you may call 1-800-443-9637. For back issues, you can write to Mothering Magazine, P.O. Box 1690, Santa Fe, NM 87504 or call (505) 984-8116.

Lactation Consultants

Regional Listings

Wellstart—the San Diego Lactation Program here in San Diego—was my main resource for health professionals who were lactation consultants. They were wonderful! They cleared up my initial problems immediately! When I started this book, I had a real concern that readers who wanted the same caliber of professional help could easily locate it. Consequently, I asked Wellstart how women across the country could find competent health professionals who were lactation consultants—consultants in whom they could have complete confidence. Wellstart gave me the following regional list. Those listed for your specific region will most likely be able to give you referrals to consultants in your immediate area.

Mom to Mom...

To get a referral, find the region which includes your state. Then, contact one of those listed on the team for a referral to a health professional in your area who specializes in breastfeeding.

Region	Areas Included	Contacts
I	Connecticut Maine Massachusetts New Hampshire Rhode Island	Maureen Savadore, MD Pediatrician, Private Practice 232 St. John Street Portland, ME 04102 (207) 772-3703 Kathy Sutton, RN, Ph.N. Dept. of Human Services 117 Maine Street Mexico, ME 04257 (207) 364-7884 Judy Gatchell, MS, LD Div. of Maternal & Child Health 151 Capitol Street Station 11 Augusta, ME 04333 (207) 289-3311
II	New York New Jersey Puerto Rico Virgin Islands	Chung Y. Kown, MD V.I. Gov't Health Dept. P.O. Box 754 Christiansted Charles Harwood Mem. Hospital St. Croix, VI 00821-0754 (809) 773-1311 Jeanette H. Lewis Maternal and Child Health St. Thomas, VI 00801 (809) 774-9000, ext. 216 Lorna Sebastian, MS, RD 5-7A Peppertree Terrace, A15 Christiansted St. Croix, VI 00820 (809) 778-5561

Indispensable Resources...

Region	Areas Included	Contacts
III	Delaware Maryland Pennsylvania Virginia West Virginia	Lina Wright, MD University of Maryland School of Medicine 22 So. Greene St., Rm. N5W70 Baltimore, MD 21201 (301) 328-6520 Susan Will, RN, MS Sinai Hospital Belvidere at Greenspring Baltimore, MD 21215 (301) 578-5193 Fay Sachs, RD, MPH Nutritional Support Services Eastern Regional Health Center 9100 Franklin Square Drive Baltimore, MD 21237 (301) 887-0317
IV	Alabama Florida Georgia Kentucky Mississippi Tennessee North Carolina South Carolina	George W. Bugg, MD Grady Memorial Hospital P.O. Box 26015 80 Butler Street, SE Atlanta, GA 30335-3801 (404) 589-4962 Kimarie Bugg, RN Grady Memorial Hospital P.O. Box 26015 80 Butler Street, SE Atlanta, GA 30335-3801 (404) 589-4932 Beth Everett, MPH, RD, LD Grady Memorial Hospital P.O. Box 26015 80 Butler Street, SE Atlanta, GA 30335-3801 (404) 589-4932

Mom to Mom ...

Region	Areas Included	Contacts
V	Illinois Indiana Michigan Ohio	Suzanne Trupin, MD 301 East Springfield Avenue Suite 104 Champaign, IL 61820 (217) 356-3736 Diana Mertens, RN, CNM, MPH Illinois Dept. of Public Health 535 W. Jefferson Springfield, IL 62761 (217) 782-2738 Doris J. McGuire Illinois Dept. of Public Health (IL Region IV Office) Cottonwood Road I270 and I59 Edwardsville, IL 62025 (618) 288-5731
VI	Arkansas Louisianna Texas New Mexico Oklahoma	Diane Kittredge, MD Oklahoma Children's Hospital 940 NE 13th Street, Rm. 3B700 Oklahoma City, OK 73104 (405) 271-6821 Dorothy Eckhart, RN, MSN, CPNP Oklahoma State Dept. Health/Pediatrics P.O. Box 73152 Oklahoma City, OK 73152 (405) 271-4471 Carol Paine-McGovern, MPH, RD Nutrition Div. Oklahoma State Dept. of Health P.O. Box 53551 Okalahoma City, OK 73152 (405) 271-4676

Indispensable Resources...

Region	Areas Included	Contacts
VII	Iowa Kansas Missouri Nebraska	M. Ahmad, MD University of Kansas Medical Center/Pediatrics 39th and Rainbow Kansas City, KS 66103 (913) 588-5919 Sallie Page-Goetz, RN, CMN University of Kansas Center/Pediatrics 39th and Rainbow Kansas City, KS 66103 (913) 588-6325 Sara McCamman CRU 39th and Rainbow Kansas City, KS 66103 (913) 588-5745
VIII	Colorado Montana Utah North Dakota South Dakota Wyoming	James Feist, MD 7 East Beall Bozeman, MT 59715 (406) 587-0174 Stephanie Nelson, RN, MS, CPNP Gallatin County Health Dept. Room 103 Courthouse Bozeman, MT 59715 (406) 585-1445 Tien-Han Ma, MA Gallan County Health Dept. Room 105 Courthouse Bozeman, MT 59715 (406) 585-1339

Mom to Mom . . .

Region	Areas Included	Contacts
IX	California Hawaii Nevada Pacific Basin Arizona	Mary O'Conner, MD, MPH San Francisco General Hospital 1001 Portrero Avenue, Rm. 6E9 San Francisco, CA 94110 (415) 821-8361 Meg Zweiback, RN, MPH, PNP San Francisco General Hospital 1001 Portrero Avenue, San Francisco, CA 94110 (415) 821-8361 Laura Finkler, MPH, RD Highland General Hospital/ Infant Feeding 411 East 31st Street Oakland, CA 94602 (415) 532-0275
X	Alaska Idaho Oregon Washington	Mary Steinberg, MD OHSU Dept. of Pediatrics 3181 SW Sam Jackson Park Rd. Portland, OR 97201 (503) 279-7300 Pam Hellings, RN, PhD, PNP Oregon Health Sciences University 3181 SW Sam Jackson Park Rd. Portland, OR 97201 (503) 279-8382 Tricia Mortell, RD OHSU Outpatient Nutrition, OP21 3181 SW Sam Jackson Park Rd. Portland, OR 97201 (503) 279-8636

Indispensable Resources...

Clips and Notes...

Mom to Mom...

Clips and Notes...

C

BIBLIOGRAPHY

Breastfeeding

Dana, Nancy and Anne Price. *The Working Woman's Guide to Breastfeeding*. Meadowbrook:Deephaven, MN. 1987. (Available from La Leche League International, P.O. Box 1209, Franklin Park, IL 60131-8209)

Dana, Nancy and Anne Price. *Successful Breastfeeding—A Practical Guide for Nursing Mothers*. Meadowbrook:Deephaven, MN. 1985.

La Leche League International. *The Womanly Art of Breastfeeding, 4th Revised Edition*. La Leche League International: Franklin Park, IL. 1987.

Lawrence, Ruth A., M.D. *Breastfeeding—Third Edition, A Guide for the Medical Profession*. C. V. Mosly Company:St. Louis. 1989.

Neville, Margaret D. and Marianne R. Neifert. *Lactation: Physiology, Nutrition, and Breast-Feeding*. Plenum Press:New York. 1983.

Pryor, Karen. *Nursing Your Baby*. Pocket Books: New York. 1973.

White, Mary. "Breastfeeding and Dental Cries," Pamphlet #31, April 1979. La Leche League International, Inc.:Franklin Park, IL.

Feeding and Meal Preparation

Jones, Elizabeth G., R.D. *Good Nutrition for Your Baby*. Slawson Communications:San Marcos, CA.

Mom to Mom . . .

La Leche League International. *Whole Foods for the Whole Family*. La Leche League International: Franklin Park, IL. 1987.

Maddon, Chris Casson. *Baby's First Helpings*. Mary Ellen Family Books:St. Louis Park, MN. 1983.

McDonald, Linda. *Instant Baby Food*. Oaklawn Press, Inc., 1318 Fair Oaks Avenue, South Pasadena, CA 91030.

Morse, Elisabeth. *First Foods*. Villard Books:New York. 1986.

Natow, Annette and Jo-Ann Heslin. *No-Nonsense Nutrition for Kids*. Pocket Books:New York. 1985.

Warner, Penny. *Healthy Snacks for Kids*. Nitty Gritty Productions, P.O. Box 2008, Benicia, CA 94510-2008.

Newletters

La Leche League International. *New Beginnings*. Bimonthly Jounal. La Leche League International, P.O. Box 1209, Franklin Park, IL 60131-8209.

Dunn and Hargitt. *Growing Parent/Growing Child*. Monthly newsletters. Dunn and Hargitt, P.O. Box 1100, Lafayette, IN 47902.

Sagall, Richard J., M.D. *Pediatrics for Parents*. Monthly newsletter. *Pediatrics for Parents,* P.O. Box 1069, Bangor, ME 04401.

Parenting Assistance

Brazelton, T. Berry, M.D. *Infants and Mothers: Differences in Development*. Revised Edition. Dell:NY. 1983.

Burmgarner, Norma Jane. *Mothering Your Nursing Toddler*. La Leche League International:Franklin Park, IL. 1986.

Bibliography...

Cosby, Bill. *Fatherhood.* Doubleday & Company: Garden City, NY. 1986.

Crary, Elizabeth. *Without Spanking or Spoiling: A Practical Approach to Toddler and Preschool Guidance.* Parenting Press, 7750 31st Avenue NE, Seattle, WA 98115. 1986.

Dobson, James, Ph. D. *Dare to Discipline.* Tyndale House Publishers. 1970.

Dobson, James, Ph. D. *Hide or Seek.* Revised Edition. Fleming H. Revell Company:Old Tappan, NJ. 1979.

Dodson, Dr. Fitzhugh. *How to Parent.* New American Library: New York. 1971.

Ferber, Richard, M.D. *Solve Your Child's Sleep Problems.* Simmon and Schuster:NY. 1985.

Gregory, Shelia and Diane Melvin. *First Fun.* Villard Books:New York. 1986.

Healy, Jane M., Ph.D. *Your Child's Growing Mind: A Guide to Learning and Brain Development from Birth to Adolescence.* Doubleday:New York. 1987.

Kuyper, Vicki J. *Parties Kids Will Love! Fun and Games for Ages 1 to 10.* Current, Inc.:Colorado Springs. 1987.

Lansky, Vicki. *101 Ways to Tell Your Child "I Love You."* Contemporary Books:Chicago. 1988.

Lansky, Vicki. *Practical Parenting Tips.* Meadowbrook, Inc.:Deephaven, MN. 1982.

Leach, Penelope. *Your Baby & Child from Birth to Age Five.* Alfred A. Knopf: New York. 1985.

Mom to Mom . . .

Leach, Penelope. *Your Growing Child from Babyhood through Adolescence.* Alfred A. Knopf:New York. 1986.

Neifert, Marianne, M.D. *Dr. Mom.* Signet:New York. 1987.

Pantell, Robert H., M.D., James F. Fries, M.D., and Donald M. Vickery, M.D. *Taking Care of Your Child, Revised Edition.* Addison-Wesley Publishing Company, Reading, Massachusetts. 1984.

Samalin, Nancy. *Loving Your Child Is Not Enough—Positive Discipline that Works.* Penguin Books:New York. 1987.

Sears, William, M.D. *Becoming a Father.* La Leche:Franklin Park, IL. 1986.

Sears, William, M.D. *Creative Parenting.* Dodd:NY. 1983.

Sears, William, M.D. *Growing Together: A Parent's Guide to Baby's First Year.* La Leche International:Franklin Park, IL. 1987.

Sears, William, M.D. *Nighttime Parenting—How to Get Your Baby and Child to Sleep.* La Leche League International:Franklin Park, IL. 1985.

Sears, William, M.D. *The Fussy Baby—How to Bring Out the Best in Your High Need Child.* La Leche League International:Franklin Park, IL. 1987.

Thevenin, Tine. *The Family Bed.* Avery Publishing Group, Inc.:Wayne, NJ. 1987.

Trelease, Jim. *The Read-Aloud Handbook.* Penguin Books, New York. 1985.

White, Burton L. *The First Three Years of Life.* Avon: New York. 1984.

Pregnancy and Childbirth

Cohen, Nancy Wainer and Lois Estner. *Silent Knife—Cesarean Prevention and Vaginal Birth after a Cesarean.* Avaliable from La Leche League International, P.O. Box 1209, Franklin Park, IL 60131-8209.

Bibliography ...

Dale, Barbara and Johanna Roeber. *The Pregnancy Exercise Book.* Pantheon Books, New York. 1982.

Eheart, Brenda Krause and Susan Karol Martel. *The Fourth Trimester.* Ballantine Books: 1984.

Eisenberg, Arlene, Heidi Eisenberg Murkoff, and Sandee Eisenberg Hathaway, R.N. *What to Eat When You're Expecting.* Workman Publishing:New York. 1986.

Eisenberg, Arlene, Heidi Eisenberg Murkoff, and Sandee Eisenberg Hathaway, R.N. *What to Expect When You're Expecting.* Workman Publishing:New York. 1988.

Engelhardt, Anne and Cheryl Sullivan. *Playful Learning—An Alternate Approach to PreSchool.* La Leche League International:Franklin Park, IL. 1986.

Faber, Adele and Elaine Mazlish. *How to Talk So Kids Will Listen and How to Listen So Kids Will Talk.* Avon:NY. 1982.

Faber, Adele and Elaine Mazlish. *Siblings without Rivalry.* W.W. Norton & Company: New York. 1987.

Feldman, George B., M.D. with Anne Felshman. *The Complete Handbook of Pregnancy.* G.P. Putnam's Sons, New York. 1984.

Gaither, Gloria and Shirley Dobson. *Let's Make a Memory.* World Books:Waco, TX. 1983.

Greene, Bob. *Good Morning, Merry Sunshine.* Penguin Books: New York. 1984.

Ingleman-Sundberg, Axel. *A Child Is Born. The Drama of Life Before Birth.* Revised Edition. Delacorte:New York. 1977.

Kelly-Buchanan, Christine. *Peace of Mind During Pregnancy: An A to Z Guide to Substances That Could Affect Your Unborn Baby.* Facts on File: Subs. of Commerce Clearing House:NY. (1-800-322-8755).

Mom to Mom . . .

Marnie, Eve. *Lovestart Pre-Birth Bonding*. Hay House, 1988. Available from all Walden and B. Dalton Bookstores and most metaphysical bookstores.

NOVA. *The Miracle of Life*. Avaliable from La Leche League International, P.O. Box 1209, Franklin Park, IL 60131-8209.

Verrilli, George E., M.D. and Anne Marie Mueser, Ed. D. *While Waiting—A Prenatal Guidebook*. St. Martin's Press, New York. 1984.

Sibling Preparation

Cole, Joanna. *How You Were Born*. Morrow:NY. 1985. (Available from La Leche League International, P.O. Box 1209, Franklin Park, IL 60131-8209)

Edelman, Elaine. *I Love My Sister (Most of the Time)*. Penguin:NY. 1985. (Available from La Leche League International, P.O. Box 1209, Franklin Park, IL 60131-8209.)

Faison, Eleanora. *Becoming*. Available from La Leche League International, P.O. Box 1209, Franklin Park, IL 60131-8209.

Pearson, Dr. Patricia and Edwina Riddell. *See How You Grow*. Barron's:New York. 1988.

$$ For YOUR TIPS and HINTS!

Mom to Mom was prepared especially for you, the mother-to-be and the new mother. It was also intended to be of considerable help for experienced mothers as well. Guiding the creation of this book was my desire for it to provide the very best help it possibly could.

This is the first edition of *Mom to Mom* and many mothers helped in putting it together, in both suggesting tips and hints that were especially helpful to them and in the suggestions they gave after reading the drafts. As long as *Mom to Mom* continues to be helpful and useful to mothers, it will be frequently revised and printed. But to ensure that it continues to be the very best helpful companion for new mothers, I need your help.

Please use the pages provided here or as many pages of your own paper as you need to send me your own valuable hints and tips that you share with your friends. Each one of your hints and tips received will be dated as it's received and will be immediately evaluated for its potential use. I will then pay $1.00 for each tip and hint slated for use in the next edition of *Mom to Mom,* scheduled to be published in late 1992. For example, if you submit ten suggestions and I use all ten, I will happily pay you $10 for sharing your creativity and for your trouble. If you submit 100 and I use 85 of those suggestions, I'll happily send you a check for $85! In the event that two or more people send in the same suggestion, payment for that suggestion will be given to the first person who submitted it, determined by the receipt date stamped on it. Submission of your ideas implies your permission to use them. If you would rather your name not be printed in the next edition, please make that clear.

In addition to payment, those who submit 20 or more ideas *that are to be used in the next edition* will receive a complimentary copy of the new edition!

If you choose to use your own paper for sending in your suggestions, *be sure to include your full name, address, area code, and phone number.*

411

Mom to Mom...

Your phone number is important because we may need to contact you to ask for more explanation on an idea that you submitted. Also, please be sure to number your suggestions and then photocopy your list so that you'll have a record of what you sent. When I respond with a note and payment, I can also easily refer to which ones are to be used simply by indicating their numbers.

I have only one other requirement for your submitted suggestions: If the hints and tips are ones you discovered through your reading, such as from an article, a book, a brochure, or a class handout, please include the source, date, author, etc., so I can write for permission to use it, if it's necessary.

Once you've completed your suggestions, please send them to me, c/o Communication Dynamics, 10601-A Tierrasanta Boulevard, Suite 201, San Diego, California 92124.

Thank you for your interest! I will appreicate any and all of your suggestions!

$$ For Your Tips and Hints . . .

SUGGESTIONS
for
the NEW EDITION of *MOM TO MOM*

Name: _____

Street or P.O. Box: _____

Apt. #: _____

City, State, Zip: _____

Area Code and Phone Number: (_____) _____

Please number your suggestions, hints, and tips:

Mom to Mom . . .

Please number your suggestions, hints, and tips:

ADDITIONAL CLIPS and NOTES . . .

You'll find that some of your "Clips and Notes . . ." sections will become quickly filled. This section will provide you some additional space to keep those new clips and notes that had no room in their appropriate chapters. This also gives you some space for those special items that didn't exactly fit into one of the chapters or sections but you wanted to be sure to keep track of them.

Be sure to record all of the clips and notes that you keep here in the index . . . these pages have page numbers, too, and it will be easier for you to find them again.

Mom to Mom . . .

Additional Notes and Clips . . .

Mom to Mom . . .

Additional Notes and Clips . . .

Mom to Mom . . .

Additional Notes and Clips . . .

Mom to Mom . . .

Additional Notes and Clips . . .

Mom to Mom . . .

Additional Notes and Clips . . .

Mom to Mom . . .

Additional Notes and Clips . . .

Mom to Mom . . .

Additional Notes and Clips . . .

Mom to Mom . . .

INDEX

A
Activated Granulated Charcoal 207-208
Activities with Toddlers and Preschoolers 273-279

B
Babysitting (See also Day Care)
    Babysitting cooperatives 264-268
    Determining your requirements 254-255
    Do's and dont's concerning sitters 267-268
    Important things to review with sitters 266-267
    Interviewing potential sitters 256-258
    Process of selecting quality sitters 258-264
    Sources of 255-256
Backyard Safety 351-352
Baths
  Infants 153-155
Before Baby's Arrival 8
    Classes recommended 50, 52, 55
    Clothing initially needed/not needed 77-80
    Diaper Service 55, 78-79, 94
    Equipment 66-77
        Baby Bathtub 70
        Bath Linens (towels, washcloths) 71
        Bassinet/Cradle and Accessories 61-63
        Bottles 76
        Buggy/Stroller (Convertible) 72-73
        Changing Table or Converter Kit 68
        Changing Table—Make Your Own 83-84
        Chest of Drawers 68
        Convertible Buggy/Stroller 19
        Crib and Accessories 63-68

Mom to Mom . . .

    Diaper Bag 75-76
    Diaper Pail/Bucket 76-77
    Front Carrier 69-70
    High Chair 77
    Infant Seat 71-72
    Lap Pads 71
    Playpen 77
    Rocking Chair 76
    Safety Seat 73-75
    Sling 69-70
    Transmitter Set 69
    Window Shade (car) 75
Hospital
    Knowing What You Want 54-55
La Leche League Meetings 53
Lamaze Birthing Class 52
Mother Support Groups 53
Nursery 80, 82
Plan for help after arrival 99
Recommended reading 46-49, 91-93
Shopping List 85-87
Sibling Preparation Class 55
Sources of couples sharing same delivery date 52
Subscriptions to consider 82-83
Things to do before going to the hospital 49-55
    Two to four weeks before 94-99
Birth
    Caesarean Birth 41-42
    Home Birth 24
    Lamaze
        Birthing "Goodie Bag" list 96-98
Birth Process 40-42
Birth Announcements 94
Bonding Process
    With Unborn Baby 23, 39-40
Books for Children 331-332
Bottle Feeding 134-136

Index...

    Equipment 134-135
    Important cautions 135
    Keys to successful 135-136
    Recommended Reading 134
Breast Pumps (Recommended) 128
Breast Pump Rentals 240
Breastfeeding 49-52, 115-134
    Benefits of 118-121
    "Bottle Mouth"—relationship to 202-203
    Breast milk storage
        Preparation for refrigeration or freezing 129-130
        Storage Guidelines 128
        Thawing frozen breast milk 130
    Breast milk—the superior food 3
    Breast pump rentals 240
    Breastfeeding the older baby and toddler 280-281
    Common *mis*information 121-122
    Correctable difficulties with 122-125
    Drugs and 132-133
    Hand expression 128-129
    Lactation consultants (regional listings) 397-402
    Nursing strike 130-131
        Causes of 130-131
        Suggestions to end strike 131
    Plugged ducts 131
    Problems with 122-125
        Evaluation of 125
        Solutions 126-127 (Also review pp. 122-124)
    Quitting—common reasons for 121-122
    Recommended breast pumps 128
    Recommended Reading 117
    Volume—to increase 126-127
    Wellstart 51
    Working mom and 133-134
        Recommended reading 133

Mom to Mom . . .

C

Caesarean Births 41-42
Cameras and Camcorders 98, 110
Car
    Safety 218, 345-346
Catalogues—recommended 393-394
Changing Table—Make Your Own 83-84
Chemical Hazards During Pregnancy 27-28
Chicken Pox—Caring for 311
Childproofing 219-225
    Bathrooms 222-223
    Dining Room 223
    General 219-222
    Kitchen 223-224
    Laundry 224
    Living Room 224
Choking Prevention 348-350
Clothing—Pregnancy 25-26
Clothing (Infant) 77-80
    Essentials 77-80
    Non-Essentials 80
    Winter wear 79-80
Clothing and Dressing Toddlers and Preschoolers 281-286
Communicating with Little Ones 149-153, 286-289
Constipation (during pregnancy) 31-32
Crying 157-162

D

Daily Care 149-172
    Baths 153-155
    Clothing and dressing an infant 155-157
    Crying 157-162
    Diapering 162-164
    Equipment
        for infants 165-166
        for older babies, toddlers 297-300

Index...

    Listening 149-152
    "Not Accomplishing A Thing" Syndrome 171-172
Day Care and Sitters (See also Babysitting)
    Determining your requirements 254
    Interviewing potential day care-givers 256-258, 290-291
    Process of selecting quality day care 258-264
    Sources of 255-256
Dehydration—Signs of 191
Dental Health (during pregnancy) 30-31
Dentist Selection 364
Diarrhea 191-192, 309-310
Diaper Bag
    Suggested contents for
        infants 234-235
        older babies 235
        toddlers 294-295
    Suggested contents for out-of-town travel 244
Diaper Service 55, 78-79
Diapering 162-164
Diapers—Washing 164-165
Dining Out 292-294
Discipline 295-297
Doctor (See Pediatrician, Pediatrician Visits)

E

Emergency First Aid Box—Contents 206-207
Emergency telephone numbers 265-266
Equipment 66-77
    Baby Bathtub 70
    Bath Linens (towels, washcloths) 71
    Bassinet/Cradle and Accessories 61-63
    Bottles 76
    Buggy/Stroller (Convertible) 72-73
    Changing Table or Converter Kit 68
    Changing Table—Make Your Own 83-84
    Chest of Drawers 68

Mom to Mom . . .

    Convertible Buggy/Stroller 19
    Crib and Accessories 63-68
    Diaper Bag 75-76
    Diaper Pail/Bucket 76-77
    Front Carrier 69-70
    High Chair 77
    Infant Seat 71-72
    Lap Pads 71
    Playpen 77
    Rocking Chair 76
    Safety Seat 73-75
    Sling 69-70
    Transmitter Set 69
        Window Shade (car) 75
Exercise (during pregnancy) 28-29

F

Family Bed 91-91, 383-388
Fears—How to handle 300-301
Feeding (See also Breastfeeding, Bottle Feeding)
    Infants 115-144
    Preparing for sitters 21
        babies on solids 22
        bottle fed babies 22
        breastfed babies 21
    Recommended Reading 116
    Toddlers and Preschoolers 301-305
Fetal Kicks 28
Fever
    Caring for 190-191
    Facts about 190-191
    Fever reducing medications 207
        Acetaminophen 207
        Aspirin 207
First Aid Box Contents 206-207
Furniture and Equipment Safety 5, 16

Index . . .

G
Grandparents 105

H
Hair Washing 279
Hand Washing—Importance of 315-316
Health
    During Pregnancy 26-31
    Of infants 187-212
    Of older babies, toddlers, and preschoolers 305-319
Heartburn during pregnancy 31
Hemorrhoids during pregnancy 32
High Chairs—Selection of 297-298
Holidays
    General 320-322
    Safety reminders 320, 352-353
Home Birth 24
Hospital for Delievery
    Knowing What You Want 54-55
    Hospital Procedures 94-96
    Hospital Stay 96, 101-103
Hospitalization
    Of infants 200-202
    Of older babies, toddlers, and preschoolers 311-314
Hot Lines for Pregnancy Information 29, 39
Hot Water Bottle 206
Humidifier 206, 209

I-J-K
Immunizations—Preparation for 189-190
Infant Seats 71-72
Insect Repellents 305-306, 317
Instincts—Following Your 105-107
Journal Writing 37-39
Jump or Bounce Seats 225

437

Mom to Mom . . .

L

La Leche League 53
Lamaze Birthing Class 52
Lactation Consultants—Regional Listings 397-402
Listening to Your Infants and Children 149-152
Lovies—Cleaning of 358-359

M

Magazines—Recommended 396-397
Medical Release Form 211-212
Medication—How to Administer 194-197, 305-308
Medicine Cabinet Contents 206-208
Medicines—Safety 344-345
Morning Sickness 31
Mother Support Groups 53

N

Nausea (during pregnancy) 31
Newsletters—Recommended 394-395
Nursery Preparation 80, 81-82

P

Pacifiers 123
Parenting Suggestions 322-326
Pediatrician
    Changing 60
    Interviews with (for selection) 57-60
    Selection of 56-60
    When to call 189, 308
Pediatrician—Visits to
    Regular check-ups 188-189
    When sick 189
Pets
    General 326-330
    Recommended reading

Index...

      Before baby arrives 81
      Pets for children 326
Plants—Poisonous 221-222
Playground Safety 351-352
Playtime
    Books for children 331-332
    For infants and babies 110-111, 167-177
    Recommended reading 167-168, 330
    Toy selection 169-170, 333-335
Potty Training 367-368
Pregnancy
    Breastfeeding 49-52
        Preparation prior to delivery 50-51
    Caesarean Births 13
    Classes to attend during 50, 52
    Common discomforts of 31-33
    Dental Health 30-31
    Fetal Kicks 28
    Health Issues 26-31
        Alcohol 26
        Chemical hazards 27-28
        Common harmful substances to avoid 27
        Diet 26
        Drugs 27
        Exercise 6
        Hot Lines 6
        Safety
            Electric Blankets 6
    Home Birth 24
    Journal Writing 37-39
    "Kick Count" 27
    Pre-Birth Bonding 23, 39-40
    Recommended Resources 22-24
    Relief of common discomforts of 31-33
    Travel 33-36
        By air 35-36

Mom to Mom . . .

    By car 34
    General 33-34
  Wardrobe 25-26
Preschool 335-339
  Preparation for 337-339
  Recommended reading 336
Products Worth Knowing About 339-341

R

Rashes—Suggested Treatments for 199-200
Recommended Reading
  Before Baby's Arrival 46-49, 91-93
  Bottle Feeding 134
  Breastfeeding
    General 46-49, 91-93
    Older babies and toddlers 280-281
    Working mom and 133
  Communicating with little ones 286-289
  Creating memories 286
  Daily care 92-93
  Feeding 116
  First Aid books 208
  Hospitalization 311-312
  Little one's arrival 91-93
  Pets 81, 326
  Play for infants and babies 167-168
  Playtime 330
  Pregnancy 22-24
  Preschool 336
  Sibling preparation for new baby's arrival 93
  Siblings 359-360
  Sleepy Time 92, 172
  Teeth and Teething 202
  Working mom and breastfeeding 133

Index...

S
Safety
- ABC's of 218
- Backyard and playground 351-352
- Balloons 354-355
- Bath 218
- Batteries 353-354
- Car 218, 345-346
- Childproofing 219-225
- Choking prevention 348-350
- Dry cleaning bags 228
- Furniture and equipment
  - High chairs 346
  - Hook-on chairs 347
  - Infant seats 225
  - Jump or Bounce Seats 225
  - Playpens 346-347
  - Toy Chests 347
  - Walkers 225-226
- Garage door openers 353
- Hiding places 355
- Holiday reminders 320, 352-353
- Important Telephone Numbers 341-342
- Literature and products 357-358
- Medicine cabinet 209
- Medicines 344-345
- Miscellaneous tips 227-228
- Pacifiers 228
- Plants—Poisonous 221
- Playgrounds 351-352
- Poisoning Prevention 342-344
- Recliner chairs 356
- Sleepy time 226-227
- Suffocation prevention 348-350
- "What-If" Game 356-357

Security Items Cleaning 358-359

441

Mom to Mom...

Self-Reliance 359
Shoes 281-283
Shopping List (preparing for baby's arrival) 85-87
Shortness of Breath (during pregnancy) 32-33
Siblings
    Preparation for new baby's arrival 37, 55, 99-100
    Recommended reading 37
    Sibling reception 102, 103-105
    Sibling rivalry 359-361
Sick Children
    Caring for infants 190-199
    Caring for toddlers, preschoolers 308-311
    Chicken Pox 311
    Diarrhea
        In infants 191-192
        In toddlers, preschoolers 308-310
        Signs of dehydration 191
    Doctor—when to call 308
    Hospitalization
        Of infants 200-202
        Of toddlers, preschoolers 311-314
    Stuffy nose
        Aspirating nose for 198-199
    Temperature—how to take 198
    Upset stomach 308-309
Sleepy Time
    Newborns 179-184
    Older babies, toddlers, and preschoolers 361-362
    Recommended reading 178
Smoke—Dangers of secondhand 314-315
Solids
    Beginning of 137-142
    Home prepared food 140-142
        Equipment needed 140-141
    Introduction of 138-139
    Recommended Reading 137-138
Spanking 295-297

Index . . .

Spit-ups—Minimizing 136
Storytelling 28
Strep Throat 310-311
Stuffy Nose 198-199
Suffocation Prevention 348-350
Sun Exposure Guidelines for Infants 209
Sunscreen 208
Support Groups 52, 53
Swimmer's Ear 317-318
Syrup of Ipecac 207

T

Teeth and Teething 202-205, 363-365
    Breastfeeding and 202-203, 363
    Care of primary teeth 202, 203, 363, 364, 365
    Caution 205
    Dentist Visits 363-364
    Dentist Selection 364
    Teething
        Signs of 204
        Signs of infection 205
    Teething discomfort—relief from 204, 205
Television 365-367
Temperature—How to Take 198
Toilet Training 367-368
Toy Selection
    First 3 months 169-170
    3 to 6 months 170
    6 to 9 months 333-334
    9 to 12 months 334
Travel While Pregnant 33-36
Travel with Baby and Toddler
    At the airport 241-242
    Breast pump rentals 240
    By car 236-237, 370
    By plane 238-243

Mom to Mom...

    Diaper bag contents
        In town 234-235
        On trips 244
        General 9
    Hotel reservations 240
    Miscellaneous Tips 368-372
    Out-of-town 238
    Overseas travel 238
    Packing list
        Blank 248-249
        Sample 244-247
    Rental car reservations 239
    Short trips around town 234-236
        General tips 236
    "Visiting bag" 369

U

Unborn Baby
    Bonding with 23, 39-40
    Health 26-30

V

Vaporizer 206, 209
Varicose Veins 33
Visual Skills Development 210

W

Walkers 225-226
Wardrobe—Pregnancy 25-26
Washing Hair 279
Weaning (child-led) 280-281
Working Mom
    Breastfeeding and 133-134
        Recommended Reading 134

Index...

X-Y-Z

Mom to Mom . . .

Index . . .

Communication Dynamics
9780 Canforero Terrace
San Diego, CA 92124
(619) 292-6949

Please ship _____ copies of *Mom-To-Mom* by Lynett Root Cablk at $14.95 each.

Order to be shipped to:

(Please print)

Name: _____

Address: _____

City, State, Zip: _____

Phone Number: (_____) _____

# of copies _____ at $14.95/book = total order: _____

SHIPPING: ($2.25 for the first book; _____
$1.25 for each additional book sent to same address): _____
(If you wish to have two-day service via UPS,
please add an additional $5.00.): _____

7% Sales Tax (CA residents only): _____

Total Amount Enclosed: _____

Thank you for your order!